D1556297

AVANT GARDE CRITICAL STUDIES

17

Dedicated to the memory of Dietrich Scheunemann
Compassionate teacher, colleague and friend
In Memoriam

AVANT-GARDE/
NEO-AVANT-GARDE

Edited by
Dietrich Scheunemann

Amsterdam - New York, NY 2005

Cover image:
Andy Warhol, *Marilyn Monroe 20 times*, 1962
© The Andy Warhol Foundation for the Visual Arts, Inc./ARS, NY
and DACS, London 2005

TM/© 2005 Marilyn Monroe, LLC by CMG Worldwide Inc., Indianapolis,
Indiana, 46256 USA www.MarilynMonroe.com

Cover design: Aart Jan Bergshoeff

All titles in the Avant Garde Critical Studies series (from 1999 onwards) are
available to download from the Ingenta website http://www.ingenta.com

The paper on which this book is printed meets the requirements of "ISO
9706: 1994, Information and documentation - Paper for documents -
Requirements for permanence".

ISBN: 90-420-1925-5
Editions Rodopi B.V., Amsterdam - New York, NY 2005
Printed in The Netherlands

Contents

III. On the Alchemy of the Word

IV. Body Arts

V. The Vanguard in Cinema and Architecture

VI. Crossing the Genres

Preface

This book and the series in which it appears would not exist had Peter Bürger not published his *Theory of the Avant-Garde* thirty years ago. It is thanks to his effort to sketch out a distinct profile of the avant-garde that a wide-ranging discourse on the achievements and shortfalls of the avant-garde movements of the 1910s and 1920s emerged. And still today Bürger's book is the inevitable starting point for every alternative prospect of the avant-garde's nature and the place that the avant-garde holds within twentieth century cultural history.

Not surprisingly, though, thirty years on a number of "blind spots" and incorrect distinctions have been marked by various critics. Also one of the consequences of Bürger's theory, the fact that it confines the scope ·of avant-gardist activities to a "fixed historical period" and presents the avant-garde as an exciting, yet by-gone revolt, has been received with critical reservation. However, while these objections hardly diminish the merits of Bürger's book as an initiating and encouraging contribution to the theory of twentieth century cultural history, greater problems arise from the critique of the basic approach on which the theory rests. From Benjamin Buchloh's review of 1984 up to our own attempt on the occasion of a research seminar at Yale University in 2000, Bürger's basic assumption that one singular intention, the intention of reintegrating art into the praxis of life, could be ascribed to the avant-garde as a whole came under attack. While the construction of an all-embracing frame had created the condition for the development of an inclusive theory of the avant-garde, its critique as an unreliable attribution applicable only to selected sections of the avant-garde called the very foundation of Bürger's theory into question. The neglect which Bürger's theory showed towards

differences and contradictions between manifested "intentions" of
the various avant-garde movements, the indifference also towards
the historical process in which traditional art concepts were
dismantled and a wealth of new art forms emerged, call for
alternative perspectives of theorising the avant-garde today.

Yet, it is not only the avant-garde of the 1910s and 1920s, but
also those attempts to reactivate its spirit and its innovative force in
the 1950s and 1960s, that deserve fresh attention. Bürger's theory
unfortunately sanctioned the short-sighted rebukes which neo-avant-
garde advances had experienced in contributions by Hans Magnus
Enzensberger, Leslie Fiedler and Octavio Paz in the 1960s and early
1970s. In particular Enzensberger and Paz had both stigmatised neo-
avant-garde manifestations as meaningless repetition of avant-
gardist gestures of yesterday. The significance of neo-avant-gardist
interventions and innovations, however, even the historical
significance of the act of "reinventing" the avant-garde after its
global destruction in the repressive decades of the 1930s and 40s,
remained as unexplored in these treatises as they did in the
sweeping rejection which the neo-avant-garde suffered in Bürger's
theory of 1974. The fact that artists of the neo-avant-garde exhibited
in museums and galleries was sufficient evidence for Bürger to
denounce the neo-avant-garde's protest gestures as "inauthentic" —
an assessment that is easily discernible as just another consequence
of Bürger's misleading definition of the avant-garde's basic
intention.

While the contributions to the seminar at Yale, published in
2002 as volume 15 in this series, were designed to explore new
avenues for the theory and study of the historical avant-garde, the
present volume, whilst continuing with this task, wishes to extend
the focus to include neo-avant-garde activities. Inevitably this raises
the intricate question of the relationship between the historical
avant-garde and the neo-avant-garde, the question also of the
specific historical function of both. Suggesting and testing some
answers to these questions is all a single volume can hope to
achieve. The contributors hope that their essays will be seen as an
invitation to others to take part in the mapping out of what is
undoubtedly a fascinating and yet widely unexplored field of
research.

The present volume is largely based on papers and discussions presented at a conference held in Edinburgh in September 2002. The volume is part of the output of the research project "The European Avant-Garde: A Reassessment", carried out within the School of Literatures, Languages and Cultures at the University of Edinburgh. I am greatly indebted to the British Arts and Humanities Research Board for the generous grant in support of the project. I am grateful to Jennifer Valcke for her assistance in organising the conference and to Kristen Albertsen and Anna Schaffner for their help in editing the present volume and providing the index.

Edinburgh, September 2004   D.S.

I.

THEORISING THE AVANT-GARDE

From Collage to the Multiple. On the Genealogy of Avant-Garde and Neo-Avant-Garde

DIETRICH SCHEUNEMANN

I.

In her charming book *Window Shopping* Anne Friedberg refers to the avant-garde as "a troubling third term" — the two other terms, supposedly troublefree, being modernism and postmodernism (Friedberg 1994: 162). Yet, having heard modernism declared dead and done with time and again, and having observed the grand notion of postmodernism losing its critical energy between the Scylla of Jean-François Lyotard's call for an end to all master narratives and the Charybdis of Fredric Jameson's retelling of such a narrative, the narrative of late capitalism, one may wonder whether the constellation in which the three terms are presented by Friedberg should not be reversed. What if the avant-garde were conceived as an energetic productive force in cultural history and modernism and postmodernism fell prey to the indistinctness of their profiles? However, two valid concerns which Friedberg raises in relation to the avant-garde stand in the way of such a reversal.

One of these concerns is, as Friedberg puts it, the "profound and lasting conflation of what is considered *modernism* and what is considered *avant-garde*" (Friedberg 1994: 163). The first *Theory of the Avant-Garde* published by Renato Poggioli in 1962 presents itself right away as a distinguished example of a wholesale confusion of the terms, presupposing "the identity and coincidence" of the modern and the avant-garde (Poggioli 1968: 15). And as Friedberg points out, the problem lingers on, not least in the most seminal contributions to the debates on modernism and postmodernism of the 1980s, in Jürgen Habermas' article on "Modernity versus Postmodernity" from 1981 and Jean-François Lyotard's response to the question "What is Postmodernism?" from 1983. In sketching out the "discipline of aesthetic modernity" Habermas presents the avant-garde as the peak of modernity. "The spirit and discipline of modernity", he writes,

> assumed clear contours in the work of Baudelaire. Modernity then unfolded in various avant-garde movements and finally reached its climax in the Café Voltaire of the dadaists and in surrealism. (Habermas 1981: 4)

However, in outlining his grandiose prospect of the "incomplete project of modernity", Habermas shifts the focus and introduces categories which Max Weber had suggested for the characterisation of "cultural modernity" (Habermas 1981: 8). The reason for this shift is twofold. Habermas had adopted Peter Bürger's diagnosis of an ultimate "failure" of the avant-gardist rebellion. To be able to hold on to the great prospects of modernity in spite of the bad omen that the avant-garde's failure would pose to it, a shift in terminology and conception was necessary. Moreover, Weber's characterisation of cultural modernity, embracing the spheres of science, morality and art, offered an extended theoretical base for the project of modernity and encouraged to envisage a wider scope of cultural activity for its advance.

The rather paradoxical insertion of the avant-garde in Habermas' article is mirrored by another, no less paradoxical insertion in the writings of his great opponent, Lyotard. Like Habermas, Lyotard closely associates the avant-garde with modernity. Unlike Habermas, however, he does not only celebrate its historical deeds, but also ascribes a highly important function to its legacy in contemporary cultural affairs. Lyotard's article on "Answering the Question: What is Postmodernism?" begins with a diatribe against those writers, art critics and architects who try to "liquidate the heritage of the avant-gardes" (Lyotard 1984: 71). Lyotard extends this critique to Habermas and counters Habermas' diagnosis of a "failure" of the avant-garde by emphasising the avant-garde's "highly responsible work". He characterises it as an investigation into "the assumptions implicit in modernity", as a "working through performed by modernity on its own meaning" (Lyotard 1985: 67f). The constellation which thus emerges could not be more stunning: both Habermas and Lyotard start from the assumption that the avant-garde forms an integral part of modernity. However, while Habermas, the apostle of modernity, testifies to the "mistakes" of the avant-garde and its supposedly self-inflicted destruction, Lyotard, the pontifex of postmodernism, celebrates the avant-garde's achievements and its indispensability as an ongoing front.

Unfortunately this is not the end of the "nominalist quagmire", as Friedberg calls it, in which modernism, postmodernism and the avant-garde are ensnared (Friedberg 1994: 163). Looking into the writings of Fredric Jameson one becomes aware of a surprising amalgamation of avant-garde manifestations with postmodern culture. In his essays "Postmodernism and Consumer Society" and "The Cultural Logic of Late Capitalism" Jameson refers to the work of John Cage and Andy Warhol as icons of postmodernism (Jameson 1983: 111; 1991: 1). Even Gertrude Stein and Marcel Duchamp now appear as "outright postmodernists avant la lettre" (Jameson 1991: 4). Characteristic features of art and literature of the historical avant-garde such as the abolishing of the "distinctive individual brushstroke" in painting and the departure from a "unique and personal style" in writing are presented here as constitutive elements of postmodern culture which according to Jameson began to emerge in the early 1960s (1991: 15). The surprising conflation of avant-gardism with postmodernism in Jameson's writings, also the idea of a decisive, epoch-making caesura in art history around 1960, results from a narrow view on American art developments and the marginality of avant-gardist activities in the United States in the 1910s and 20s. What Jameson takes for a ground-breaking rupture between modernism and postmodernism, i.e. the reaction of pop art to abstract expressionism, is nothing more than the repetition of a corresponding reversal 40 years earlier in the days of the original expressionist movement and the dadaist revolt against it. To reflect upon the reasons for the repetition of this dialectical process is a highly exciting task. However, to ignore the avant-garde's legacy and present Andy Warhol's *Diamond Dust Shoes* as the dawn of a new era in cultural history puts the stakes too high — too high also in terms of the claims made here to just another meta-narrative.

In his article "Who's Afraid of the Neo-Avant-Garde?" Hal Foster reminds us that "to pose the question of repetition" in twentieth century cultural history is to pose "the question of the neo-avant-garde" (Foster 1996: 1). Unlike Jameson, who conflates neo-avant-garde and postmodernism, Foster insists on the value of an "independent construct of the avant-garde" and the need for "new narratives of its history"(Foster 1996: 5). No other conclusions can be drawn from Anne Friedberg's observations. Both critics put the construction of "new genealogies" of the avant-garde on the agenda, genealogies that "complicate its past and support its future". Such a construction must meet two requirements: firstly, to elaborate an independent profile of the avant-garde characterising it as a cultural force in its own right and with its own mission, and secondly, to provide an answer to the question of repetition and reinvention, continuity and rupture, re-appropriation and new departure, in short explore the nature of the relationship between the historical and the neo-avant-garde in a more substantive and imaginative manner than has hitherto been attempted. The all too familiar diagnoses of the "mistakes", the "failure", the "decline" and "death" of the avant-garde have clearly acted as a blockade preventing for decades by now a fresh look at the innate relationship between avant-garde and neo-avant-garde activities. Removing these obstacles, however, will not be enough. A more comprehensive and more solid theoretical grounding of the avant-garde is required than the one provided by the still authoritative text, the *Theory of the Avant-Garde* by Peter Bürger. And this is the second concern which Anne Friedberg indicates.

Bürger's theory has contributed significantly to the elaboration of an independent profile of the avant-garde. By developing his widely accepted definition of the avant-garde as an "attack on the autonomous status of art in bourgeois society" and an attempt to "reintegrate art into the praxis of life", Bürger has established a unified and politically specific platform for the discussion of the avant-garde movements of the 1910s and 1920s (Bürger 1984: 49f). Not surprisingly, Friedberg gives him all the credit in the world for correcting the "coexistensivity between the avant-garde and modernism" as assumed by other critics (Friedberg 1994: 163). However, taking cinema as her testing ground, Friedberg soon finds out that Bürger's distinctions "do not fit" the aims, means or prospects of avant-garde cinema. As Friedberg points out, one of the "implicit agendas" of French avant-garde film of the 1920s was "to have the cinematic medium taken seriously as an art form". Indeed, critics and avant-garde filmmakers alike discussed their cinema in terms of "an autonomous art", as "pure cinema". In her account of "The Aesthetics of Avant-Garde Cinema" Germaine Dulac insists that avant-garde film "must reject every aesthetic principle which does not properly belong to it and seek out its own aesthetic in the contributions of the visual" (Dulac 1978: 47). Not an attack on the status or the institutions of art was intended here, but attaining recognition for cinema as a high art form with its very own aesthetic principles was the goal. Investigating the aesthetic potential of the new medium became the hallmark of the experiments of Man Ray, Fernand Léger and Marcel Duchamp as well as those performed simultaneously by the German avant-garde filmmakers Hans Richter, Viking Eggeling and Walther Ruttmann.

But it is not only the filmmakers whose work so strikingly contradicts Bürger's definition of the avant-garde. Cubist painting, expressionist literature or the movement of *De Stijl* can also not be subsumed under the formula of attacking the autonomy of art in bourgeois society. Since Bürger published his theory in 1974, a number of blind spots, inexact descriptions, and flawed observations have been marked by critics. But more importantly is the fact that as Benjamin Buchloh and Hal Foster have pointed out Bürger's definition of the avant-garde is "overly selective" (Buchloh 1984: 19; Foster 1996: 8). The definition is based only on a small section of the historical avant-garde's activities. In a footnote to his theory Bürger concedes that "the concept of the historical avant-garde movements" developed in his book applied primarily to dadaism, early surrealism and the Russian avant-garde after the October Revolution (Bürger 1984: 109). Only within "certain limitations", Bürger admits, does it apply to the formative movements of the avant-garde, to cubism, futurism, expressionism and the Russian avant-garde before the October Revolution. The *Black Square* by Malevich does indeed neither attack art as an autonomous institution nor does it reconcile art with life. However, a theory of the avant-garde that excludes the formative movements that generated the

avant-gardist impetus and gave shape to its initial artistic innovations, and excludes the whole art form of avant-garde film — such a
theory is certainly in need of extensive repair, if not replacement.

As Buchloh pointed out in his early review, Bürger's attempt to
"reduce the vast differences and contradictions" of the avant-gardist
art practice to a *single unifying intention*, i.e. the intention to reintegrate art into the practice of life, poses a further problem (Buchloh
1984: 19). Given the variety and divergence of the intentions of
cubist and futurist, expressionist, dadaist and surrealist artists, such
one-dimensional approach necessarily leads to doubtful generalisations and attributions. Foster questions the implied assumption of
Bürger's approach in similar terms, rejecting the idea "that *one* theory can comprehend *the* avant-garde, that all its activities can be
subsumed under the project to destroy the false autonomy of bourgeois art" (Foster 1996: 8). Without giving up his unifying approach, Bürger has in a subsequent article reconsidered some aspects of his theory. With regard to his diagnosis of the "failure" of
the avant-garde Bürger now concedes that "such a judgement itself
remains caught within the logic of the either – or". Drawing on Ernst
Bloch's "principle hope", he supplements his previous notion with
an illuminating interpretation:

> It seems questionable whether a Utopian project can ever fail
> since it is so intimately connected with that hope that can never
> be disappointed, according to the dictum of Ernst Bloch. We can
> also express this idea in another way: failure is the mode in
> which the avant-garde artist reaffirms the Utopian quality of the
> project. (Bürger 1992: 153)

Igniting the flame of utopian hope appears here as the function and
task of the historical avant-garde. Such a prospect represents a significant modification of the historiographic armature of Bürger's
theory with eminent consequences for the assessment of the neo-
avant-garde. Initially dismissed by Bürger as an "inauthentic"
repetition of the protest of the historical avant-garde, the neo-avant-
garde can now be conceived as another bearer of the flame of hope,
re-igniting it and passing it on after a period of darkness. The trajectory of this argument is tempting. Yet the problem remains that
the utopian project to which Bürger refers is still the same simplistic, formulaic assumption that the avant-garde intended to reconcile

art and the practice of life. The invention of the whole arsenal of revolutionary new art forms and artistic techniques from collage and montage to assemblage, from the readymade to automatic writing, from monochrome painting to the geometrically constructed grid and the multiple cannot be deduced from such a platform.

In a "Postscript to the Second Edition" of the *Theory of the Avant-Garde* Bürger alludes to the origin and the historical role of the formulaic description proposed in his initial attempt. He notes that the *Theory of the Avant-Garde* was written in 1974, "after the events of May 1968 and the failure of the student movement in the early seventies" (Bürger 1974b: 134). Quite obviously, the *Theory* established historical parallels to the hopes and prospects of '68 — at the very moment of their waning. The formula designed to characterise the "intention" of the historical avant-garde as well as the anticipation of its failure were prefigured by the experiences with the utopian project proclaimed in the streets of Berlin and Frankfurt, Paris and Berkeley in May 1968. The avant-garde movements of the 1910s and 20s, however, cannot stand in for this project.

On re-reading the manifestos and programmatical statements of the avant-garde one encounters a wide-ranging spectrum of possible stances in the question of art's relationship to life from renewed claims on the autonomy of art in all sections of abstract painting and avant-garde cinema to art's unequivocal utilisation in the "production art" of Russian constructivism, from a rejection of any link to everyday life in statements of expressionist writers to an emphatic call for the reflection of life's "simultaneous confusion of noises, colours and spiritual rhythms" in dadaist manifestos (Huelsenbeck 1992: 46). The single one-dimensional "intention" of the avant-garde is as much one of its myths as is the related assumption of its "failure". It is not in a joint strategy or political direction of the artists that a common ground of the avant-garde movements can be found, but rather in external challenges that fundamentally affected the production situation of the artist, the means of artistic production and the overall notion of art. To become aware of this challenge it is necessary to re-affirm the weight of Walter Benjamin's insights into the situation of the work of art in the age of technological reproduction. It is the advance of new means of technical production and reproduction that called into question the traditional practice and traditional notions of art. The advance of photography, of the phonograph and the filmstrip undermined traditional functions of art and challenged the very techniques of artistic production.

In his seminal essay on "The Work of Art in the Age of Mechanical Reproduction" Benjamin had raised the question whether "the very invention of photography had not transformed the entire nature of art" (Benjamin 1973b: 229). With this question Benjamin grasped one of the major concerns shared by artists across all avantgarde movements from cubism, futurism and expressionism to dadaism, constructivism and surrealism. In statements and through their work they made it clear that the invention of photography and its latest manifestation, the filmstrip, had indeed altered the conditions and the "entire nature" of artistic production. Not that they developed one unifying strategy as to how to combat this challenge. The differences in their responses constitute the variety of the avantgarde movements and the variety of their programmatical orientation. What they have in common, though, and what distinguishes them from traditionalist as well as modernist trends of the time, is the constructive and innovative response to this challenge.

II.

"I have discovered photography", Pablo Picasso is said to have once exclaimed, "now I can kill myself" (Baldassari 1997: 17). Luckily, he did not follow through with his resolution, but instead introduced a whole system of fundamental changes to the conventions of painting. It was not a new style or technical finesse that he developed in close co-operation with George Braque, but rather a series of innovations which prepared the ground for much of twentieth century art. At the centre of the cubist project was, as Edward Fry has convincingly shown, the abandonment of the linear perspective, the abolishing of the convention of the "spatial illusionism of the one-point perspective" (Fry 1966: 13). The convention of the linear perspective had been an obligatory part of the painters' tool box for almost 500 years, ever since Brunelleschi and Alberti established its rules and principles. Erwin Panofsky has described the significance of the linear perspective in terms of a "symbolic form" (Panofsky 1991). In a painting that observes the rules of the linear perspective, all architectural lines converge in one central point, the focal point of the viewer. This furthers an interpretation of the technique that sees the viewer elevated over the objects viewed and the individual observer defined as the centre of the view of the world. It is against this background, the legacy of 500 years of painting in the Western World and its implications, that the abandonment of the linear perspective in cubist painting assumes its full weight. The renunciation of the traditional perspective represents a revolution in the conventions of perception, including a destruction of the traditional spatial illusionism in painting and encouraging a wide-ranging exploration of alternative modes of depicting objects and human figures. The technique of combining multiple view-points into a single image, first introduced by Picasso in his famous painting of the *Demoiselles d'Avignon*, was soon accompanied by other devices supporting the break-up of spatial illusionism. These include the fragmentation and geometricalisation of the objects and figures depicted, the blurring of distinctions between foreground and background of the image and a variety of ways of emphasising the flatness of the canvas, explored initially through the insertion of letters into the paintings and eventually through sticking a ready-made piece of oil-cloth or snippets of coloured papers onto the canvas. The invention of the new artistic technique and art form of collage was the pinnacle of this rapid process of innovation designed to take painting away from the illusionism of "realist" photographic representation.

Artists of the avant-garde did not make a secret of the fact that the strategies developed by the cubist painters were driven by the desire to depart as decisively as possible from photographic imagery. "Each God creates in his own image, and so do painters", Apollinaire wrote in his early account of *The Cubist Painters*. "Only photographers", he added, "manufacture duplicates of nature" (Apollinaire 1962: 11). "Photography has completely distorted the idea of form", complained Albert Gleizes. New ways in painting, he believed, "must perforce be antagonistic to the photographic image" (cf. Scharf 1983: 252). And for Louis Aragon there was no doubt that "cubism was a reaction of painters to the invention of photography. The photograph and the cinema", he wrote, "made it seem childish to them to strive for verisimilitude" (cf. Selz 1963: 326). The problem with this statement is only that Aragon seems to link verisimilitude to the one-point perspective.

No one, however, has underscored the relationship between the cubist innovations and the advance of technological reproduction in the form of photography in a more pronounced way than Picasso himself in *Still Life with Chair Caning*, the first collage in the history of painting. At the birth of this genuine avant-gardist art form Picasso juxtaposed a cubist notation of common objects — a newspaper, a pipe, a sliced lemon, a glass and a scallop shell — with a piece of oil-cloth that bears an industrially produced photographic reproduction of chair caning. Bürger mistakes the cloth for an actual "piece of basket" and celebrates it as a reality fragment within a picture. The nature of the reality, however, is photographic reproduction, the perfect illusion of chair caning. By bringing together

Pablo Picasso: *Still-Life with Chair Caning* (1912)

within one frame a characteristic cubist notion of objects and a piece of photographic reproduction, Picasso staged an encounter between the challenger photography and the response which the cubist paint-ers had given to the challenge. The cause is confronted with its re-tort. The notation of objects displays all the innovations which the cubist painters had introduced in their pictures since the *Demoiselles d'Avignon*: the objects are fragmented and composed of geometrical shapes; the glass is depicted from multiple perspectives; the distinction between foreground and background is dispensed with in favour of an inscription of the objects on the flat canvas; and the letters JOU, the fragmented title of a journal, lend additional emphasis to the flatness of the canvas, since letters, as Braque stated, "are flat by their very nature"!

Statements of futurist artists were hardly far removed from those accompanying cubist painting. "With the perfection of photography, static traditional painting has completely fallen from repute", Giacomo Balla notes in an exhibition catalogue (cf. Apollonio 1973: 206). "Given the existence of photography and cinema", he adds in a manifesto on colour, "the pictorial representation of the truth does not and cannot any longer interest anyone" (cf. Scharf 1983: 253). The same driving force is identified for the break with the conventions of painting as in comments on cubist painting. However, the reference to the *stasis* of traditional painting foreshadows the different direction which the experiments of the futurist painters ultimately took. Not the conventions of the traditional linear perspective, but another age-old convention, the conviction of the static nature of painting, became the focus of the futurist's energetically promoted break with tradition. In his treatise on the *Laocoon*, G.E. Lessing had defined painting as the art form that extends in space, and poetry as the form that extends in time. And he had derived recommendations for the proper choice of subjects for the writer and painter from this distinction. While the writer could select subjects that move in time, painters were confined to the depiction of static objects or alternatively to a single "moment of an action" (Lessing 1874: 150). The preference for still-lifes, landscapes and portraits throughout the history of painting supports the general conclusions which Lessing and also Diderot had drawn. Breaking with this tradition and opening up the medium of painting for the depiction of the "universal dynamism" of the modern world became one of the central aims which the futurist painters proclaimed in their manifestos. Had Marinetti sung his praise of the "new beauty of speed" by comparing a roaring racing car with the *Victory of Samothrace*, giving the former the advantage over the latter in spite of the *Victory's* energetic posture (cf. Apollonio 1973: 21), so the painters emphasised on their part the break with the representation of any "fixed moment". "The gesture which we would reproduce on canvas shall no longer be a fixed moment", they proclaimed in their "Technical Manifesto" of 1910 (cf. Apollonio 1973: 27). The "universal dynamism" was to be rendered "as a dynamic sensation" communicating the energy, the force, the power of objects in motion.

Although expressionist painters were not at all interested in the "force-lines" by which the futurists inscribed the energy of objects and environments into their paintings, the familiar pattern emerges here as well. "Today photography takes over exact representation. Thus painting, relieved from this task, gains its former freedom of action", Ernst Ludwig Kirchner pronounced in a credo on his working method (cf. Buchheim 1956: 174). Line, plane, colour and also the "technical aid of perspective" thus became compositional means designed to transpose "a sensuous experience" into an artwork. "The most important point in the question of form", Vassily Kandinsky adds, is "whether or not it springs from inner necessity" (Kandinsky 1968: 158). Convinced of the "impossibility" and "uselessness of attempting to copy an object exactly" he made use of lines, shapes and colours as expressive means of inner urges of the artist (cf. Scharf 1983: 253). No one abandoned the mimetic function of painting and paved the way towards abstract painting as energetically as Kandinsky. Colours and lines became increasingly independent, autonomous means of composition in his pictures hovering freely on an indeterminate plane. Kandinsky shaped the idea of abstract painting, soon to be followed by Kasimir Malevich's suprematist experiments and Piet Mondrian's geometrical colour compositions.

Art historians like to explain the emergence of abstract painting as "the inevitable result of the reaction against naturalism" (Bowness 1972: 129). Apparently the "reaction against naturalism" does not require any explanation. Avant-garde artists, however, do not hesitate to name the historical forces that instigated the development of a range of alternatives to the traditions of painting, including the move towards abstract painting. Whether it is the depiction of volumes on a flat canvas, the portrayal of motion and dynamic energies in the static medium of painting or the use of perspective and colour for the communication of "sensuous experience" — at their most fundamental all seem to express the desire to move away from photographic imagery and develop functions for artistic production which lie beyond the traditional mimetic task of all arts.

In the introduction to an exhibition of paintings by Max Ernst André Breton provided an excellent summary of this phenomenon maintaining that

> the invention of photography has dealt a mortal blow to the old modes of expression, in painting as well as in poetry [...]. Since a blind instrument now assured artists of achieving the aim they had set themselves up to that time, they now aspired, not without recklessness, to break with the imitation of appearances. (Breton 1948)

Breton's statement is of particular value because he included his own métier, poetry, in this account. Evidently, the revolution in painting which the cubist, futurist, expressionist and the Russian cubo-futurist movements caused, did not leave the other arts, in particular poetry, unaffected. Apollinaire, the mediator and promoter of Picasso and Braque, began to experiment with "the new genre of visual poetry", as Tristan Tzara noted in the first issue of *Cabaret Voltaire* (Tzara 1916). With "Lundi Rue Christine", a poem composed of snippets of overheard conversation mixed with authorial reflections, Apollinaire made another significant contribution to the transfer of artistic principles from painting to poetry. The enthusiasm which Apollinaire had expressed in his treatise on "The Cubist Painters" over the invention of the new art form of collage suggests that the insertion of fragments of ready-made overheard speech was a direct transfer of the collage technique from painting to literature.

While Apollinaire explored the visual aspect of language and experimented with the collage technique, it was Gertrude Stein, another close friend of Picasso's, who started to explore the aural aspect of everyday American English. The poems she published in the collection *Tender Buttons* drew their poetic effect as well as their provocation from the fact that the meaning of the words assembled was subordinate to the sounds and the rhythm of the language. Stein was the first of a significant number of writers who made the new genre of oral poetry an important part of the avant-garde's poetic production. These included in particular the Russian cubo-futurist Velimir Khlebnikov's "Incantation to Laughter" and Hugo Ball's renowned contribution to the opening of the Cabaret Voltaire,

"Karawane". While Apollinaire and Stein developed their poetic experiments with the visual and aural properties of language in the wider context of cubist painting, all subsequent movements of the avant-garde embraced painters and poets equally. The questioning of traditional borderlines between the arts and a lively interaction, including the transfer of new techniques and aesthetic principles from one art to another, became, not accidentally, one of the outstanding features of avant-gardist art production.

III.

While the formative phase of the avant-garde was dominated by attempts to develop counterstrategies to the advance of photographic reproduction, entailing a radical questioning of the mimetic function of all arts and a wide-ranging exploration of the properties of artistic materials, the advent of dadaism and surrealism brought about a fundamental change in the direction of avant-garde experiments. Not that the largely aesthetic orientation of the formative years suddenly gave way to a dominance of social and political concerns, although the World War and the Revolutions of 1917 and 18 left their imprint on dadaist and constructivist manifestations. Neither can one observe attempts at "reintegrating art into the praxis of life" to be undertaken on a wider scale — with the significant exception of activities of the Russian avant-garde. For obvious reasons the call for the utilisation of art for the formation of a new society became the hallmark of programmatical statements and manifestations of the Russian avant-garde, spearheaded by Boris Arvatov's concept of *production art* and Vladimir Tatlin's constructivist plans and projects. Duchamp's *readymades*, however, and the Berlin dadaist's invention of the *photomontage*, the two outstanding innovations in artistic technique of the avant-garde in the years since 1913, indicate different concerns.

The provocation and puzzlement which Duchamp's readymades pose have elicited a range of radical interpretations. Peter Bürger draws upon several of them. The readymade is portrayed by him as an attack on "art as an institution" including the organisational forms of the museum and exhibition, as an attack on the art market where "the signature counts more than the quality of the

Marcel Duchamp: *Bicycle Wheel* [replica of lost work from 1913] (1964)

work", and finally as an attack on the "category of individual production" (Bürger 1984: 51f.). However, the comments with which
Duchamp himself accompanied the production of his readymades,
shifts the focus elsewhere. In response to the unfavourable treatment
of his "Fountain" by the exhibition organisers, Duchamp noted in an
article in *The Blind Man*:

> Whether Mr. Mutt with his own hands made the fountain or not
> has no importance. He CHOSE it. He took an ordinary article of
> life, placed it so that its useful significance disappeared under the
> new title and point of view — created a new thought for that ob-
> ject. (cf. Dachy 1990: 83)

This comment suggests nothing less than a fundamental change of
the notion of art. It anticipates an understanding of artistic activity to

which Duchamp had already committed himself in his own practice. Having abandoned oil, palette, brush and canvas, he submitted an "ordinary article of life" to an exhibition. This was not at all meant as an attack on the institution of art exhibition, nor as an attempt at sublating art into life — rather the opposite: explored in this act are the conditions under which an ordinary article of life transforms into a work of art. What makes an object a work of art, is the provocative question raised.

The *Fountain* does not only raise the question, it also suggests an answer to it. It is not the handicraft of the artist, but the selection and placement of the ordinary object that are identified as the defining features of creative activity. The *Fountain* mocks the traditional idea of artistic creativity bound to the imprint of the hand or the brushstroke of the artist. The *Fountain* propagates a new idea, a notion of art that implies the use of ready-made, industrially produced materials and defines creativity in terms of the selection and placement of such materials. It is a notion of artistic creativity well suited to the age of technological reproduction. More than two decades before Walter Benjamin undertook to work out the theoretical implications of the work of art in the age of technological reproduction, Duchamp exhibited them in the form of his readymades. Not surprisingly, the lack of *uniqueness* of the work of art in the modern age and the outdatedness of the category of the *original* were emphasised by both, the artist and the critic.

While Duchamp's readymades, works of aesthetic reflection in the first place, raised the question of the status of the work of art in the age of technological reproduction, the Berlin dadaists made the next step *avant garde* by putting the radical change in the notion of art suggested by the readymades into artistic practice. The invention of the photomontage by the Berlin dadaists marks a new stage in the development of the avant-garde, a dialectical inversion of its beginnings. While initially the differentiation from photography and photographic imagery fuelled a range of artistic conceptions whose common ground was the abandonment of the age-old mimetic function of all arts, the photomontage now incorporated photographic imagery into artistic production. Ready-made, mass-produced photographic snippets cut out from illustrated magazines and newspapers became the material basis of the new art form. In addition, the photomontage is not only an art form based on material produced through technological reproduction; it is also one "designed for reproducibility". Any reproduction of a photomontage communicates its meaning and reveals its aesthetic significance as precisely as the original does. Photomontages share this feature with Duchamp's readymades. The term *original* has since lost its traditional value and significance.

Bürger presents the photomontage as a reading picture constructed in the rigid fashion of a Baroque emblem. This is appropriate if one refers to the political work of Heartfield in the early 1930s in which the original dadaist form of the photomontage was simplified and more clearly organised for political effect. However, in 1932 dada had been dead for at least eight years. Indeed, the dadaist photomontage had displayed an entirely different organisation. It was chaotic, anarchic. This applies to Heartfield's early works as well as to those by George Grosz, Raoul Hausmann and Hannah Höch. In his definition of the photomontage Hausmann hailed its anarchic form as the appropriate reflection of "the chaos of an age of war and revolution". By describing the composition of photomontage in its early form as an "explosive mixture of different points of view and levels" (cf. H. Richter 1965: 116), Hausmann made it clear that the incorporation of the new photographic material did not signal a return to realist, representational functions of the arts. By combining multiple angles and view points, juxtaposing elements that emphasise the flatness of the surface with others indicating depth, and by using disparate, fragmented snippets for the composition of the picture, the photomontage appropriates and upholds many of the innovations introduced by the avant-garde painters before. But the use of photographic material meant that technological reproduction became an integral part of the avant-garde's artistic production. And this was more than just an expansion of artistic materials.

The separation between art and technology, one of the cultural divisions of the late eighteenth and nineteenth centuries that Habermas in his project of fulfilling the idea of modernity clearly wishes to see overcome, was thus eliminated. One of the "barriers", this is how Benjamin put it, that "inhibited the productive capacity" of the artist, had been brought down (Benjamin 1983: 95). It would therefore be mistaken to consider the linking of art and technology as an attack on the institution of art with a view to destroying it. It is a radical change in the traditional notion of art and a radical change of its practice. Just as the proclamation "the King is dead, long live the King" does not imply the abolition of the monarchy, so did the board with the wording "art is dead, long live the new machine art of Tatlin" held up by Heartfield and Grosz at the Dada Fair of 1920 not at all anticipate the end of art, but a new and timely notion of art, a changed conception of its techniques and a new understanding of the artists themselves. It was again Hausmann who left no doubt about the latter: "We regarded ourselves as engineers, and our work as construction", he noted, "we *assembled* (in French: *monter*) our work, like a fitter" (cf. H. Richter 1965: 118).

Two of the early photomontages, *Life and Activity in Universal City at 12.05 Midday* by Grosz and Heartfield and *Dada Cino* by Hausmann, pointedly allude to cinema in their titles. In *Life and Activity* Grosz and Heartfield even inserted pieces of a film strip into the picture along with cut-outs of movie star images and literal references to Fox and to "photoplays", the old name for film in the Hollywood studios. The significance of the references is clear enough. The new art form of photomontage, based on technological reproduction, celebrates another new, technically conditioned medium, film. At the same time, it draws attention to the fact that photomontage, like film, consists of multiple images of different proportions, framing and points of view, thus celebrating its own complex organisation. Not surprisingly, Hausmann therefore refers to photomontage as a "motionless moving picture" (H. Richter 1965: 118). Indeed, dadaist photomontage is hardly the political weapon into which commentators so often transform it. It is first and foremost the initial exploration of an unfamiliar terrain of artistic activity based on materials produced by technological reproduction.

A close ally of Heartfield and a collaborator of Eisenstein, Sergei Tretiakov, clearly understood the technological context from which the photomontage emerged and the formal anarchy to which it initially subscribed. Speaking on Heartfield's work he points out that "the kitchen of photomontage was above all the cinema", the "mechanical sequence of filmic images" (Tretiakov 1977: 169). Moreover, he distinguishes succinctly between the "dadaist photomontages" of Heartfield consisting of a "multitude" of cut-out photographic fragments assembled in the fashion of an "abstract composition", and his later work in which only "a small number of elements", often not more than two photos or texts, are combined to form an effective political message. No doubt, Tretiakov's sympathies lie with the latter, and he is glad to announce that "the dadaist period in Heartfield's works did not last long" (Tretiakov 1977: 169). Yet, to arrive at a well-grounded account of the avant-garde's activities and of the historical forces that shaped the invention of the genuine new forms of expression, it is important to take into account the distinctions made by Tretiakov between the photomontage as invented and practised by the dadaists and the political as well as commercial use to which this innovative technique was put when dada was dead.

Duchamp's readymades and the photomontage of the Berlin dadaists represent the peak of the avant-gardist rebellion in the arts. Their processing of industrially produced objects and mass-produced pre-processed images provided artistic production with a new material basis and moved it on to a plane where it was no longer in opposition to procedures characteristic of other spheres of life, but communicated with them. The implications of such practice were enormous. Long-cherished aesthetic categories such as the *originality*, *uniqueness* and *autonomy* of artistic production, the value of the *individual brushstroke* and of *handicraft*, the traditional idea of *creativity* and the fundamental mimetic function of all arts were radically called into question. Moreover, the waves of this rebellion in the visual arts reverberated in literary production. While in the early avant-garde the destruction of the syntax and the exploration of aural and visual qualities of language had been at the forefront of the experiments, Tzara and Breton now recommended scraps and headlines from mass-produced and mass-circulated newspapers as the material basis of dadaist poetry, while Schwitters collected the highly poetic lines of "Anna Blume" from wooden planks, grammar books and prize questions in magazines. Döblin proposes right away a "cinema style" of writing with the aim of "breaking the hegemony of the author" (Döblin 1963: 17f.), while Isherwood, although more conventional in his practice, has his narrator proclaim, "I am a camera with its shutter open, quite passive, recording, not thinking" (Isherwood 1977: 11).

Avant-garde cinema that emerged in the wake of the dadaist rebellion with the work of Hans Richter, Viking Eggeling, Walther Ruttmann, Man Ray, Fernand Léger and Duchamp adds just another facet to this picture. Its main features have succinctly been described by Adams Sitney in his introduction to *The Avant-Garde Film*. Concentrating on abstract forms or on mechanical objects set in motion the avant-garde filmmakers explored, as Sitney phrases it, "the empty screen, black and white alternation, the disappearance and re-emergence of simple shapes" and "the creation of deep and shallow space" (Sitney 1978: xi–xii). Exploring the aesthetic properties of the new medium was the joint effort of the avant-garde films of the early 1920s. This characterisation "fits" well into the picture developed here of the avant-garde as a whole. And correspondences between avant-garde painting and avant-garde film are not at all confined to the "multiplicity of viewpoints" on which Standish Lawder focuses in his comparison between avant-garde film and cubist painting. Other characteristics include the prismatic fracturing of images and the floating interpenetration of moving objects in Léger's *Ballet mécanique*, the interplay of planes and the spatial ambiguities in Richter's *Rhythmus* films, the optical experiments with light and shadow in Man Ray's *Return to Reason* and the technical manipulation of visual perception in Duchamp's *Anémic Cinèma*. Indeed, avant-garde cinema appropriates a whole range of features from the formal vocabulary and the principal anti-mimetic stance of the early avant-garde movements and transfers them onto a new plane, one that easily embraces beauty and technology, abstract animation and the use of optical and technical means of artistic production. The photomontage of the dadaists is avant-garde cinema's sympathetic companion.

IV.

While the liberation from mimetic functions with the advance of mechanical means of reproduction represents the core of the first phase of avant-gardist endeavours, the second phase marked by the readymade and the photomontage and their half-sister, the surrealist concept of automatic writing, represents a dialectical reversal of the initial trend. Industrially produced materials and the technical media of photography and film were incorporated into art production. Any attempt to continue with the construction of the genealogy of the avant-garde beyond this threshold, however, meets with two major difficulties.

The first of these is of a historical nature. Since the late 1920s and manifestly since the early 1930s the avant-garde is in obvious retreat. The "long depression" of which Lyotard speaks, that lasted "from the thirties until the end of the 'reconstruction' in the mid-fifties" (Lyotard 1993: 254), did not offer the space, let alone the incentive, for radical artistic experimentation. Just the opposite. A massive and severe clamp-down on all modernist and avant-gardist art concepts and techniques occurred almost simultaneously from various sides. The onslought originated from the fascist campaign against "degenerate art" following the seizure of power by Hitler in 1933, and at the same time from the socialist campaign against "formalist, decadent" art concepts accompanying the launch of the doctrine of "socialist realism" at the First All-Union Congress of Writers in Moscow in 1934. The books that burnt on the night of 10 May 1933, and the pictures that were shown at the infamous exhibition of "Degenerate Art" in Munich in 1937, branded works from the whole spectrum of the expressionist and dadaist art movements. And discussions of the concept of "socialist realism" very soon directed its fiercest attacks on the genuine avant-gardist technique of montage. The dispute between Georg Lukács and Ernst Bloch in the context of the expressionism debate was the pinnacle of this persecution of avant-gardist techniques. The combined onslaught of fascist and socialist cultural politics sealed the fate of the avant-garde.

In addition, we know that the exile of many writers and artists during the 1930s and 40s was not the school for exciting new experiments, but rather the place where familiar, traditional concepts tried and tested for many times were reactivated. Even such a tantalising moment as the joint formulation of the manifesto "For an Independent Revolutionary Art" by Breton and Trotsky in Mexico in 1938 bore more the hallmark of a helpless gesture far away from the political and cultural struggles of the day than any real prospect of fulfilment. The progressive politicisation of the arts for which Benjamin had still hoped for in 1936 did not take place. The aestheticisation of politics ruled the day. Strangely enough, critics of such enlightened political stature as Hans Magnus Enzensberger, Octavio Paz, Peter Bürger and Jürgen Habermas have come to speak of the "anachronism", the "death" and the "failure" of the avant-garde without making any reference to the repressive political context in which the avant-garde vanished (Enzensberger 1980; Paz 1989; Bürger 1984; Habermas 1981). These assessments placing the avant-garde in a political vacuum did not only generate questionable speculations about the reasons for its decline, but they had also severe consequences for the way in which the neo-avant-garde of the 1950s and 60s was approached. And this represents the second complication in creating a clear trajectory of the avant-garde's genealogy.

If one assumes that the historical avant-garde perished because of its own "aporias" and "mistakes", then its repetition or reactivation in the 1950s and 60s cannot make any historical sense. Not surprisingly, therefore, Enzensberger and Paz, Bürger and Habermas unanimously dismiss the neo-avant-garde as "anachronistic", "inauthentic" , a mere "ritual repetition" of the "deeds and gestures of 1917". However, if one takes it that the avant-garde initially forfeited some of its innovatory edge in adapting to effective political activities in the late 1920s and was eventually quashed in its existence and artistic presence by the combined forces of fascist and socialist cultural politics, then the re-appropriation of artistic strategies and techniques of the historical avant-garde in several neo-avant-gardist movements of the post-war period turns into a highly important historical operation. In his "Theses on the Philosophy of History", which clearly bear the mark of the "dark days" of 1940, Benjamin reminds us that "in every era the attempt must be made anew to wrest tradition away from a conformism that is about to overpower it" (Benjamin 1973a: 257). The inappropriateness of this remark lies only in the fact that the "tradition" here at stake is none other than the avant-garde. What the neo-avant-garde of the 1950s and 60s achieved, even if it were merely repeating the deeds and gestures of 1917, was to reconnect the contemporary development of the arts with the lost practice of the early decades. Hal Foster and Benjamin Buchloh have recently promoted such a constructive perspective for the understanding of neo-avant-garde activities (cf Foster 1996; Buchloh 2000).

The elaboration of a sound conception of the relationship between the historical avant-garde and the neo-avant-garde is one of the crucial requirements of any theory of the avant-garde. Foster discovers such a conception even at the bottom of Bürger's theory, notwithstanding the dismissive attitude in which Bürger approaches the neo-avant-garde. It is the famous model of the repetition of all great events in world history which Karl Marx put forward in "The Eighteenth Brumaire of Louis Bonapart". The model attributes distinct characteristics to both occurrences of the repeated event. It appears "the first time as tragedy, the second time as farce" (Marx 1960: 115). One may indeed see a faint imprint of the old mentor's historiography in Bürger's diagnoses of the "failure" of the avant-garde in the first instance and the "inauthentic gestures of protest" attributed to the neo-avant-garde in the second. Yet, Foster finds Marx's model insufficient and Bürger's analysis questionable in several respects. He therefore offers an alternative historiographic model based on the Freudian concept of "deferred action". Repetition here brings to the fore traumatic events that had been repressed and opens up the possibility of working them through.

However, since I find the concept of "deferred action" rather at odds with the actual manifestation of the avant-garde in the 1910s and 20s, at odds also with the meaning of repetition as an act of re-cuperating a lost, but advanced artistic practice, I prefer to follow a suggestion which Benjamin outlined in his "Theses on the Philosophy of History". Distinguishing between the chronological approach of the "historicist" and the "constructive principle" observed by the "historical materialist", Benjamin writes:

> Historicism contents itself with establishing a causal connection between various moments in history. But no fact that is a cause is for that very reason historical. [...] A historian who takes this as his point of departure stops telling the sequence of events like the beads of a rosary. Instead, he grasps the constellation which his own era has formed with a definite earlier one. (Benjamin 1973a: 265)

To "blast open the continuum of history" and "fan the spark of hope in the past" is described by Benjamin as the task of the historian (Benjamin 1973a: 257, 263). The artist of the neo-avant-garde is such a historian in relation to preceding tradition. To him the historical avant-garde was neither a tragedy nor a trauma, but represented the most advanced position artists had achieved in the practice and understanding of artistic production in the modern age. To re-ignite this position after a long period of recess is the task to which he set himself.

Reconnecting with the lost practice of the historical avant-garde put the neo-avant-garde "ahead" of the deeply conservative and conformist trends of the 1950s. Yet, one may wish to put the stakes of avant-gardism higher than that. The neo-avant-garde will fully live up to its name only when the reconnection with the past proves to be the motor to a distinct own advance of the practice and understanding of artistic production. Little preliminary work has been done to explore this terrain. It is again above all to Buchloh's and Foster's credit that not only the question of the relationship between the avant-gardes, but also the question of the "specificity" of the neo-avant-garde have been clearly posed and pursued in a number of essays. What follows is an attempt to add to these a few comments on a particularly illuminating, particularly exemplary case of a reconnection with the past and a specific advance of the artistic practice beyond the thresholds of the historical avant-garde.

V.

The work of Andy Warhol has often been linked to Duchamp's concept of the readymade. In particular the silk-screened pictures of Marlon Brando and Elvis Presley, Marilyn Monroe and Elizabeth Taylor, Jackie Kennedy and the Mona Lisa which Warhol produced since 1962 have been described as an "extension" of the dadaist legacy of the readymade. So it seems that after the "dark days" of the 1930s and 40s, during which the avant-garde vanished under the pressure of political persecution, Duchamp's attack on the traditional categories of the "originality" and "uniqueness" of the work of art and his critique of the reliance of the traditional notion of art on the skill of the artist's hand were re-appropriated for contemporary artistic production in and through Warhol's work. Duchamp himself has endorsed this view. In a remarkable statement illuminating in respect of both the understanding of his own work as well as the interpretation of the image repetition in Warhol's pictures he characterises pop art as a "return to 'conceptual' painting". "If you take a Campbell's Soup Can and repeat it 50 times", he explained, then "you are not interested in the retinal image. What interests you is the concept that wants to put 50 Campbell's Soup Cans on a canvas" (cf. Beyeler 2000: 8).

But what is the concept behind putting 50 Campbell's Soup cans or 112 green Coca-Cola bottles on a canvas? It is the concept of serialisation, a concept that undermines the notion of the uniqueness of the artwork more radically than the invention of the readymade and its replicas had done. Serialisation appears in Warhol's work in two forms, as repetition of the same motif in a series of pictures and as multiple reproduction of the same image on one canvas. Surprisingly, serialisation became a feature of Warhol's pictures even before the practice of multiple mechanical reproduction became his main working method. The Campbell's Soup cans and the Coca-Cola bottles were hand-painted. This was certainly not in the trajectory of Duchamp's conceptual thinking. However, the content of the pictures anticipated the radical change which Warhol would introduce to his working method in the coming years. The introduction of the photographic silk-screening process was the decisive step by which Warhol aligned his working method with the content of his paintings. It was through this step that he made a conspicuous and quite specific contribution to the advance of avant-garde art.

The first move towards the production of the silk-screened pictures was the selection of a ready-made, two-dimensional image. The image was not composed, invented or created. It was taken from a pre-processed mass-produced source, at best a press photograph. All of Warhol's pictures are thus "multiples", all of them defy the category of original. Though he portrayed several glamorous Hollywood stars, Warhol made no effort to maintain or even heighten the "aura" of the depicted person. Just the opposite. Through the choice of the images he rather undermined the cult value of the stars. The images are coarse, offering hardly more than the contours of the person's face or body. They were mechanically produced and reproduced. At the outset of the composition thus stands, as Buchloh puts it, "mechanically reproduced ready-made imagery" (Buchloh 2001: 15). Already in the selection of his source material Warhol was thus alluding to the legacy of Duchamp. Also in his conceptual thinking he soon moved closer to the concept of the readymade. While for Duchamp the readymade functioned as an alternative to painting, Warhol now also declared that "hand painting" was a matter of the past:

> In my art work hand painting would take much too long and
> anyway that's not the age we live in. Mechanical means are
> *today*, and using them I can get more art to more people. Art
> should be for everyone. (Cf. Buchloh 2001: 5)

Yet, while they agreed on the obsolete nature of hand painting, the
alternative perspectives developed by Duchamp and Warhol differed. While Duchamp gave up painting altogether and replaced it
with the procedures of selecting and (dis-)placing ready-made objects, Warhol opened up new possibilities for the production of
images, experimenting with the integration of mechanical means and
mechanical working methods "of the age" into image production.

Even in retrospect Warhol remembered the excitement that accompanied the introduction of the photographic silk-screening
process into his work:

> In August '62 I started doing silk-screens. The rubber-stamp
> method I'd been using to repeat images suddenly seemed too
> home-made; I wanted something stronger that gave more of an
> assembly-line effect. With silk-screening, you pick a photograph,
> blow it up, transfer it in glue onto silk, and then roll ink across it
> so the ink goes through the silk but not the glue. That way you
> get the same image, slightly different each time. It was all so
> simple — quick and chancy. I was thrilled with it. (Warhol 1980:
> 22)

It is through both the choice of the mass-produced photographic
source material and the introduction of the largely mechanical
working process of the silk-screening that Warhol extended
Duchamp's concept of the readymade to the realm of painting.
Rather than give up painting altogether, he developed a novel practice of image production in which "mechanical methods of today"
dominate the working process. Even the hand of the artist had some
minor tasks to fulfil in the process of creating the multiple, such as
applying different background colours to the canvas, tracing the
outlines of individual colour areas with pencil and rolling and
pressing the ink with a squeegee through the fabric of the silk. The
working process thus implied neither a "cutting off" of the artist's
hand as Duchamp had suggested (cf. Naumann 1999: 19), nor a
celebration of the personal touch of the artist as a mark of his subjectivity to which the New York School of abstract expressionist

painters had just returned. The basis of artistic production, however, are no longer oil, palette and the skill of the hand, but means and methods of mechanical reproduction: photography and silkscreen printing.

Andy Warhol: *Marilyn Monroe (Twenty Times)* (1962)

Warhol did what he could to foreground the specific nature of the production of his multiples. With the coarse application of colours to individual areas of the picture and the variations in the sharpness and "blackness" of the eventual imprint of the image the pictures maintained a touch of hand-made quality. However, through the selection of images of clearly photographic origin, through the serial use of the same ready-made source material over and over again and through the multiple reproduction of the same image on a single canvas the pictures variously draw attention to their reproductive nature and achieve the desired "assembly-line effect". Thus we encounter the same image of Marilyn in a series of innumerable colour variations, and we encounter four and twenty and one hundred Marilyns in one frame. Already in 1962 Warhol also introduced the form of a diptych presenting 25 Marilyns in colour and 25 in black and white, thus juxtaposing images produced with the full artistic armature, including pencil tracing, stencils and various colour applications, with others made purely by pressing the black ink through the prepared screen. In "Gold Marilyn" and "Silver Liz" he produced a variation on this procedure. A panel showing nothing but the golden or silver background colour is juxtaposed with a panel that shows the same colour imprinted with the familiar images of Marilyn and Liz. With the serial repetition of Marilyn's image these forms of juxtaposition share one overwhelming effect: "The spectator's attention", this is how Simon Wilson puts it, "is directed away from the image as such and towards a consideration of what the artist has done with it" (Wilson 1999: 316). Warhol himself confirms this observation: "The more you look at the same exact thing, the more the meaning goes away" (Warhol 1980: 50).

Ultimately, what Warhol did with the ready-made image is twofold. Firstly, he drained the image of its aura, the semblance of its uniqueness. "Thirty Mona Lisas are better than one", is the ironic title comment by which Warhol underscores this aspect. Secondly, with the silk-screening process he transformed the notion of painting forever. None other than Gerhard Richter confirmed this: "Warhol legitimised the mechanical", he remarked (G. Richter 2003: 32). The Marilyns and Lizs, Jackies and Mona Lisas stand out as manifestations of a new form of image production that offered an alternative not only to the traditional art of hand painting, but also to the various modes of abstraction as developed by the early avant-garde as well as to the grand subjective rhetoric of abstract expressionism. Warhol's work redefined painting as a working process in which a ready-made image is transformed into an artwork by means of photographic technique, silkscreen printing and the application of background colour. In Warhol's work painting's traditional devotion to an outdated artisan practice with all its inherent allegiances to originality and uniqueness, authenticity and individual authorship had finally given way to the new practice of the multiple, a practice that maintained a lively communication and exchange with the mechanical and serial processes dominant in other spheres of contemporary life. Not surprisingly, Richter confirmed this reorientation of the age-old art of painting: "I am a painter. I love to paint. Using photographs was the only possible way to continue to paint" (G. Richter 2003: 32).

VI.

If neither Marx's model of "tragedy" and "farce", nor the Freudian reading of repetition as a condition for the working through of traumatic events, provide adequate guidance for the construction of the avant-garde's genealogy, how else can this course of innovations and disruptions be summarised in a meaningful manner — for the sake of illustration as well as for the purpose of further testing? It seems to me that the tripartite structure of the dialectical processes of all matters and ideas that Hegel has left to us describes the phases of the avant-garde's advances rather well.

The avant-garde was "ahead" of mainstream developments in art, literature and film in the modern age due to its awareness that the advent of technical media of representation posed a radical challenge to the age-old function of all arts and due to its constructive response to this challenge. The response unfolded in three stages. The avant-garde initially abandoned the traditional mimetic task of the arts and replaced it with an exploration of the properties of the artistic materials and a range of alternative, widely abstract forms of artistic composition. The traditional emphasis on the autonomy of the work of art was here upheld throughout.

In its second phase the avant-garde moved towards an opposite, antithetical response. Opening up the realm of art and incorporating mechanically produced and reproduced objects and images as source materials of artistic production was the outstanding characteristic of this phase. It was marked by the inventions of the readymade, the photomontage and the programmes of dadaist poems made from "scraps and headlines of newspapers".

What followed once the "dark days" of the 1930s and 40s had been overcome was neither a meaningless repetition of the gestures of yesterday, nor an independent and unrelated revolution in the American arts world. In its best moments the neo-avant-garde re-appropriated a lost practice and advanced it to a new level where ready-made images and forms of hand painting, the technology of photography and mechanical printing procedures easily communicate with each other in the production of images. For the future of the avant-garde and its status as an "ongoing", if discontinuous, project such communication augurs well. The semblance of the autonomy of the artwork, however, has vanished forever.

BIBLIOGRAPHY

Apollinaire, Guillaume
1962   *The Cubist Painters*. New York: Wittenborn.

Apollonio, Umbro (ed.)
1973   *Futurist Manifestos*. London: Thames and Hudson.

Baldassari, Anne
1997   *Picasso und die Photographie*. Munich: Schirmer/Mosel.

Benjamin, Walter
1973a   "Theses on the Philosophy of History". In: Benjamin, *Illuminations*. Fontana, 255–266.

1973b   "The Work of Art in the Age of Mechanical Reproduction". In: Benjamin, *Illuminations*. Fontana, 219–253.

1983   "The Author as Producer". In: Benjamin, *Understanding Brecht*. London: Verso, 85–103.

Beyeler, Ernst, et al.
2000   *Andy Warhol. Series and Singles*. Basel: Fondation Beyeler.

Bowness, Alan
1972   *Modern European Art*. London: Thames & Hudson.

Boccioni, Umberto, et al.
1973   "Futurist Painting: Technical Manifesto 1910". In: Apollonio 1973, 27–31.

Breton, André
1948   "Max Ernst". In: Max Ernst, *Beyond Painting*. New York: Wittenborn, 177.

Buchheim, Lothar-Günther
1956   *Die Künstlergemeinschaft Brücke*. Feldafing: Buchheim.

Buchloh, Benjamin
1984   "Theorizing the Avant-Garde". In: *Art in America*, November 1984, 19–21.

2000   *Neo-Avantgarde and Culture Industry. Essays on European and American Art from 1955 to 1975*. Cambridge, Mass.: MIT Press.

2001   "Any Warhol's One-Dimensional Art: 1956–1966". In: *Andy Warhol*, ed. Annette Michelsen. Cambridge, Mass.: MIT Press, 1–46.

Bürger, Peter
1974a   *Theorie der Avantgarde*. Frankfurt am Main: Suhrkamp.

1974b   "Nachwort zur zweiten Auflage". In: *Theorie der Avantgarde*. Frankfurt am Main: Suhrkamp.

1984   *Theory of the Avant-Garde*. Minneapolis: University of Minnesota Press.

1992   *The Decline of Modernism*. Cambridge: Polity.

Dachy, Marc
1990   *The Dada Movement 1915–1923*. New York: Rizzoli.

Döblin, Alfred
1963   "An Romanautoren und ihre Kritiker. Berliner Programm". In: Döblin, *Aufsätze zur Literatur*, 15–19.

Dulac, Germaine
1978   "The Avant-Garde Cinema". In: *The Avant-Garde Film. A Reader of Theory and Criticism*, ed. P. Adams Sitney. New York: New York University Press, 43–48.

Enzensberger, Hans Magnus
1980   "Die Aporien der Avantgarde". In: Enzensberger, *Einzelheiten II. Poesie und Politik*. Frankfurt: Suhrkamp, 50–80.

Foster, Hal
1996   "Who's Afraid of the Neo-Avant-Garde?" In: Foster, *The Return of the Real. The Avant-Garde at the End of the Century*. Cambridge, Mass.: MIT Press, 1–32.

Friedberg, Anne
1994   *Window Shopping. Cinema and the Postmodern*. Berkeley: University of California Press.

Fry, Edward F.
1966   *Cubism*. London: Thames and Hudson.

Habermas, Jürgen
1981   "Modernity versus Postmodernity". In: *New German Critique* 22, 3–14.

Honnef, Klaus
1992   "Symbolic Form as a Vivid Cognitive Principle. An Essay on Montage". In: *John Heartfield*, ed. by Peter Pachnicke and Klaus Honnef. New York: Harry N. Abrams, 49–64.

Huelsenbeck, Richard et al
1992   "Dadaistisches Manifest". In: *The Dada Almanac*. London: Atlas Press, 44–49.

Isherwood, Christopher
1977   *Goodbye to Berlin*. London: Granada.

Jameson, Fredric
1983   "Postmodernism and Consumer Society". In: Hal Foster (ed.), *The Anti-Aesthetic Essays on Postmodern Culture*. Seattle: Bay Press, 111–125.

1991   "The Cultural Logic of Late Capitalism". In: Jameson, *Postmodernism and the Cultural Logic of Late Capitalism*. London: Verso, 1–54.

Kandinsky, Vassily
1968   "On the Problem of Form". In: Herschel B. Chipp (ed.), *Theories of Modern Art*. Berkeley: University of California Press, 155–170.

Lawder, Standish D.
1975   *The Cubist Cinema*. New York: New York University Press.

Lessing, Gotthold Ephraim
    1874   *Laocoon*, trans. Robert Phillimore. London: MacMillan.

Lyotard, Jean-François
    1984   "Answering the Question: What is Postmodernism?" In: Lyotard, *The Postmodern Condition: A Report on Knowledge*. Manchester: Manchester University Press, 71–82.

    1985   "Note on the Meaning of 'Post-'". In: Lyotard, *The Postmodern Explained: Corresponce 1982–1985*. Minneapolis: University of Minnesota Press, 64–68.

    1993   "The Sublime and the Avant-Garde". In: *Postmodernism. A Reader*, ed. Thomas Docherty. New York: Harvester Wheatsheaf, 244–256.

Marx, Karl
    1960   "Der achtzehnte Brumaire des Louis Bonaparte". In: Marx / Friedrich Engels, *Werke*, vol. 8. Berlin: Dietz, 115–207.

Naumann, Francis M.
    1999   *Marcel Duchamp. The Art of Making Art in the Age of Mechanical Reproduction*. New York: Harry N. Abrams.

Panofsky, Erwin
    1991   *Perspective as Symbolic Form*, trans. Chrostopher S. Wood. New York: Zone Books.

Paz, Octavio
    1989   "Der Tod der Avantgarde". In: Paz, *Die andere Zeit der Dichtung*. Frankfurt: Suhrkamp, 188–206.

Poggioli, Renato
    1968   *The Theory of the Avant-Garde*. Cambridge, Mass.: Harvard University Press.

Richter, Hans
    1965   *Dada. Art and Anti-Art*. London: Thames and Hudson.

Richter, Gerhard
    2003   *Atlas. The Reader*. London: Whitechapel.

Scharf, Aaron
    1983   *Art and Photography*. Harmondsworth: Penguin.

Selz, Peter
  1963   "John   Heartfield's   Photomontages".   In: *The
              Massachusetts Review*, vol. 4, 309–336.

Sitney, P. Adams
  1978   "Introduction". In: *The Avant-Garde Film. A Reader of
              Theory and Criticism*, ed. P. A. Sitney. New York: New
              York University Press, vii–xiv.

Tretiakov, Sergei
  1977   "John   Heartfield   montiert".   In: *Montage: John
              Heartfield*, ed. Eckhard Siepmann. Berlin: Elefanten
              Press, 168–175.

Tzara, Tristan
  1916   "Note pour les Bourgeois". In: *Cabaret Voltaire*, ed.
              Hugo Ball. Zurich, 6–7.

Warhol, Andy, and Pat Hackett
  1980   *POPism. The Warhol '60s*. New York: Harcourt Brace
              Jovanovich.

Wilson, Simon
  1999   "Pop". In: *Modern Art. Impressionism to Post-Modern-
              ism*, ed. David Britt. London: Thames & Hudson, 305–
              357.

Wilhelm Worringer and the Historical Avant-Garde

RHYS W. WILLIAMS

It may seem paradoxical to contribute to a volume which seeks to explore the multi-facetted interrelationships between the historical and neo-avant-garde by focussing attention on a relatively obscure German art historian whose connections even to the historical German avant-garde are at best tenuous. Certainly, the case of Worringer seems to confirm neither Peter Bürger's theory, nor the counter-argument which emphasizes the technical advances of the new media. My justification is supplied by Dietrich Scheunemann's essay on "Photography and Painting", which introduced the volume *European Avant-Garde: New Perspectives*. Here Scheunemann writes:

> It is the abandonment of the age-old spatial conception of the Renaissance in cubist painting, not the literary celebration of roaring racing cars in the futurist manifesto, nor any ideological project resembling the proposed intention of sublating art into the practice of life, that marked the beginning and served as a constant reference point of the avant-garde's epochal innovation. (Scheunemann 2000: 16)

I shall argue that Worringer was a key figure in that "abandonment of the age-old spatial conception of the Renaissance" and that his cultural theories helped to shape thinking about modernism and the avant-garde in surprising ways. From the outset, I should like to acknowledge the work of Neil H. Donahue, whose excellent essay collection *Invisible Cathedrals. The Expressionist Art History of Wilhelm Worringer* (1995) was the first major attempt to tease out the ramifications of Worringer's approach for the avant-garde.

Wilhelm Worringer is one of the very few members of the academic community who could boast that his doctoral dissertation was in print throughout his own life and beyond. Indeed, it is still in print today. That thesis, entitled *Abstraktion und Einfühlung: Ein Beitrag zur Stilpsychologie*, was submitted in 1906 and first published in Neuwied in 1907 as a dissertation. Somewhat unusually, it was recommended to, and reviewed favourably by, the writer Paul Ernst, whose article in *Kunst und Künstler* was the first to argue that the work provided a historico-philosophical explanation for the cultural manifestations of the present and swiftly led to its publication in book form the following year. That a doctoral thesis should have had such a profound impact, not only for art historians and theorists, but also for generations of creative writers and intellectuals, is, I think, unprecedented. All the more surprising is that it does not deal, even indirectly, with contemporary art and is wholly historical in its focus. Yet, as a number of critics have pointed out, Worringer's work addresses with urgency and no little rhetorical panache the artistic and cultural concerns of his day. And it is for his contemporary relevance, rather than as a disinterested academic scholar, that Worringer is remembered.

After clearing the ground by insisting that the work of art has organic integrity equal to nature, but is wholly independent of nature, *Abstraktion und Einfühlung* takes as its starting-point Theodor Lipps's theory of empathy: the notion that the work of art maximizes our capacity for empathy, that beauty derives from our sense of being able to identify with an object. While conceding that a mimetic urge exists in man, Worringer denies any necessary connection between *mimesis* and all art: if Egyptian art was highly stylized, he argues, this was not because its artists were incompetent and failed to reproduce external reality accurately, but because Egyptian art answered a radically different psychological need. The psychological disposition of a given period, Worringer argues, always seeks its fullest realisation in art. The art of a given period, then, will be the stylistic expression of the psychology of that period, the relationship which exists in that period between man and his surroundings. In mimetic works, he argues, we derive satisfaction from "objectified delight in the self"; the aim of the artist is to maximize our capacity for empathising with the work. This kind of art springs, psychologically, from a confidence in the world as it is, a satisfaction in its forms, which is embodied in Classical and Renaissance art. But Worringer insists that this art of empathy is but one pole of aesthetic experience:

> Just as the urge to empathy, as a prerequisite of aesthetic experience, finds its gratification in the beauty of the organic, the urge to abstraction finds its beauty, in turn, in the life-denying inorganic, in the crystalline, or, more generally, in abstract laws and necessity. (Worringer 1976: 49)

The urge to abstraction, exemplified variously by Egyptian, Byzantine, Gothic, or primitive art, articulates a wholly different response to the universe: it expresses man's insecurity and seeks to answer transcendental or spiritual needs:

> What are the psychological prerequisites of the urge to abstraction? We have to look for them in the psychological response of those people to the cosmos, in their sense of the world. While the drive for empathy is conditioned by a happy pantheistic familiarity between man and the world which surrounds him, the drive for abstraction springs from a great inner anxiety of man in the face of the external world and corresponds in the religious sphere to a transcendental colouring of all ideas. I should like to call this condition an immense spiritual dread of space [*eine ungeheure geistige Raumscheu*]. (Worringer 1976: 49)

In certain historical periods, Worringer argues, man is confidently assertive and finds satisfaction in "objectified delight in the self" and can abandon himself in contemplation of the external world; but, in periods of anxiety and uncertainty, man seeks to abstract objects from their contingency, transforming them into permanent, absolute, transcendental forms. It is the world feeling [*Weltgefühl*], the psychological state in which mankind finds itself, which leaves its imprint on the work of art. It follows that "what might appear to us as the greatest distortion must have been for the producer of that art the highest beauty and the fulfilment of his artistic urge" (1976: 47).

It is clear that Worringer regards style as the expressive reification of artistic volition [*Kunstwollen*]. While it is the psychological
drive which is paramount, this inscribes itself into the artistic possibilities available at any given time. Thus to explore a style should
enable us to reconstruct the world feeling which it expresses. The
dangers of circularity of argument are all too apparent, but
Worringer confines his attention to two broad styles corresponding
to the two distinct kind of world feeling: empathy, which produces
an art reflecting man comfortably at home in a familiar world, and
abstraction, which is determined by man's sense of being lost or
overwhelmed by the world. Abstract art, then, is an expression of
man's primordial fear of open space in an inexplicable and threatening universe. Worringer's enthusiasm for primitive abstraction is
shot through with the visionary possibility that the modern age is
about to embark on a phase of abstraction, conditioned not by instinct, but by the realization of the limits of rational cognition:

> To employ an audacious comparison it is as though the instinct
> for the "thing in itself" is strongest in primitive man. The in-
> creasing intellectual domination of the outside world and
> familiarity with it signify a blunting, a dimming of this instinct.
> Only after the human spirit, after a thousand years of develop-
> ment, has run the whole course of rationalistic cognition, will his
> feeling for "the thing in itself" reawaken as the final renunciation
> of knowledge. What was once instinct is now the ultimate prod-
> uct of knowledge. Cast down from the arrogance of knowledge
> modern man faces the world, just as lost and helpless as primitive
> man. (Worringer 1976: 52)

The prophetic vision makes it easy to appreciate the fascination
which Worringer's theory held for the writers and intellectuals of the
expressionist generation in Germany. He supplied a theoretical justification for the revival of interest in Early German art and for the
simultaneous discovery of primitivism. His theory also had a socio-
logical and epistemological dimension. He seemed to be offering a
parallel between the experience of primitive man and that of the citizen of a modern industrial society. The fear and alienation which
"primitive man" had experienced in the face of a hostile universe
had, he argued, prompted an urge to create fixed, abstract, and geometric forms. While Renaissance individualism had later weakened

the capacity for abstraction, the modern experience of industrialisation, the sense that individual identity was threatened by a hostile mass society, had rekindled the need for abstract forms to counteract a sense of what Marx, among others, had defined as alienation. It seemed to many that Worringer's thesis offered a new blueprint for a modernist aesthetic. Although derived in essence from a skilful appropriation and intermingling of the very different aesthetic theories of Lipps and Riegl, it offered a justification for the formal distortion of post-impressionism and expressionism. As Worringer himself asserts in the closing pages of *Abstraktion und Einfühlung*: "What we are today alienated by as distortion is not the fault of technical inability, but the result of a completely different intention."

The reception of Worringer in England is not my main focus, though T. E. Hulme's essay "Modern Art and its Philosophy", published in *Speculations* (1924) is, to all intents and purposes, a reiteration of Worringer's position, as its author readily acknowledges: "what follows is practically an abstract of Worringer's views" (Hulme 1924: 82). Having summarised Worringer's position, Hulme concludes his essay by taking the argument a step further in relation to Jacob Epstein's sculpture:

> The tendency to abstraction, the desire to turn the organic into something hard and durable, is here at work. Not on something simple. Such as you get in more archaic work, but on something much more complicated. It is, however, the same tendency at work in both. [...] The point that I want to emphasise is that the use of mechanical lines in the new art is in no sense merely a reflection of mechanical environment. It is a result of a change of sensibility which is, I think, the result of a change of attitude which will become increasingly obvious. [...] It seems to me beyond doubt that this, whether you like it or not, is the character of the art that is coming. (Hulme 1924, 107–9)

For Hulme, the re-emergence of abstraction marks the end of Western humanism since the Renaissance and implies a return to a new religious phase. While Worringer's argument remains confined to rather abstract aesthetic and psychological principles, Hulme employs it to reinforce anti-humanist and conservative views. But in extolling what W. Wolfgang Holdheim nicely terms "the abstract charms of machinery" (1979: 344), Hulme's position seems to move towards one which could with ease encompass Italian futurism.

Worringer's second major publication, *Formprobleme der Gotik* (1911), translated by Herbert Read as *Form in Gothic*, developed the closing section of his earlier thesis into a fully-fledged account of Gothic art and architecture. Once again, Worringer operates with a definition of the Gothic which is all-embracing: "Gothic", for him, is all the art of the Western world which was not shaped by classical Mediterranean culture, all art, in short, which was not a direct reproduction of nature. Worringer's remarks on primitive man are of particular interest:

> Confused by the arbitrariness and incoherence of appearances, primitive man lives in a relationship of gloomy spiritual fear to the outer world. [...] Under the pressure of his intense metaphysical anxiety, primitive man brings all his acts and his doings into an encumbering relationship with religion [...]. His art is also an outcome of these secret exorcising ceremonies inasmuch as it endeavours to dam back the arbitrariness of the visual world by the intuitive creation of absolute values. (Worringer 1964: 16–17)

Primitive man was drawn to two-dimensional representation as the appropriate expression of his artistic intention, and even when he engaged in plastic representation, in sculpture, he sought "the greatest possible adherence to cubic compactness [...] by means of a modelling that excludes all spatial, incomprehensible, fortuitous elements. The result of this avoidance of any approximation to life in stylistic purpose was an approximation to abstract cubic elementary forms" (19). Starting with the latent Gothic in early Northern ornament, with its repetition, its geometric pattern, its flowing line, Worringer moves on to examine cathedral statuary, and finally Gothic architecture, with its "will to expression, striving towards the transcendental". As Magdalena Bushart has convincingly argued, Worringer's study of Gothic stimulated an intense fascination with the subject among German artists, critics and publicists. While Worringer was never explicit about the connections between Gothic art and expressionism, his arguments, and perhaps even more significantly his passionate rhetoric, touched a raw nerve in Germany in the period shortly before the First World War. It stimulated a range of discussions about the German cultural tradition, which saw itself embattled in an increasingly threatening political and cultural encirclement. Intellectuals like Wilhelm Hausenstein and Paul Fechter wondered aloud whether a new culture might emerge which was transcendent, in Worringer's sense, and in which the religious and mystical might coalesce with the collective.

Worringer's ideas were accepted with equal enthusiasm on the Right and the Left, among art historians, cultural theorists, and, above all, by artists and writers. I propose here to offer some illustration of that influence. What is striking is that Worringer's impact on his contemporaries has not yet been fully documented. The reasons for that omission are themselves fascinating. Where Worringer attempts to locate his theoretical abstractions in specific historical contexts, the twenty-first century reader may be uncomfortably reminded of the later misuse of such terminology on the extreme Right under National Socialism. Statements like: "the land of the pure Gothic is the Germanic North", a formulation which reflects Worringer's fondness for employing antithetical terms, like North/South, Gothic/Renaissance, abstraction/empathy, have acquired unfortunate ideological connotations. Perhaps this factor helps to explain why Worringer's work has suffered from comparative critical neglect, for despite the undeniable importance of his early writings, and despite many passing references to his achievements, there is, notwithstanding Neil H. Donahue's essay collection, no full-length critical study devoted to him. A secondary factor in his neglect is, paradoxically, rooted in his sheer success: his rehabilitation of abstraction as an aesthetic principle was so enthusiastically received and so widely disseminated as to become a commonplace of German modernism, a fact which ironically tended to obscure his unique contribution to acceptance of that principle.

The most striking example of Worringer's impact on the avant-garde emerges in Carl Einstein's *Negerplastik* (1915). Einstein had been a regular visitor to France before 1914 and thanks to his links with the gallery owner Daniel-Henry Kahnweiler, he gained immediate access to the current work of Picasso and Braque. It is possible that Einstein's interest in African art had been stimulated by the Parisian art scene, by the first cubist paintings and the discovery of African masks by the *Fauves*: Vlaminck, Matisse and Derain. We know that Einstein began amassing material for his *Negerplastik* as early as 1912, but when the study appeared in 1915, it was clear that Einstein's approach and language had been shaped by Worringer's. In a series of short essays in 1914 entitled *Totalität I–V* Einstein outlines the approach which underlies *Negerplastik*. In these essays Einstein maintains that art is not mimetic—its objects do not exist in the empirical world—that each object is constituted in and through an act of seeing. The work of art has, as its end, not the depiction of an object, but the structuring of a way of seeing. The work of art alone succeeds in isolating an object from the web of causal connections in which it is enmeshed and reconstituting it as an object in its own right, returning it, as it were, to a "Ding an sich". The totality in which such a work consists is transcendent, for while causal scientific rationality reduces the individual object to a mere example or illustration, a quantitative extensive model, totality constitutes the qualitative uniqueness, the intensity, of an object. African art, for Einstein, embodies the totality thus defined. Its discovery, contemporary with the arrival of cubism and clearly inspiring cubism, has enabled modern man to resolve the crisis in Western art which has existed since the Renaissance. For Einstein (as for Worringer before him) the Renaissance saw the development of perspective. The spectator was presented with an object which was the product of the artist's point of view and invited to identify with that perspective. The result was the neglect of what Einstein calls "cubic space" [*kubischer Raum*], a dimension which the cubists rediscovered and which made them predisposed to appreciate the potential of African art. Because African art is religious it involves, for Einstein, an inbuilt transcendence which precludes the tacit collusion between artist and viewer characteristic of Western art. Further more, the religious function of the cultic object determines its formal properties which Einstein analyses in a highly technical section of his essay. African art does not present a frontal perspective combined with a suggestion of depth; rather, through surface distortion, it presents a simultaneity of perspectives apprehended in a single act of perception. The static quality of African art results from the way in which movement, successive variousness, is translated into formal spatial qualities. Primitive art (Einstein's illustrations to the volume indicate that he did not distinguish between African and Polynesian art) is once again interpreted with Worringer's psychological theory and stylistic consequences drawn from that theory. And once again religious transcendence is related to the art object. It is clear that Einstein is bent upon relating the revolutionary aesthetic of cubism to African sculpture. As he was later to argue in his *Die Kunst des 20. Jahrhunderts* (1926), "the significance of cubism was this: the translation of the three-dimensional experience of movement into two-dimensional form, without attempting to create the illusion of depth" (69), precisely the terms which he had earlier used of primitive art.

I have argued the case elsewhere for Worringer's writings as the source of Einstein's aesthetic terminology. The fact that Einstein does not explicitly mention Worringer is no evidence of a lack of influence. Not only was Einstein himself notoriously lax in his attributions, but Worringer's thesis had become part of an accepted and commonplace view. It is thanks to Worringer that Einstein attaches religious connotations to his new mode of seeing, which he variously terms Vision, Wunder, Totalität, das Absolute, das Halluzinatorische (or any tautological combination of these). The new way of seeing is intuitive and transcendent; it has the power to overcome the rationalism which has dominated Western Europe since the Renaissance. Einstein's cultural pessimism and his rejection of scientific positivism involve a new positive reappraisal of both the primitive and the medieval. The pre-civilised and the pre-industrial are brought together as a new possibility for twentieth-century man, and they are imbued with quasi-religious intensity and visionary quality. Versions of this vision are found scattered through expressionist theory and practice, from Gustav Landauer's anarcho-socialist anti-industrial revolution to Gottfried Benn's incantatory poetic evocation of a South Sea idyll.

In the interests of exploring some of the parallels between at least the German literary avant-garde and Carl Einstein's notion of primitivism, we need only to cite Einstein's letter to Kahnweiler of 1923: "I have known for a long time that what we call cubism goes far beyond painting". The rejection of a naturalistic, mimetic art, which explains Einstein's enthusiasm for African art (and Worringer's for Gothic art) opens up new possibilities not only for the visual arts, but also for literature. Einstein believed that his own highly experimental text Bebuquin (written between 1906 and 1909 and published in 1912) had succeeded in embodying such a possibility: time and space do not correspond to any empirically perceived reality, but are constituted in and through the narrative. Although Einstein's linguistic dislocation and distortion do not go as far as those of some of his expressionist contemporaries, he clearly views dislocation as a valuable means of disrupting the conventional response to literature. Embodied in his own literary efforts are the cubist presuppositions which he restates in Negerplastik. Seldom have the visual arts and literature been so closely integrated as in the expressionist period; seldom have writers sought more enthusiastically to transpose techniques from painting and sculpture into prose.

Negerplastik has also its thematic repercussions. The motif of a regression to a pre-civilised mode of vision (linked to a non-rational mode of apprehending the world and implying a rejection of what are deemed the bourgeois values of conformism, capitalism and social levelling) is ubiquitous in the literature of expressionism, especially after 1914. The impact of the War is a factor in the reception of Negerplastik. It seemed to many intellectuals, particularly those associated with the anti-war journal Die Aktion, that the War was an inevitable consequence not only of the German, but also of the European intellectual tradition, and that a radical break with that tradition offered the only way forward. The rejection of conventional habits of thought and the advocacy of a new way of seeing, a new epistemology, were associated variously with quasi-religious conversion or political revolution. In Einstein's language Vision was associated with the suspension of the subject-object dichotomy and characterised by "intensity" and "simultaneity", two notions which dominate the early avant-garde. The formal distortion of African art seemed to guarantee both intensity and perspectival simultaneity. In their efforts to define the essence of man, to project the image of the new man, the expressionists had before their own eyes examples of pre-civilized, pre-rational, essentially religious existence which they called primitive, locating it indiscriminately in the world of Gothic art, in the South Seas, or in Africa. The motif of regression, expressed in its most extreme form in Gottfried Benn's lines: "O daß wir unsere Ururahnen wären / Ein Klümpchen Schleim in einem warmen Moor" (Benn 1959–61: 125), the peeling away of the layers of bourgeois civilisation, is the thematic correlative of the formal distortion of syntax and perspective which the expressionist quest for intensity and simultaneity produced. The Pathos, the intensity, of expressionist dramatic language is the equivalent of the "fixed ecstasy" [fixierte Ekstase] which Einstein defined as the essence of the African mask. The taste for the African is but one element of modernism, but, in his definition of African art which owes much to Worringer, Einstein manages to smuggle in most other aspects.

It is difficult within the scope of this paper to do justice to the influence exerted by Worringer over the expressionist generation in Germany, suffice it to say that his definition of abstraction, with all the implications which attended it, dominated expressionist ideas about the medieval and the primitive. Why, then, should Worringer's contribution have been so neglected? There are a number of reasons which I shall rehearse here. First of all, Worringer's theory addresses contemporary art only by implication. Charles W. Haxthausen makes the point explicitly: "So far as I have been able to determine, not once in the criticism he wrote on the modern movement between 1911 and 1925 did he mention the name of a single German artist, of a single avant-garde group; not once did he name, let alone discuss, a single German work" (Donahue 1995: 127). Direct evidence of his engagement with the avant-garde is quite simply absent. Secondly, Worringer chose in 1920 to distance himself emphatically from expressionism in an essay "Questions about Contemporary Art" [Künstlerische Zeitfragen]. In that essay, Worringer's bleak assessment is that modern plastic art had failed to give expression to the spirit of the time and had become marginal to modern life. expressionist art was, for him, the last desperate attempt to claim that painting and sculpture were sociologically relevant. For Worringer, it was scholarship alone which could carry out this task. But Worringer's sometime friend Georg Lukács was to seize upon this essay to support his famous denunciation of expressionism in 1934. It seemed, then, that Worringer was now repudiating the very thesis which he had advanced so successfully in the pre-war period, though a closer reading suggests that it is only art which has failed and not expressionist writing. The polarization of German politics during the late 1920s seemed to place Lukács on the opposite side of the fence to Worringer, however closely their original perspectives had been. Thirdly, as Neil Donahue has shown in his excellent article "From Worringer to Baudrillard and Back", Worringer was capable in his study Egyptian Art (1927) of radically revising his original view of Egyptian art as the purest form of abstraction, viewing it in the latter years of the Weimar Republic as an art which embodies the threatening forces of urban-technological modernity. Here, Egyptian art clearly stands as a cipher for the kind of American commercialisation which Worringer now wished to attack. Finally, the language Worringer employs has been discredited by its subsequent associations. When Worringer writes, at the end of his Form in Gothic, that Gothic is "a phenomenon not belonging to any age but rather in its deepest foundations an ageless racial phenomenon, deeply rooted in the innermost constitution of Northern man, and, for this reason, not to be uprooted by the levelling action of the European Renaissance", the reader of the twenty-first century cannot feel entirely comfortable, even if Worringer adds: "In any case we must not understand race in the narrow sense of racial purity: here the word race must include all the peoples in the composition of which the Germans have played a decisive part. And that applies to the greater part of Europe." (Worringer 1964: 180)

Worringer himself was not unaware of the fact that his two earliest works overshadowed all that he subsequently wrote. After spending the whole of the First World War on active service, he subsequently taught at the University of Bonn, before moving to Königsberg in 1928, where he remained until 1945, when he was forced to flee. He relocated to the University of Halle in the Soviet Zone. In 1950, a year after the founding of the German Democratic Republic, he left East Germany for the West, settling in Munich, where he died in 1965. For the 1948 edition of *Abstraction and Empathy* he supplied a foreword which was no doubt intended to lend his work a more socially relevant tenor. He notes how the inspiration for his dissertation came to him in the Musée du Trocadéro in Paris when he witnessed the great German sociologist Georg Simmel entering the museum. Over forty years after the event he foregrounds not the ethnographical exhibits (the same exhibits, incidentally, which are featured in Einstein's *Negerplastik*), nor even the topical associations with contemporary French art, but Simmel's chance presence at the conception of his great work. It would be churlish to suggest that Worringer is merely seeking to ingratiate himself with the cultural functionaries of the Soviet Zone. He is attempting, I think, something much more significant, namely, to suggest that his analysis of the crisis faced by modern man in the metropolis, and projected by him into his definition of primitive man, is more sociologically acute than readers at the time appreciated. He is, as it were, claiming for himself the kind of social analysis which Simmel displays in essays more or less contemporary with *Abstraktion und Einfühlung*. Simmel opens his essay "The Metropolis and Mental Life" (1903) with the following assertion:

> The deepest problems of modern life derive from the claim of the individual to preserve the autonomy of his existence in the face of overwhelming social forces, of historical heritage, of external culture, and of the technique of life. The fight with nature which primitive man has to wage for his *bodily* existence attains in this modern form its latest transformation. (Simmel 1997: 174–5)

In defining the art of primitive man as a necessary psychological response to overwhelming forces, Worringer was simultaneously seeking to offer modern man in the metropolis an aesthetic possibility, through distortion and abstraction, of preserving the autonomy of his existence. In so doing he makes his valuable contribution to the German avant-garde.

BIBLIOGRAPHY

Benn, Gottfried
  1959–61 *Gesammelte Werke in vier Bänden*, ed. Dieter Wellershoff, Wiesbaden: Limes.

Bushart, Magdalena
  1990 *Der Geist der Gotik und die expressionistische Kunst*, Munich: S. Schreiber.

Einstein, Carl
  1926 *Die Kunst des 20. Jahrhunderts*, Berlin: Propyläen Verlag.

Donahue, Neil H. (ed.)
  1995 *Invisible Cathedrals: The Expressionist Art History of Wilhelm Worringer*, Ann Arbor: University of Michigan Press.

Holdheim, W. Wolfgang
  1979 "Wilhelm Worringer and the Polarity of Understanding". In: *Boundary*, vol. 2, 339–358.

Scheunemann, Dietrich
    2000   "On Photography and Painting. Prolegomena to a New Theory of the Avant-Garde". In: Scheunemann (ed.), *European Avant-Garde: New Perspectives.* Amsterdam, Atlanta, GA: Rodopi.

Simmel, Georg
    1997   "The Metropolis and Mental Life". In: *Simmel on Culture: Selected Writings,* ed. David Frisby and Mike Featherstone, London: Sage.

Worringer, Wilhelm
    1976   *Abstraktion und Einfühlung. Ein Beitrag zur Stilpsychologie,* Munich: Piper (first published in 1908). Quotations from the text refer to this edition and have been translated by the author.

    1964   *Form in Gothic,* translated by Herbert Read, London: Alec Tiranti (first published in 1927).

On the Historiographic Distinction between Historical and Neo-Avant-Garde

HUBERT VAN DEN BERG

I.

When aesthetic avant-garde movements of the 20th century are discussed in literary and art historical studies, it has become common practice, in particular in a German context, to distinguish between so-called "historical" and so-called "neo-avant-garde" movements. This distinction is sometimes made explicitly, but in many more cases implicitly, simply by the fact that studies pretending to be studies on *the* avant-garde are actually confined to the period before the Second World War, the period of the so-called historical avant-garde.

On first sight the distinction between a historical and a neo-avant-garde in 20th-century European (here: also including American) art (here: also including literary) history might be regarded only a question of chronology, a matter of periodization: a dichotomy between avant-garde movements before and avant-garde movements after the Second World War. Two observations may favour this chronological distinction.

First of all, there can be no doubt that the European aesthetic avant-garde movements of the 20th century had their heydays in two distinct periods. A first wave of avant-garde activity started in the

1910s and ended in the 1930s, with a peak in the first years after the First World War, a second wave started in the 1950s and ended more or less in 1970s, with a peak around the tumultuous year 1968.

Secondly, there can be no doubt that the cultural field, in which the avant-garde movements operated, underwent a profound change in the middle of the 20th century. Setting aside the more principle matter, put on the agenda by Theodor Adorno, whether one might still write poetry after Auschwitz, the status and position of avant-garde art and artists changed substantially after the war. The avant-garde before the Second World War had operated generally in the margins of the respective national literary and artistic fields in Europe. For several reasons not to be discussed here, this same avant-garde obtained after 1945 a position more and more in the centre of the cultural field. For many artists, who had been involved in the avant-garde in the first half of the 20th century and who had survived, the period after the Second World War was, in a way, their harvest time. Simultaneously, the work by avant-garde artists after 1945 found its market and entered the museum much sooner than the oeuvre by pre-war avant-garde artists in the period before the war. Next to this changed position and appreciation of the avant-garde, there cannot be any doubt either that new, post-war avant-garde initiatives, be it Cobra, the *Internationale Situationiste*, Fluxus, pop art or, for example in music, developments represented by John Cage, differed profoundly from pre-war avant-garde isms, not least on an aesthetic level.

At the same time, several, if not all of the avant-garde formations in the second half of the 20th century share as artistic movements some basic characteristics with their avant-garde precursors from the first half of the 20th century, not only a self-understanding as avant-garde, but notably also — in broad terms — the combination of radical aesthetic innovations with the attempt of revolutionizing not only artistic practices, but society as whole (cf. Drijkoningen 1982:20–24, Asholt/Fähnders 2000:14–15). It is certainly not accidental that the two peaks in aesthetic avant-garde coincide with the revolutionary period in the wake of the First World War and the protest movements of 1968, in which several aesthetic avant-garde movements participated themselves.

II.

The dichotomy between a historical avant-garde before and a neo-avant-garde after the Second World War might be regarded as a neutral chronological distinction. It involves, though, in many studies a value judgement, in which the first is regarded as the true avant-garde and the latter as an epigone repetition of the first historical version. This frequently recurring assessment is, not only in a German context, often based on the way, in which Peter Bürger has attributed different qualities to the historical and neo-avant-garde in his *Theorie der Avantgarde*.

Although Bürger's *Theorie der Avantgarde* focuses primarily on what he called the historical avant-garde, he also discusses, or rather discredits the post-war neo-avant-garde as a shallow, inauthentic imitation of the historical avant-garde. The main objective of this avant-garde before the Second World War had been the attempt to revolutionize art through — in positive terms — the *Überführung*, the transportation, the transition of art in the realm of life-praxis or — in negative terms — the overcoming, the annihilation of aestheticism, of the autonomous, the institutionalized status of art, or even, as assumedly in the case of dada, the overcoming of art itself. Since the avant-garde of the first half of the 20th century had failed to achieve its aims and, what is more, since this attempt had historically turned out to be an impossibility, according to Bürger, any later attempts by later avant-garde movements to achieve the same can only be considered as inauthentic repetitions of an outdated avant-garde gesture, which has lost its ground as historical possibility, even though the intentions of these later avant-garde artists may have been genuine and sincere:

> Da inzwischen der Protest der historischen Avantgarde gegen die Institution Kunst als Kunst rezipierbar geworden ist, verfällt die Protestgeste der Neoavantgarde der Inauthentizität. (Bürger 1974: 71)

> Die Wiederaufnahme der avantgardistischen Intentionen mit den Mitteln des Avantgardismus kann in einem veränderten Kontext nicht einmal mehr die begrenzte Wirkung der historischen Avantgarden erreichen. Insofern die Mittel, mit deren Hilfe die Avantgardisten die Aufhebung der Kunst zu bewirken hofften,

inzwischen Kunstwerkstatus erlangt haben, kann mit ihrer An-
wendung der Anspruch einer Erneuerung der Lebenspraxis le-
gitimerweise nicht mehr verbunden werden. Pointiert formuliert:
Die Neoavantgarde institutionalisiert die Avantgarde als Kunst
und negiert damit die genuin avantgardistischen Intentionen. Das
gilt unabhängig von dem Bewußtsein, das die Künstler mit ihrem
Tun verbinden, und das sehr wohl avantgardistisch sein kann.
(Bürger 1974: 80)

In particular Bürger's concession, that the intentions of the neo-
avant-garde might have been genuine and sincere, immunizes his
pejorative assessment of the neo-avant-garde against any refutation,
as far as the revolutionary intentions of later avant-garde movements
are concerned. Even if one would point at the revolutionary programme of neo-avant-garde movements like Cobra or the *Internationale Situationiste*, this would remain a quite inadequate alternative to Bürger's dismissive assessment of the neo-avant-garde in his
Theorie der Avantgarde. It would, in fact, not alter anything, since
Bürger does not deny at all that avant-garde movements in the second half of the 20th century may indeed have had revolutionary intentions. He is rather suggesting — put in simple terms — that these
movements may have been subjectively revolutionary, yet objectively — as part and in the light of his materialist analysis of the
20th-century avant-garde — were lacking such a revolutionary character, because the historical avant-garde revolt had turned out to be a
failure and an impossibility. As far as the observation of this apparent impossibility of change leads automatically to the accusation of
inauthenticity, one might argue, that Bürger neglects the fact that
resistance, a revolt or a revolution, is not necessarily meaningless,
when there is little or no chance of success or victory. The fundamental question rises here, whether the relevance of resistance
should only be measured by its chance of success. Does not resistance, does not a revolt possess always a moral dimension as well?

III.

Apart from this fundamental debate on the morality of resistance
and opposition, another question remains, namely: how to refute
Bürger's accusation of inauthenticity of the neo-avant-garde, which
seems to be based in particular on the assumption that the post-1945

neo-avant-garde movements repeated and imitated the historical avant-garde. Even though their intentions might have been genuine and sincere, they were still — this fact seems to remain — repeating what had been done before, yet still claiming to be avant-garde and revolutionary (at least in the cultural field). They still remain just "neo".

The origin of this (dis-)qualification is often attributed to and can often be retraced, indeed, to Bürger, as suggested in the outline of the research project, of which this book is part, but also, for example, by Hal Foster (1994:10) in his article "What is Neo about the Neo-Avant-Garde?". And it is indeed true that most later studies on the avant-garde addressing in one way or another the neo-avant-garde have Bürger's *Theorie der Avantgarde* or its American translation as a point of reference. Bürger's accusation of the neo-avant-garde being an inauthentic repetition of apparently authentic avant-garde gestures from the first half of the 20th century is, however, not without precedent.

It should be noted here that Bürger's *Theorie der Avantgarde*, aiming at the development of a broad framework and some general lines for the interpretation of the 20th-century avant-garde, was based only to a relatively small extent on a precise historiographical examination of source material as far as the historical avant-garde is concerned, not least in the case of dada, which is at the heart of Bürger's assessment of the historical avant-garde.

A fundamental historiographic problem concerning in particular the study of dada in the 1960s and early 1970s was the fact that these studies had still to a considerable extent to rely on information supplied by former dadaists still living then, like Richard Huelsenbeck, Raoul Hausmann, and Hans Richter, who started to promote their youth sin again. Whereas nowadays most of the original, authentic documents concerning dada has been retraced and made accessible, a quarter of a century ago anyone who wanted to know more about dada, was by and large dependent on the memories of the former dadaists and on material released by them (cf. van den Berg 1999:438–443). Also Bürger draws in his *Theorie der Avantgarde* as far as dada is concerned mainly on later, post-1945 self-interpretations of dada by artists who had been involved in historical dadaism several decades earlier.

Returning to Bürger's verdict on the neo-avant-garde: his judgement may be typically Bürger as far as the specific ideology-critical articulation and vocabulary are concerned. At the same time, it should be noted, though, that Bürger's verdict in 1974 was anything but a novelty. Bürger's assessment of the neo-avant-garde possesses, actually, some quite remarkable intertexts, in terms of Bürger: from representatives of the historical avant-garde.

To be more precise: as part of his critique of the neo-avant-garde, Bürger argues in his *Theorie der Avantgarde*:

> Selbstverständlich gibt es auch heute Versuche, die Tradition der Avantgardebewegungen fortzusetzen [...]; aber diese Versuche, wie z.b. die Happenings — man könnte sie als neoavant-gardistisch bezeichnen — vermögen den Protestwert dada-istischer Veranstaltungen nicht mehr zu erreichen, und das unab-hängig davon, daß sie perfekter geplant und durchgeführt sein mögen als diese. (Bürger 1974: 80)

> Daher rührt der Eindruck des Kunstgewerblichen, den neoavant-gardistische Werke nicht selten hervorrufen. (Bürger 1974: 71)

Setting aside the fact that several happenings of the neo-avant-garde had a provable impact much larger than most, if not all historical dada happenings (at least judging by the media coverage as well as by visitor numbers), setting aside as well the fact that a combination of arts and crafts — *Kunst und Handwerk* or *Kunstgewerbe* — was one the main objectives of the Zurich dadaists and of Swiss and German constructivists around 1920 (cf. van den Berg 1999: 380–390), Bürger's just quoted remarks also show a striking similarity with arguments previously forwarded by several former dadaists in publications from the 1960s and early 1970s. One might even say that Bürger actually reproduces their polemics against "neo-dada", which can be found, for example, in two essays by Raoul Hausmann, entitled "Post-Dada" and "Ansichten oder Ende des Neodadaismus", collected 1972 in the volume *Am Anfang war Dada* (mentioned in the bibliography of *Theorie der Avantgarde*), and by Hans Richter in a final chapter, entitled "Neodada", in his influential monograph *Dada — Kunst und Antikunst*, first published in 1964:

> DADA war neben vielem anderen auch eine Protesthaltung ge-genüber den bürgerlichen und intellektuellen Traditionen. Der

NeoDADAismus ist dies entschieden nicht: er macht sich die
Existenz nach bekannten Beispielen leicht und einfach. Zu einfach, manchmal so einfach, daß man von Plagiat sprechen
könnte.

Die Lautgedichte gewisser NeoDADAisten ahmen bis auf die
Typographie die ersten Lautgedichte von 1916 und 1920 nach.

Die neoDADAistischen Materialbilder sind zu oft Nachahmun-
gen von Duchamp und Man Ray.

Sie wollen nichts angreifen, nichts erschüttern, nichts verhöhnen,
sie sind kein Protest, sie zeigen nur, daß man ein Rezept kennt,
und daß man weiß, wie das gemacht wird.

Einfach die geistig-klimatische Hochdruckatmosphäre ist nicht
die gleiche, um von der Erfindungsnotwendigkeit nicht zu sprechen. (Hausmann 1972:155)

Die anti-ästhetische Deklaration des Readymade, die Blas-
phemien Picabias erscheinen im Neo-Dada jetzt wie in
Kreuzstich oder in Holzbrand, als Comic Strips oder als zusam-
mengepreßte Auto-Karosserien. Sie sind nicht A- oder Anti-
Kunst, sondern Genußobjekte geworden. Was sie in der Fantasie
der Betrachter anregen, hält sie auf der Höhe der guten alten
Ankerschen Steinbaukasten und der Gartenzwerge. (Richter
1978: 209)

Es handelt sich also überhaupt nicht um eine Rebellion, sondern
um das Gegenteil. (Richter 1978:203)

Both Hausmann and Richter may not have been engaged in a
polemics against something called neo-avant-garde — they were
targeting at something called neo-dada. This neo-dada was, however, in their opinion, like Bürger's neo-avant-garde, an inauthentic,
commercialized repetition of its historical precursor — dada, yet
without the authentic revolutionary character of the original.

Bürger, in a way, exchanged the label neo-dada for neo-avant-
garde, in line with the pivotal role of dada in his discussion of the
historical avant-garde in *Theorie der Avantgarde*, namely as *pars
pro toto* and simultaneously as the most radical formation of the
historical avant-garde. And certainly: Bürger is not simply copying

or repeating Hausmann or Richter, he also adds something of his own, namely his repeated claim that the historical avantgarde ended in a failure — something Richter and Hausmann would never have admitted openly.

IV.

The intertext of Richter's and Hausmann's polemics against neo-dada is in particular interesting, because it points at the fact that Bürger follows the immanent logic of the (self-)understanding of the 20th-century aesthetic avant-garde movements as vanguard, as ultimate vanguard in the field of the arts. Bürger's verdict on the neo-avant-garde, thus, leads to another basic problem in studies of the avant-garde: a better understanding of the artistic practice of these movements requires — on the one hand — that one has to take in consideration also the programmatic writings, pamphlets, manifestos etc. of these movements, since they, and only they allow an insight in the historical intentions of those involved leading to rather hermetic works, like Kazimir Malevich's *Black Square* or a dadaist sound poem by Hugo Ball, Kurt Schwitters or Raoul Hausmann, whereas — on the other hand — much of these programmatic writings should be encountered with more than one pinch of salt, in particular as far as the (self-)positioning of the avant-garde in the cultural field is concerned. As Tristan Tzara (1979:67) already wrote in his "Dada manifeste sur l'amour faible et l'amour amer" in the early 1920s:

> Il y a des gens qui ont antidaté leurs manifestes pour faire croire
> qu'ils ont eu un peu avant l'idée de leur propre grandeur.

In regard to this self-positioning, the French sociologist Pierre Bourdieu (1992) has pointed at the fact that in the modern European cultural field the (self-)presentation as avant-garde had an obvious strategic character in relationship with the attempts of new artists and writers to conquer and consolidate a position of their own in the artistic and literary field. One of the key aspects of this (self-) positioning as avant-garde is self-evidently the claim to be new, to be the first, as in a definition of the avant-garde by Theo van Doesburg, editor of the constructivist review *De Stijl*:

Avant-garde! Voorhoede! Ziedaar de leuze waaronder alle moderne en ultra-moderne groepen van de geheele wereld in de richting van een geheel nieuwe uitdrukkingswijze in alle vormen van kunst, opmarcheeren. (1921: 109)

In short: the avant-garde claims to be "vanguard", "completely new", "modern", "ultra-modern", put differently: to be original. As Rosalind Krauss points out in her article "The Originality of the Avant-Garde" from 1981, this claim to be original is essential to the (self-)understanding of avant-garde movements:

> The avant-garde artist has worn many guises over the first hundred years of his existence: revolutionary, dandy, anarchist, aesthete, technologist, mystic. He has also preached a variety of creeds. One thing only seems to hold fairly constant in the vanguardist discourse and that is the theme of originality. (Krauss 1986:157)

Krauss goes even a step further, arguing that "the very notion of the avant-garde can be seen as a function of the discourse of originality" (Krauss 1986:157). In the light of the apparent necessity of the avant-garde to be original, to be innovative or — alternately — to be disqualified as a second-hand imitation, the purport of Hausmann's and Richter's polemics against neo-dada is obvious. They wanted to show that they themselves were the "real" avant-garde, whereas neo-dada was only a poor imitation, for a very clear and simple reason. They wanted or rather: they *had* to secure their avant-garde status, they *had* to confirm once more their and *only their* originality in the post-1945 cultural context to secure their position in the cultural field, to secure the market value of their art, which was in danger of being outmoded and overruled by new competitors, new initiatives, by new avant-garde movements. These movements did *not* understand themselves as a rule — this should be stressed here — as neo-avant-garde, but simply as avant-garde (cf. also Bürger 1974:75, note 18). A post-modern, self-ironical exception constitutes the case of so-called "Neoism" and "Plagiarism" in the early 1980s (cf. Home 1995). In the case of the historical dadaists attacking neo-dada, one might argue, though, that their polemics against neo-dada started already by name-tagging avant-garde developments after the Second World War as "neo-".

V.

Although the prefix "neo" may seem perfectly in line with the belief in progress, innovation and the new, typical for Western modernity, so typical that it even survived the post-modernist end of history (as the recent hype about a "*new* economy" may indicate), the discernment of neo-movements, currents and styles — at least in art — has another dimension. It implies that the movement, current or style involved is not simply new, but rather a new edition, a new appearance of something old, of something previous. As a consequence, neo-styles always possess an aura of the retrograde, the repetition, the epigone, of the *Ewiggestrige*, of living in the past, of trying to revive a past style. As such, something "neo" is from the outset — at least nominally — at odds with the core avant-garde business of being original, of conquering new territories, of presenting something unprecedented. And it is certainly no accident in this context that many if not all commonly distinguished neo- movements, currents and styles can be qualified as conservative or as expressions of a conservative or a retrograde aesthetic stand (be it in art e.g. Neo-Gothic, Neo-Romanticism, Neo-Classicism etc.).

Likewise, the term historical avant-garde may also cause some unease. But is an avant-garde of yesterday still not much more acceptable and to be preferred above a re-edition of yesterday's avant-garde, above an avant-garde, which is *not* original, as the contradiction in terms neo-avant-garde is implying? Whereas the term historical avant-garde can be read as avant-garde, performing an historical act, the act of being original, innovative etc., in other terms as an avant-garde that delivered a historical contribution to the innovation of artistic practices, the qualification neo-avant-garde, instead, particularly in contrast with a historical avant-garde, that delivered such a historical contribution, does not only lack this aspect of delivering an historical contribution, but also indicates that the involved artists and writers produced nothing more than a shallow repetition of something previous, without any historical merit. Although: in the case of Bürger's *Theorie der Avantgarde* one should observe that his assessment of the historical avant-garde is quite negative as well. Whereas the neo-avant-garde is dismissed as an inauthentic copy-cat project, Bürger stresses from the outset that the historical avant-garde failed to meet its (or maybe more precise:

Bürger's) objectives. And: what is better? What is preferable? To be an authentic failure or an inauthentic success?

VI.

In short: the term neo-avantgarde is already in itself a disqualification and this disqualifying aspect is even endorsed by its usage as second term in an assumed dichotomy between a historical and a neo-avant-garde.

Certainly: when the terms neo-dada and neo-avant-garde came into circulation after the Second World War, and when these terms were used by Hausmann, Richter and later-on by Bürger, the terms might have had a purport slightly differing from the purport of the term in current discussions and historiography of this so-called neo-avant-garde, now at the beginning of the 21st century. Then, in the second half of the 20th century, the term referred to contemporary avant-garde initiatives, in a way to the avant-garde of the day, and in this constellation the term neo-avant-garde may have been more than a simple disqualification. In a way it also pointed at the aspect of a new emergence of the avant-garde, yet with a quite pejorative edge. In the meantime, the neo-avant-garde has become a historical phenomenon itself, a historical avant-garde from a previous century. As a consequence, the pejorative edge of the neo- disqualification is even endorsed by the fact that the — in the meantime no less historical (historical here in contrast to contemporary) — neo-avant-garde is denied its status as historical phenomenon in the dichotomy historical versus neo-avant-garde.

Since the disqualifying connotation of the term neo-avant-garde makes its historiographic merit quite dubious, much favours the abolition or at least the avoidance of the term neo-avant-garde as a historiographic term in studies on 20th-century avant-garde movements. As far as the distinction between a historical and a neo-avant-garde may be intended, used and interpreted only as a temporal distinction, as a periodization attempt, one may ask: why use *these* terms, which imply almost automatically a certain quality of the movements, currents and styles classified as neo-avant-garde? Why not simply describe the temporal aspect in temporal terms, for example by speaking of avant-garde movements before and after the Second World War?

BIBLIOGRAPHY

Asholt, Wolfgang, and Walter Fähnders
2000   "Einleitung". In: Wolfgang Asholt/Walter Fähnders (eds.): *Der Blick vom Wolkenkratzer. Avantgarde — Avantgardekritik — Avantgardeforschung.* Amsterdam: Rodopi, 9–27.

van den Berg, Hubert
1999   *Avantgarde und Anarchismus. Dada in Zürich und Berlin.* Heidelberg: Winter.

Bourdieu, Pierre
1992   *Les règles de l'art. Genèse et structure du champ littéraire.* Paris: Seuil.

Bürger, Peter
1974   *Theorie der Avantgarde.* Frankfurt am Main: Suhrkamp.

van Doesburg, Theo
1921   "Revue der Avant-garde." In: *Het Getij*, vol. 6, 109–112.

Drijkoningen, Ferdinand
1982   "Voorwoord". In: Ferdinand Drijkoningen/Jan Fontijn (eds.): *Historische Avantgarde.* Amsterdam: Huis aan de drie grachten, 5–51.

Foster, Hal
1994   "What's Neo about the Neo-Avant-Garde?" In: *October* 70,5–32.

Krauss, Rosalind
1986   *The Originality of the Avant-Garde and Other Modernist Myths.* Cambridge, Mass.: MIT Press.

Hausmann, Raoul
1972   *Am Anfang war Dada.* Steinbach/Giessen: Anabas.

Home, Stewart
1995   *Neoism, Plagiarism & Praxis.* Edinburgh/San Francisco: AK.

Richter, Hans
1978   *DADA — Kunst und Antikunst. Der Beitrag Dadas zur Kunst des 20. Jahrhunderts.* Cologne: Dumont.

Tzara, Tristan
1979   Lampisteries. Sept manifestes DADA. Paris: Pauvert.

II.

REVIEWING THE AUTONOMY OF ART

Abstraction, Sublation and the Avant-Garde: The Case of *De Stijl*

MICHAEL WHITE

> I have often thought how interesting a magazine paper might be written by any author who would — that is to say who could — detail, step by step, the processes by which any of his compositions attained its ultimate point of completion [...] Most writers — poets in especial — prefer having it understood that they compose by a species of fine frenzy — an ecstatic intuition — and would positively shudder at letting the public take a peep behind the scenes. (Poe 1875: 267)

The extract above is taken from an essay published by Edgar Allan Poe in 1846 entitled *The Philosophy of Composition*. In this text he actually went about producing exactly what he called for and gave a detailed description of the process by which he composed his poem *The Raven*. His point was to demonstrate that "no one point in its composition is referable either to accident or intuition — that the work proceeded step by step, to its completion with the precision and rigid consequence of a mathematical problem" (Poe 1875: 268). Curiously, this step by step approach was initiated, according to Poe, by the construction of the final stanza: "Here then the poem may be said to have had its beginning, at the end where all works of art should begin" (Poe 1875: 273). Having predetermined the outcome, Poe then claims to have aimed for originality, but this is a quality which he describes "demands in its attainment less of invention than negation" (Poe 1875: 274).

This is not an essay about Edgar Allan Poe, however. Rather, it concerns abstract painting and, more specifically, a very similar attempt at exposition made some 63 years after Poe's essay. I will be examining an article published by Theo van Doesburg, the editor of the journal *De Stijl*, in which he outlined a procedure in painting of uncanny similarity to that which Poe described regarding poetry. As with Poe, much of what Van Doesburg claimed about his working method is questionable. Some of it may even have been intended to be satirical. However, there remains much that can be read between the lines, so to speak.

My reason for turning to this historical explanation of abstract painting is to test a number of assertions concerning the relationship between what is currently understood as modernism and avant-garde. Since the publication of Peter Bürger's *Theory of the Avant-Garde*, it has now become commonplace to distinguish these two terms. In order to emphasise the radical nature of the latter, the former has been ceaselessly subject to an ideological critique which has aimed to demonstrate its affirmative nature. To give a recent example, Hal Foster in *The Return of the Real* carefully picks apart Bürger's dismissal of the neo-avant-garde by undermining the historicist model he uses (Foster 1996: 1–32). However, Foster does not dispute *at all* that the avant-garde (and subsequently the neo-avant-garde) can be defined as the calling into question of the conventionality of the art object accepted by modernism. While Foster avoids some of the trickier aspects of the concept of autonomy developed by Bürger, he maintains an essential separation between conservative and oppositional tendencies in twentieth-century art without even feeling the need to justify it. Paradoxically, though, at one point he places *De Stijl* in the category of avant-garde but subsequently uses Mondrian as the purest example of modernism (Foster 1996: 16, 77). This indicates to me a fundamental confusion concerning the relation of abstract painting to avant-gardism that I hope to expose in this essay and I will be returning to Foster's argument later. Before moving on much further, though, it is necessary to say a little more about Bürger's analysis.

Bürger proposes not only that what he terms modernism can be distinguished from the avant-garde but also that it necessarily precedes it. In his argument, modernism is described as the point where the autonomy of art, understood as the separateness of art from life, reaches its most developed stage. The avant-garde attempts to negate autonomy but also inherits the dissatisfaction with life as it is which has brought it about:

> Aestheticism had made the distance from the praxis of life the content of art [...] Now it is not the aim of the avant-gardistes to integrate art into *this* praxis. On the contrary, they assent to the aestheticists' rejection of the world and its means-ends rationality [...] In this respect also, aestheticism turns out to have been the necessary precondition of the avant-gardiste intent. (Bürger 1984: 49)[1]

In the examination of abstract painting which follows, I want to test two of the presumptions made here. The first is the historical model in which the thesis of autonomy is followed by its antithesis, the avant-garde. The second is the definition of aestheticism Bürger offers. Notoriously, Bürger included very few concrete examples to elucidate his theory of the avant-garde, and certainly not a single one to identify what an aestheticist work of art might be. On his behalf, therefore, I am offering an abstract painting, together with a contemporary explanation of it which might justify the description. What I aim to demonstrate, however, is that abstract painting was about more than the making of "the distance from the praxis of life the content of art." It is my view that the concept of autonomy was a retrospective projection on the part of the theorists of the avant-garde. In this last group I include not only Bürger but Van Doesburg himself, and maybe even Poe.[2]

The object of this analysis, then, is an article published by Van Doesburg in 1919 in the magazine *De Hollandsche Revue*, a monthly journal which covered art, literature, theatre and other cultural matters. Although he was editor of the journal *De Stijl*, Van Doesburg frequently placed articles outside of it, taking full advantage of the opportunity for the broader exposure of his ideas. The text in question, titled *Van "Natuur" tot "Kompositie": Aantekeningen bij de ontwikkeling van een abstract schilderij* (From "Nature" to "Composition": Notes on the development of an abstract painting), was intended to provide a straightforward account of the transformation from naturalistic to abstract painting. The tone of the

article suggests that Van Doesburg had in mind a readership of educated skeptics whom he aimed to persuade of the value of abstract
painting. He used plainer language than could be found in *De Stijl*
and included eight illustrations. These images formed an explicit
diagram of the process of abstraction. As Van Doesburg made clear
in his introductory remarks, these successive stages demonstrate
both a rejection of naturalistic representation and of the "spontane-
ous expression of feeling, as was once considered by the Impres-
sionists and made into a dogma by the Expressionists" (Doesburg
1919: 471). As in Poe's *Philosophy of Composition*, a patient and
mediated process is shown to characterise the making of abstract
painting.

The theme introduced by Van Doesburg of an inevitable historical passage to abstraction is derived wholeheartedly from idealist
philosophy and repeated many times elsewhere by him and other *De
Stijl* associates. *From "Nature" to "Composition"* includes a description of an essential conflict between the human spirit and the
physical world. Van Doesburg describes the achievement of abstract
painting to be the overcoming of natural constraints by the spirit:
"These reproductions show the *process of liberation of the spirit
from the bonds of nature*" (his italics) (Doesburg 1919: 473). This
comes very close to Bürger's later conception of modernism; Van
Doesburg argued that abstract painting was not the extraction of the
essence of life but a rejection of life. Similarly, this rejection is
combined with the rhetoric of liberation.

The images that Van Doesburg chose to represent the "process
of liberation" began not with a naturalistic painting but with a photograph, captioned by the text *Meisje in atelier* (Girl in a Studio).
The subsequent image illustrated a painting derived from the photograph which was captioned *Portret-kompositie* (Portrait Composition). This was followed in turn by a simplified version captioned
Eerste doorbeelding portret-kompositie (First Decomposition of
Portrait Composition). The fourth illustration showed the portrait
further disintegrating and was captioned *Destruktieve voorstudie
voor Kompositie 16* (Destructive Study for Composition 16), naming
the painting that was to be the final result of the process. The next
three illustrations are all titled *Voorstudie voor Kompositie 16*
(Study for Composition 16) with *Kompositie 16* (Composition 16)
itself as the last image.

1. *Girl in a Studio*   2. *Portrait Composition*

As these captions suggest, the gaps between the first four stages are very crucial and they receive the lengthiest description in Van Doesburg's article. As he states, between the photograph and the first painting there is already quite a jump. This he suggests is the difference between the mechanical view of the camera lens and nature seen by a living person. A major difference he chose not to emphasise is the cropping of the image and its reconfiguration from standard portrait proportions to a square format. Thus much of the studio setting becomes harder to read. The mirror in the top right hand corner is reduced to a series of framed edges, as is the painting which hangs in the top left. The armrest of the chair on which the figure sits disappears and the canvas turned against the wall is also severely reduced. Both Mondrian and Van Doesburg had adopted square format canvasses around this time as a means of eradicating portrait and landscape associations, giving greater impact to the shape of the stretcher itself.

Van Doesburg then introduced two stages of "decomposition" and "destruction." These are explained in the text as part of a natural historical process whereby, "nothing is created without the annihilation of something else. Annihilation and construction are complementary" (Doesburg 1919: 472). "Decomposition" is illustrated more as a means of formal simplification but the next stage involved something much closer to an obliteration of the figure, cancelled out

3. *First Decomposition of Portrait*   4. *Destructive Study for Composi-*
   Composition   *tion 16*

under large diagonal strokes. The character of these diagonals is not
suggested by the forms of the original image. However, despite the
destruction of the figure, Van Doesburg describes the preservation
of some features through these two stages, such as, "the psychic
moment that was given expression in fig. 2 primarily in the face,
now is spread over the whole painting" (Doesburg 1919: 475). Although he was able to use only black and white illustrations, Van
Doesburg also assured his readers that the colours of the final
painting maintained their derivation from the original source.

Once again it should be clear how this rationalization of the process of abstraction has its roots in a quasi-Hegelian view of historical progress; on more than one occasion Van Doesburg used the
word *opheffing*, the Dutch equivalent of *Aufhebung*, to explain the
sequence of transformations. The word translates awkwardly into
English as "sublation" and is used in this context to suggest how
certain values are preserved through change. As such it fits quite
neatly with Bürger's idealist world view whereby the shifts from
courtly art to bourgeois art to the avant-garde follow similar moments of self awareness, overturning and preservation. However, it
is obvious from my summary of Van Doesburg's article that this
process was produced in a highly artificial way and I will now begin
to unravel this neat model.

5. *Study for Composition 16*   6. *Study for Composition 16*

There are several problems with Van Doesburg's explanation of the generation of *Composition 16*. The first is the question of whether the illustrations he used did actually represent his working practice. A large number of drawings and preparatory works survived Van Doesburg's death in 1931. These show that he often did experiment with breaking a motif into constituent parts. However, there is no comparable example of anything quite so formulaic or protracted. Aside from the *Portrait Composition* and *Composition 16* itself, all trace of the other paintings has vanished. We have no idea what state of finish they ever achieved nor even the materials they were executed in. Van Doesburg's correspondence also reveals great inconsistencies. In a letter to Georges Vantongerloo at the beginning March 1919 he mentions starting a "composition in dissonances" which was an alternative title for *Composition 16* (Hoek 2000: 246). By the start of April he was recounting to another friend "working through the portrait of a woman. After 8 studies I came to a satisfactory result" (Hoek 2000: 246). By mid May he wrote to the same friend about completing *Composition 16 with dissonances* (Hoek 2000: 246). The precise relation between the "portrait of a woman" and the final composition is unclear. He published eight illustrations with his article but by definition only five of them were studies. It seems, then, as if Van Doesburg was working both projectively and retrospectively. He must have begun the final work and then linked it with studies derived from the portrait. There is also an

7. *Study for Composition 16*   8. *Composition 16*

obscure relation between the photograph and the first painting which represent differing viewpoints. Was the photograph a restaging of the painting for the benefit of the article? The artifice of Van Doesburg's explanation of abstraction does not perhaps need such careful exposure but by doing so we may come closer to understanding what the mask of rational progress is covering.

It is worth pointing out at this stage that the motif of the "girl in the studio" was itself a restaging of an earlier painting, *Lena in an interior* of 1917. This earlier work depicts Van Doesburg's second wife, Helena Milius, seated in his studio in Leiden. The structure of mirror, fireplace, painting on the wall behind was identical, although the previous work shows more of the figure and furnishings of the interior. The elements of restaging and repetition are further complicated by the inclusion of *Composition XIII* (1918) hanging behind the sitter in the later portrait which also had the subtitle "woman in the studio" and was derived from another seated portrait of Helena Milius. In this painting, one can just make out a figure seated in profile to the right. This complements the subject of the *Portrait Composition* who is turned left. When we consider the other items included in the restaged portrait, a canvas turned to the wall and the mirror, we realise that Van Doesburg has included a whole sequence of references to reflections (literal and metaphorical), doublings and the artifice of representation.

One aspect lost between the sequence of paintings of women in an interior and the first painting is that in the original work Lena Milius appeared to be reading. The books lined up on the mantlepiece at least encouraged this suggestion, as did the orientation of her head, although it was difficult to see if she holds anything in her hands. To me this invites comparison with the well established genre theme of the woman in an interior reading (either a letter or a book) which was established in seventeenth-century Dutch painting. A rich comparison could be made, perhaps, with Gabriel Metsu's *Woman Reading a Letter* where an incredible interplay is developed between the subject's attention to the piece of paper she holds and a range of representational surfaces. Again we have a painting on the back wall, this time being revealed by a maid. A mirror placed behind the sitter does not reflect what we want it to, namely the text, but the window frame. Even the maid's bucket is covered in signs but we are not sure of what they point to. The abundance of superficial information is contrasted with the paucity of an explicit narrative, with the hardest surface to read being the woman's emotionless face. Van Doesburg's attraction to this motif could well have been for precisely the problems of intersubjectivity tackled in it.

As Poe said, most poets "would positively shudder at the prospect of letting the public take a peek behind the scenes." And like Poe, Van Doesburg presented his working method as supremely rational. From the first to the last stage, creativity was shown to involve a sequence of deliberate decisions (or negations). Every effort was made to demonstrate the exclusion of chance and even emotion. Abstraction in painting was explained as the achievement of a subjectivity in total control of itself. However, as has been pointed out regarding Poe, the greater the need to convince the public of his sanity, the greater was the likelihood of the failure of his reason (Bonaparte 1971: 96). Similarly, the perversity of Van Doesburg's article is its backward looking aspect. For all the effort to show abstract painting as a series of progressive stages towards the liberation from subject matter, the reader cannot help but look for what connects *Composition 16* with the portrait. The act of restaging that seems to have occurred, visible in the article in the disparity between photograph and portrait, and noticeable in Van Doesburg's oeuvre in the reappearance of the motif of a woman in the studio, quickly undoes all that should be confirmed. If, according to Bürger, modernist art (in his terms) is the mechanism via which "the atrophied bourgeois individual can experience the self as personality," what kind of personality is being offered here? (Bürger 1984: 13)

It is now time to start rethinking Van Doesburg's strategies and thereby the established definitions of modernism and avant-garde. First of all, it is necessary to comment briefly on how the rhetoric of Van Doesburg's demonstration of abstract painting was clearly situated in relation to contemporary art theory in the Netherlands. It was, in my view, partly motivated as a response to the criticisms made of abstract painting by the director of the Rijksacademie, Richard Roland Holst, who had used his inaugural speech in 1918 to launch a stinging attack on *De Stijl*. Roland Holst specifically connected abstract painting with industrialisation and mass culture, accusing it of destroying individuality and leading to a "mechanization of the spirit" (Roland Holst 1923: 167). Van Doesburg reviewed this speech in *De Stijl* where he used a similar strategy of cultural analysis to denounce Roland Holst's own art nouveau inspired painting as an indication of degeneracy (Doesburg 1919b: 102–104). He explicitly encouraged an opposition between geometric abstraction and curvaceous ornament along the lines of mechanical versus natural, male versus female, progressive versus regressive. The rigid emphasis in *From "Nature" to "Abstraction"* on the rationality of his practice was specifically intended to mark his difference from the predominant theories of the day which tended to connect art with the irrational. The forcible eradication of the human figure he demonstrated in his illustrations was completely bound up with the annihilation of humanistic values.

Closer to home, Van Doesburg was also responding to his colleague, Piet Mondrian, who had submitted a lengthy article to *De Stijl* entitled *Natuurlijke en abstracte realiteit* (Natural Reality and Abstract Reality). This famous text, written as a three way conversation between a layman, naturalistic painter and abstract painter, was a retrospective dramatization of Mondrian's career to date which attempted to explain his transition from naturalistic to abstract painting as the gradual revelation of a progressive path to the future. Mondrian's article contained two significant aspects for Van Doesburg. The first was the idea that, although rejecting representation, abstract painting maintained some connection to natural appearance and the second, that the path to abstraction was an evolutionary process. Both of these issues reappeared rehashed in *From "Nature" to "Composition."* Furthermore, Mondrian described the connection between abstract form and natural appearance as "the search for plastic harmony between the aesthetically inward or intuitive and memory of the outward" (Holzmann & James 1987: 108). The act of restaging and repetition in the production of Van Doesburg's *Composition 16* can be read as a direct engagement with this notion of remembering. At the point where subject matter was shown to be disappearing from art, both Mondrian and Van Doesburg enacted its evaporation but clung to its vestigial trace as memory.

Let me return now to the theory of the avant-garde. For Hal Foster and others, the trace of representation within abstract painting is an indication of its resistance to the "arbitrariness of the sign" (Foster 1996: 103). In his words, abstraction *sublates* representation, that is it maintains representation at the same time as it proposes to go beyond it. This characterization of abstract painting is used a means to distinguish it from the avant-garde, exemplified by such forms as cubist collage and dada photomontage, where signification runs wild. Foster's summary concludes that abstract painting puts autonomy in place of arbitrariness whereby the art object itself takes the place of the referent. In my view, *From "Nature" to "Composition"* reveals something different. For the act of destruction Van Doesburg demonstrated as the process of creation of *Composition 16* is not so simple. Indeed Foster's adoption of the very term sublation tacitly instates the historicist model he is trying to work a way out of. The trace of representation in *Composition 16* is not so much a reminiscence of the object itself but the repetition its disappearance. To recall Van Doesburg's own words, what is preserved through the destruction of the figure is not a figural reference but a 'psychic moment.' We should perhaps be thinking less about sublation here than sublimation.

So far, I have tracked Van Doesburg's 8 illustrations forwards and backwards. I have shown how his simple description of the order in which the images were created concealed inconsistencies and that, like Poe, he worked with a process "less of invention than negation." In conclusion, I want to propose that his diagram also has a circular pattern, or rather that the photograph he begins with and the abstract painting with which he concludes, bracket the other illustrations. For it is clear that the photograph does not stand for the "nature" mentioned in the title, nor does its position before *Portrait Composition* give it priority in terms of representational power (thus the need for an explicit caption). Instead it marks the problem of representation in modernity and the anonymity of the image. It stands as the alternative origin of *Composition 16* which can be seen to sublate/sublimate the problematic qualities of photography: flatness, reproducibility, arbitrariness and the mechanical.

There are always those who search for the real behind abstract painting. Van Doesburg's readers in 1919 were tempted to follow this path as a way of alleviating the discomfort of its illegibility. Later commentators, such as Foster, have been more sophisticated and looked for the sublation of representation in abstraction. As I hope has become clear now, this reading has only been another way of establishing the notion of the autonomy of art. In turn, autonomy has been used as a means to distinguish abstract painting from the avant-garde and establish the act of overturning that latter is supposed to have performed. The avant-garde and its theorists have set up a straw man to demolish. In my view, all of these readers have followed the path of the signifier to closely. They have seen something a little too self evident. If we follow the construction of the theory of autonomy rather more carefully, in such instances as the Van Doesburg article I have examined here, the distinction between modernism and avant-garde collapses. My hope is that once the avant-garde has lost the modernist shadow from which it has persistently derived its myths of originality and invention, its other qualities may come into greater focus, those which Poe identified so early on: negation, denial, revision and repetition. These are all present in Van Doesburg's *Composition 16* (and in his description of it). In this painting the bourgeois subject may well see himself mirrored but not necessarily affirmed.

NOTES

[1] Several crude summaries of Bürger's argument have failed to recognise the negative position in the "aestheticists' rejection of the world" which is so crucially carried over into his concept of the avant-garde. Even a sophisticated commentator such as Paul Wood has recently transcribed

Bürger's account as, "art-for-art's sake is seen as the affirmative art of bourgeois culture, an art which co-exists with the status quo," which is clearly an oversimplification (Wood 1999: 227).

[2] In the case of Van Doesburg, it is notable that his most resolute account of the autonomy of art is produced in 1929–30. It is a concept which hardens over the course of the 1920s rather than weakens. Nancy Troy argues in *The De Stijl Environment* (Troy 1983) that the history of *De Stijl* can be read as the movement away from collaboration to the separation of painting from architecture, rather than towards the integration of art with three dimensional space.

BIBLIOGRAPHY

Bonaparte, Marie
    1971   *The Life and Work of Edgar Allan Poe: A Psychoanalytic Study*. New York: Humanities Press.

Bürger, Peter
    1984   *Theory of the Avant-Garde*. Minneapolis: University of Minnesota Press.

Doesburg, Theo van
    1919a   "Van 'Natuur' tot 'Kompositie'". In: *De Hollandsche Revue*, vol. 24, no. 8, 470–476.

    1919b   "Moderne Wendingen in het kunstonderwijs". In: *De Stijl*, vol. 2, no. 9, 102–104.

Foster, Hal
    1996   *The Return of the Real*. Cambridge MA & London: MIT Press.

Hoek, Els, et al.
    2000   *Theo van Doesburg. Oeuvre Catalogus*. Bussum: Uitgeverij Thoth.

Holtzmann, Harry and Martin James (eds.)
    1987   *The New Art — The New Life: The Collected Writings of Piet Mondrian*. London: Thames and Hudson.

Poe, Edgar Allan
    1875   *The Works of Edgar Allan Poe*, vol. III: *Poems and Essays*. Edinburgh: Adam and Charles Black.

Roland Holst, Richard
    1923   *Over   kunst   en   kunstenaars.   Beschouwingen   en
               herdenkingen.* Amsterdam: Meulenhoff.

Troy, Nancy
    1983   *The De Stijl Environment.* Cambridge MA & London:
               MIT Press.

Wood, Paul et al.
    1999   *The Challenge of the Avant-Garde.* New Haven &
               London: Yale.

Sameness and Difference: Duchamp's Editioned *Readymades* and the Neo-Avant-Garde

DAVID HOPKINS

It is generally accepted these days that Peter Bürger's formulation of the fundamental concerns of the early twentieth century avant-garde is seriously flawed. There has been an equally broad-based move against Bürger's blanket denunciation of the legitimacy of the 1960s neo-avant-garde, pre-eminently in the writings of American critics such as Benjamin Buchloh and Hal Foster (Buchloh 1986, Foster 1996). However, despite Bürger's massive generalisations and factual simplifications, his monolithic theory still provides a useful starting-off point for a consideration of the way in which the historical avant-garde, and its post-war spin-offs, is to be understood.

I want to begin this essay by acknowledging Dietrich Scheunemann's observation that one of Bürger's fundamental theoretical blind spots, not least in the case of Duchamp's *Fountain* — which is taken by Bürger to be exemplary of avant-garde production — is "the question of whether art should continue to be based on handicraft in an age where other spheres of life are determined by mechanical production and industrial reproduction processes" (Scheunemann 2000: 35–6). In Scheunemann's view, Bürger downplays the structural incursions of serial production and mechanical reproduction into modern art practice, such that Scheunemann will claim that "a dialectical process of demarcation from technological reproduction and its eventual integration into the practice and concept of art characterises the avant-gardist response to [...] technological advances" (42). Scheunemann correctly, I think, disparages Bürger's blithe vision of avant-gardism as a "sublation of art into the practice of life" as merely reminiscent of the "calls of May 1968" (43). However, Scheunemann himself appears to feel that both the historical and the neo-avant-gardes, in their embrace of industrial methods, have performed a form of emancipatory rapprochement with the forces of modernity. Hence he writes that "new techniques, above all the technique of montage [...] achieved [...] the formation of modes of perception and construction that are more in tune with other fields of activity and other spheres of life" (43), adding elsewhere that their invention has "worked towards bridging the gap between art and technology, between handicraft and industrial production, between the culture of taste and the culture of technical skills" (43).

In many ways the theme of this essay is precisely the extent to which a trio of central avant-garde figures — Marcel Duchamp, Yves Klein and Andy Warhol — turned themselves almost literally into figures of serial production or commodification. But it seems to me that, contra Scheunemann, we should be careful here to preserve some sense not so much of Bürger's own viewpoint, which may in the final analysis not be so very far removed from Scheunemann's, but of Bürger's evident sensitivity to Adorno's position on the category of "the new" in art. Basically Bürger castigates Adorno for failing to perceive that his formulation of the "tradition of the new" in modernism — his vision, in other words, of a constant negation of tradition in favour of an increasingly rapid turnover of new styles which is congruent with the logic of the turnover of capital — is problematic, mainly because, in Bürger's words "not only [...] is it too general and unspecific but [...] it provides no criteria for distinguishing between faddish (arbitrary) and historically necessary newness" (1984: 63).

Bürger himself skirts around the problem of how we are to perceive the stirrings of historical necessity in a situation where no agreed criteria for artistic innovation are in operation. At the same time, he fails, I think, to make full use of a perception of Adorno's which may be used productively to pinpoint an urgency at work in neo-avant-garde art production, and which does not reduce the art merely to the terms of a rapprochement with technological change.

At one point Bürger attempts an even-handed exposition of Adorno's dialectical position on the new in art (59–63). On the one hand, the Frankfurt School theorist held that "Modernism is art through mimetic adaptation to what is hardened and alienated" (Adorno 1970: 39, as cited by Bürger 1984: 62). On the other hand, he felt that modernist art could be understood as internally resistant to the forms it mimics, a kind of ironic adaptation to the status quo and a mutely parodic replaying of the operations of the prevailing Doxa. Art in the age of commodity capitalism may become alienated and hardened, but this hardening is also its shield. It holds something in reserve behind it.

For a moment Bürger wants to hold onto Adorno's perception, which can be aligned so interestingly with Warhol, that "no general judgement can be made whether someone who does away with all expression is the mouthpiece of reified consciousness or the speechless, expressionless expression that denounces that consciousness" (Adorno 1970: 179, as cited by Bürger 1984: 62). But Bürger quickly lets this slip away, not least because of his horror at having to grasp the dialectical nettle. What I now want to do is to reassert the importance of Adorno's crucial and seemingly imponderable dialectic, partly to hammer another nail into the coffin of Bürger's theory, but also to caution against a too-easy defence of the neo-avant-garde in terms of its technologism. As I have said, my case histories are paradigmatic ones: Duchamp, Klein and Warhol. But I hope in the course of what follows to inflect these figures and their gestures rather differently historically, hence returning the problematic of the avant-garde and the neo-avant-garde — or more exactly, the relationship between the two — to some sense of the historical contingencies in which it should be framed. It would be unfair, incidentally, to expect such contingencies to have been appreciated in their fullness by Adorno, although Bürger cannot be exonerated from blame so easily.

I want to start with Duchamp. First of all it is necessary to appreciate how fundamentally Bürger got him wrong. For Bürger the great achievement of a readymade such as *Fountain* of 1917 was that it was an unrepeatable and deeply ironic exposé of the bourgeois assumptions inherent in the idea of artistic authorship (Bürger 1984: 51–3). Scheunemann is surely correct for pointing out that for Duchamp himself the readymade was just as much about his authorial right to pluck an object out of circulation, thereby choosing to invest it with new meanings, as it was about a dissolution of authorship (2000: 34–5). But it could equally be asserted, by virtue of pointing to the sheer variety of readymades produced by Duchamp, that the idea was never a singular one. Between 1913 and the early 1920s he produced numerous readymade propositions — both material and textual — in which a number of disparate and often paradoxical ideas are put into play. Authorial lack and authorial over-investment are as much at stake in these objects and proposals as are a range of other concepts, such as notions of deferral of gratification or of the possible links between aesthetic and bodily reflex in the case of, say, *In Advance of the Broken Arm* of 1915. [1]

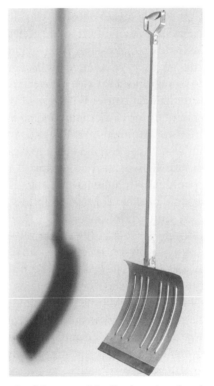

Marcel Duchamp: *In Advance of the Broken Arm* (readymade: wood and galvanised-iron snow shovel, replica made under the artist's supervision from photographs of the lost original). Edition of 8, Milan (1964)

Broadly speaking, the readymades could be said to constitute a set of experimental test cases for the possibility of art — but they are hardly reducible to one idea, i.e. that of "the readymade" conceived of as a single-track challenge to dominant aesthetic assumptions.

More importantly — and this is where Bürger's historical blind spots let him down irredeemably — Duchamp never understood the readymade to constitute a definitive statement in temporal terms. Properly understood, the concept resists being located in, say, 1917, at a moment of historical self-realisation in the unfolding of the historical avant-garde's destiny, and continues to unravel precisely at that point when the "neo-avant-garde" is fully in motion, and when Bürger has lost interest in the avant-garde project. For Duchamp the readymade idea was a kind of genre in which he could be responsive to fluctuations that existed both internally, so to speak, in terms of his own thought processes, and externally, in terms of the material conditions on which his practice was contingent. Consequently the so-called "classic readymades" of 1913 to the early 1920s were only the beginning of an ongoing investigation that continued — in line with Duchamp's increasingly sophisticated ruminations about the technological processes of mass production and the cultural commodification of the artistic gesture — well into the 1960s.

Two of the crucial later stages of the idea are the series of *Boîtes-en-Valises*, assembled in the first "de luxe" edition of twenty four between 1935 and 1941, and the so-called "editioned readymades" — exact replicas of fourteen selected examples from the original sequence chosen between 1913 and the early 1920s — which were ironically mass-produced in a series of artist's editions of eight in 1964. In the case of the *Boîtes* — once described by Duchamp as dealing with "mass production on a modest scale" — an overall principle of miniaturisation is deployed such that objects that were originally "readymade" have been carefully scaled down as exquisite sculptural objects, whilst works which were once original paintings have been submitted to small-scale mechanical reproduction. In the case of the editioned readymades the notion of machine production is neatly conflated with the idea of the artist's edition. All in all, of course, Duchamp appears to have pre-empted Bürger's thesis. He opens himself up, with his customary conceptual succinctness, to the idea of self-commodification, inauthenticity, and

Marcel Duchamp, *La Boîte-en-Valise* (The Box in a Valise), miniature
replicas and colour reproductions of works by Duchamp contained in a
cloth-covered cardboard box enclosed in a leather valise (1935–41)

so on. Of course what he has in abundance, and what Bürger appears
to lack, is a sense of humour. And what the continuation of the
readymade project into the 1960s tracks, with both inexorable precision and bitter acceptance, is the technological determinism, the
unholy aesthetic confluence of disinterestedness and commodification, and the curious inversions of value that modulate the identity
of art under late capitalism.

There is, to put it simply, a developmental logic inherent to the
concept of the readymade which aligns it with the permutations that
the aesthetic and the manufactured object simultaneously undergo
under capital. Duchamp thus ends up becoming as much an em-
bodiment of the so-called "neo-avant-garde" as of the "avant-garde"
proper. As such he quickly slips out of Bürger's grasp. This post-
war Duchamp has never really been theorised adequately in relation
to the avant-garde concept, not least because he so obviously con-
founds what Bürger would like to think is its all-embracing mission,
namely a model of the possibility of a non-instrumentalised aesthetic
praxis. Duchamp's whole post-war position is predicated on an ac-

knowledgement of his alienated, reified consciousness. There are no heroics on offer although, as I have suggested, there is a distinctive cast of humour, and this should not be underestimated. But just as Bürger fails to understand Duchamp comprehensively so art historians have failed to appreciate one element of his late take on the readymade idea that potentially modifies the extent of his capitulation to capital, however elegantly rueful it may have been.

At this point I want to think more closely about the editioned readymades of 1964 and propose a new reading of them. The idea of producing an edition of eight of each of fourteen selected readymades was probably arrived at whilst Duchamp was in the company of the Italian gallerist and dealer Arturo Schwarz in Milan in June 1964. Although the details are unclear, Duchamp appears to have entered a contractual financial agreement with Schwarz whereby each of the selected readymades would be painstakingly replicated on the basis of a draughtsman's drawing produced after exacting study of available photographs of the now-vanished objects.

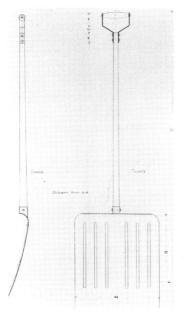

Marcel Duchamp: Working drawing for replica of the readymade *In Advance of the Broken Arm*. BIGI Art Space, Tokyo: July 1964.

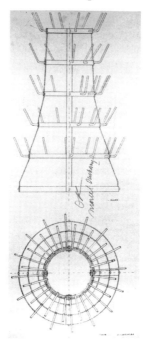

Marcel Duchamp: Working drawing for replica of *Bottlerack* readymade.
Private Collection, Paris: May 1964.

Duchamp agreed to "sign off" on the draughtsman's drawings in the
way in which an architect signs off on blueprints, and undertook not
to sign any other replicas beyond those currently being editioned.
The point about withholding his signature on future occasions seems
particularly significant given that over the previous fifteen years or
so Duchamp had gladly acquiesced to the production of one-off replicas of his readymades, and even of his *Large Glass*, largely for the
purposes of exhibition. Usually these replicas were far from accu-
rate, insofar as documentation of the original objects was not taken
into account, and Duchamp seems unfailingly to have given his
blessing to them, blithely signing them in full knowledge, as he once
remarked, that he was "devaluing" them. [2]
    In the case of the Schwarz editions he may, of course, have sud-
denly been motivated by financial considerations, but all the
evidence suggests that in some way it was the fanatically precise
replication of the objects that interested him. In the case of the Bot-

tlerack readymade, for instance, we know that although such objects could still be purchased easily in Paris, Duchamp wanted the replicas to be galvanised in precisely the manner of the lost original of 1914. Consequently each one in the edition had to be handmade by an Italian craftsman who specialised in metalwork (Nauman 1999: 249). In some important way such painstaking replication added a final twist to the readymade idea. Obviously the idea in question might simply have been bound up with serial production, the condition from which most of the originary readymades had emerged; but the fact that they were now being produced by craftsmen as artist's editions was clearly integral to some more elaborate strategem.

In comments Duchamp made at the time, he chose in fact to stress the art context. He said that the great artists from many epochs in the past had made copies of their paintings and that much sculpture was never a unique original but a cast (Lebel 1967: 77). This latter point is particularly revealing since there is an extremely important strand of Duchamp's output in which he constantly gave overt prominence to the relationship between the notion of the original, the mould, and the cast (namely his writings). The generalised understanding of Duchamp promoted in theoretical texts such as Bürger's frequently fails to take account of the textual dimension of his work, but the notes Duchamp produced for the *Large Glass* between 1912 and 1918 or in the context of the production of the *Boîtes-en-Valises* in the late 1930s are of primary importance in appreciating his concerns. The late 1930s notes on the idea of what Duchamp described as the "infra-mince", or infra-thin, are particularly pertinent to the present discussion. Some of these notes are frankly amusing. They are concerned with providing examples of various liminal conditions or states of interface in which two entities are virtually indistinguishable. Among the examples on offer are: "The warmth of a seat (which has just / been left) is an infrathin" (Duchamp 1983: unpaginated), or "When the tobacco smoke smells of the / mouth which exhales it, the 2 odors / marry by infra-thin" (1983: unpaginated). However, other notes elaborating on the concept deal with the relationship between moulds and casts in a way that may have a direct bearing on the discussion of the editioned readymades. Hence one note reads: "the difference / dimensional / between 2 mass produced objects (from the same mould) is an infra-thin? when the maximum precision is / obtained" (1983: unpagi-

nated). That such speculations have an almost metaphysical dimension is suggested by another note, which reads: "Sameness / similarity / the same (mass produced) / practical approximation of
similarity. In time the same object is not the / same after a 1 second
interval — what / Relations with the identity principle?" (1983: unpaginated).

From notes such as these it is surely appropriate to suggest that
the editioned readymades operate as a kind of "infra-thin" between
the phenomenon of the artist's edition and the mass produced commodity. Insofar as an "infra-thin" difference separates each of the
readymades in each edition — each of which amounts to being an
infinitesimally different cast from the same mould — a kind of
ironic "infra-thin" residue of uniqueness clings to each. Hence, the
artist — or rather his authorial identity — is ironically preserved at
the very point at which he is lost to the processes of mass production.

I hope that something of my determination to preserve Adorno's
dialectical understanding of modernism's "mimetic adaptation to the
hardened and alienated" in the face of Bürger's pious horror at the
possible collapse of art's critical distance into the instrumentalised
world is borne out by this reading of the late Duchamp. But I don't
want to leave things alone here. The force of my point, and the
specificity of Duchamp's late reformulation of the readymade idea,
can be made more vivid in the context of two preceding historical
gestures by Yves Klein and Andy Warhol — figures who are virtually synonymous with the Bürgeresque understanding of the failure
of the neo-avant-garde, although strictly speaking it is only Warhol
that he cites as an example.

The fact is that Duchamp's editioned readymades may in fact
have been a form of response to Klein and Warhol, both of whose
work he would have been well aware of by 1964. Knowing that they
would have grown up with an awareness of his earlier dada readymades, Duchamp may well have felt that these younger artists stood
to gain the credit for the subtler implications of his ideas before he
himself was properly appreciated, and chose therefore to trump them
with a final gesture. In the past apologists for the editioned readymades have attempted to see them as a kind of despairing, highly
perverse gambit spurred on by Duchamp's famous condemnation of
the "neo-dada" trend in a letter to Hans Richter of 1962: "In Neo-

Dada they have taken my readymades and found aesthetic beauty in them. I threw the bottlerack and the urinal in their faces as a challenge and now they admire them for their aesthetic beauty" (Richter 1965: 208). On one reading, therefore, Duchamp may have felt that the only outrageous thing that remained for to him to do would be to turn the readymade back into art — which would effectively align Duchamp's attitude towards post-war artists with that of Bürger. However, it seems to me, in line with the esoteric interpretation of the editioned readymades I have outlined, that Duchamp was more fully attuned to the complexities of the works of the younger "neo-dada" generation. Some detail is now required to clarify this point.

In 1957, Yves Klein, at that time a relatively unknown French artist with a peculiar penchant for showmanship and mystical philosophy, had an exhibition at the Galleria Apollinaire in Milan. He showed eleven monochrome panels, all of the same blue and all identical in size, although there were very slight variations in facure as some were lightly inflected with a ripple pattern. For Klein their physical presence was ultimately unimportant; what counted was that they transmitted the essence of his key artistic principle, "immateriality". He believed his own expressive input was similarly of no consequence; personal ego was, he claimed, tantamount to a moral plague infecting Western art. Although the canvases were ostensibly identical, Klein asserted that each had its own distinctive "aura". This led him to adopt a highly eccentric pricing policy for the works which he describes as follows:

> Each of the blue propositions, all similar in appearance, were all recognised by the public as very different, one from the other. The amateur passed from one to the other as it suited him and penetrated the world of blue in a state of instantaneous contemplation.

> But each blue world of each painting, although the same blue and treated in the same way, presents a completely different essence and atmosphere.

> The most sensational observation was from the "buyers". They chose among the eleven exhibited paintings, each in their own way, and each paid the requested price. The prices were all different of course. On the one hand this shows that the pictorial quality of each painting was perceptible by something other than

the material and physical appearance. On the other hand, it is evident that those who chose recognised this state of things that I call the "pictorial sensibility." (Klein 1983: 173)

Now we might be inclined to see in this a gesture of charlatanism. In this respect it is significant that Klein's carefully stage-managed debut within the Paris art world, trumpeting his so-called "monochrome adventure", had been a booklet of 1954, entitled "Yves Peintures", which had contained a non-text (consisting of a sequence of ruled lines standing in for lines of print) by an invented critic named Pascal Claude and a set of colour reproductions which ostensibly referred to paintings produced by Klein in various cities over the previous few years but which were in fact simply commercially inked sheets of paper.[3] What seems likeliest here is that Klein had at some point seen one of Duchamp's *Boîtes-en-Valises* in which there is a similar play on the relationship between the commercially manufactured and the "unique", as well as a conflation of the miniaturised set of samples and the artist's catalogue raisonné. Not surprisingly, Klein made little of this debt. But if we take the later 1957 exhibition a little more seriously — and this I think is important as a minor corrective to Benjamin Buchloh's excellent reading of Klein, which has asserted that his repetition of the earlier avant-garde use of monochromy, in Rodchenko for instance, is to be understood primarily as symptomatic of a shift in the cultural status of the artist — we might see Klein intuiting the more esoteric side of Duchamp's thought in the post-war period regarding the readymades (Buchloh 1986). Klein's concern in 1957 to establish essential qualitative differences among a set of works which, though they were handmade, had the appearance of machine-produced replicas surely has a whiff of that concern with pinpointing "infra-thin" differences within apparent sameness that Duchamp was later to explore in his editioned readymades.

Klein cannot have known about the "infra-thin" idea. Duchamp's notes on the topic were not published until the early 1980s. But he could easily have appreciated that the idea of the readymade had metaphysical connotations. Interestingly, a young American artist seems to have been pondering the concept of the readymade — along with Duchamp's *Boîte-en-Valise* — at about the same time. Five years later this artist, Andy Warhol, came up with a remarkably similar response to the Duchampian heritage, though tellingly stripped of Klein's metaphysics and almost bleakly materialist in its implications. Let us turn finally then to Warhol's 1962 exhibition of thirty-two paintings of Campbell's Soup cans at Irving Blum's Ferus Gallery in Los Angeles.

When they are reproduced in books, these paintings, each identical in terms of the basic motif of the soup can but each labelled differently in terms of the flavour of the product (one rogue label also proclaims that the "cheddar cheese soup" it contains is "great as a sauce too"), are normally arranged in a series of rows to make up a large rectangular block. In fact, as can be seen from installation shots, the paintings were originally displayed at the Ferus Gallery in a long line along a shelf at just below head height, asserting that they were, very much, products to be bought. The number of paintings, thirty-two, had in fact been determined by the range of Campbell's soup flavours then available. Warhol thus asserted an absolute identicality between his activity as an artist and the production of commercial products. Most importantly, in terms of the comparison with Klein, his products were all priced equally. The implacable democracy of mass culture had become triumphant in art as in supermarket food-products.

At this stage, Warhol had not actually taken up silkscreen printing as a means of standardising his technique in conformity with mechanical reproduction. The schema for each soup can was produced by a template and the images were then hand-painted. The only printed element was the *fleur-de-lis* motif along each can's bottom edge, but even here home-made gum-rubber stamps were used.[4] In many ways the images were almost reassuringly home-made. Over the next couple of years, Warhol would submit his images, as far as he was able, to a principle of production line impersonality.

It might seem that there is little room for the "infra-thin" here, or for the concern with infinitesimal degrees of difference within sameness that applied to the Duchampian fascination with the relationship between cast and mould; but it is, of course, significant that what most obviously establishes each painting's difference from the others in the set is its ostensible "flavour" — the fact that it purports to be chicken noodle, cream of mushroom, green pea, asparagus or whatever. The key word here, of course, is "purports". It is as though the "infra-thin" has lost any metaphysical substance — the sense in which it could exist as some ineffable guarantor of value even when installed in the most apparently standardised of objects — and literally been reduced to a label signifying difference within a pre-determined "range."

It is significant, though, that in talking about the ossification of the "infra-thin" principle in Warhol's soup can paintings we are, from a historical viewpoint, speaking in advance of the fact. Duchamp was not to produce his editioned readymades — which seem so clearly to embody the "infra-thin" concept — until two years after Warhol. As has been indicated earlier, he had been playing with the idea in scribbled notes for years, and it is surely possible now to appreciate the extent to which, seeing younger artists bringing his ideas to fruition to partial degrees, he must have felt the need to make one final gesture of conceptual authority. The issue of the partiality of Klein's and Warhol's gestures is surely the key point. I have implied throughout my discussion of their two exhibitions of 1957 and 1962 that there is a clear-cut split between them — which crudely translates as spirituality versus materialism. Another way to talk about the difference would be in terms of stages in the assimilation of the traditional idea of the artist-creator to a model of mechanisation. Klein's 1957 exhibition could be seen as a last-ditch attempt to preserve an almost theological model of the artist-creator, whilst Warhol gladly sheds any sense of the uniqueness of the artist's spiritual agency. In a sense, what Duchamp does in his editioned readymades is to bring their gestures together firmly under his own name. The idea of a sleight-of-hand elision of the artist's edition (with the minor differences in individual examples involved) and mass production — as an acknowledgement of the originary conditions under which the readymades came into existence — neatly collapses Klein into Warhol.

What Duchamp's late gesture also neatly achieves — or at least this is my hope in terms of the larger theoretical project underpinning this essay — is an "infra-thin" interface between personal autonomy and technological determinism — which responds to Adorno's dialectical reading of modernism as bound up with the "mimetic adaptation to what is hardened and alienated". Duchamp's editioned readymades literally mimic the processes of artistic commodification. He commodifies his own previous critique of the commodity form in its relation to art — whilst preserving, courtesy of the "infra-thin" thematics of the relation between cast and mould, an ironic distillation of the artistically "unique."

To that extent critique inheres in the very signifiers of capitulation. Difference is installed in sameness. It goes without saying that for me at least, Klein and Warhol fail to achieve the dialectical finesse of Duchamp. He was a better chess player; he won out in the end. But what is particularly important is that Duchamp's post-war practice was heavily dependant on Klein and Warhol in terms of its unravelling. To that extent, these fascinating figures, whose works are disparaged by Bürger in such cavalier fashion, become players in a post-war coda to the historical avant-garde's project. There is no qualitative distinction to be made, I would argue, between the early avant-garde and the neo-avant-garde, just as, properly understood, the Duchampian readymade occupies an historical moment stretching from 1913 to 1964 (and arguably afterwards in a kind of after-life).[5] Possibly in the interplay between Duchamp, Klein, and Warhol a story of the interface between art and technology under modernism is brought to a form of conclusion. But to reinforce an important point from earlier, it does not seem to me that this can be read as a form of rapprochement, although what does seem striking to me about Duchamp, Klein and Warhol is the peculiarly bitter-sweet quality of their humour. Resistance to technological determinism is squeezed into Duchamp's late readymade project until that resistance itself becomes a form of the "infra-thin". But it is there. And until decisive structural changes occur within our culture, the slow demise of modernism can probably achieve little more.

NOTES

[1] For a discussion of the readymades (*Fountain* included) as concerned with interactions between physical and aesthetic "reflex", see my essay "Marcel Duchamp's Readymades and Anti-Aesthetic Reflex". In: Paul Smith and Carolyn Wilde (eds.), *A Companion to Art Theory*. Oxford: Blackwells, 2002, 253–263.

[2] For a full discussion of these instances see: Francis Nauman, *Marcel Duchamp: the Art of Making Art in the Age of Mechanical Reproduction*. Amsterdam: Ludion Press, 1999, chapters 6–8.

[3] For a detailed discussion of the 1954 "Yves Peintres" brochure see: Sidra Stich, *Yves Klein.* London: Hayward Gallery, 1995, 42–47.

[4] For a thorough technical description of these paintings alongside a discussion of the 1962 exhibition as a whole, see: Kirk Varnedoe. "Campbell Soup Cans, 1962". In: Heiner Bastian (ed.), *Andy Warhol: Retrospective.* London: Tate Modern, 2001, 40–45.

[5] To a degree my argument here can be aligned with that of Hal Foster in the essay "Who's Afraid of the Neo-Avant-Garde." In: Hal Foster, *The Return of the Real.* MIT Press, 1996, 1–34. Towards the end of this essay Foster attempts to overturn Bürger's crude "before and after" model of twentieth century avant-gardism by arguing for what he characterises as a "deferred action" in the avant-garde's historical effects such that originary meanings and potential become "realised" via repetition at a later date: "Historical and neo-avant-gardes are constituted in a similar way, as a continued process of protension and retension, a complex relay of anticipated futures and reconstructed pasts – in short, in a deferred action that throws over any simple scheme of before and after, cause and effect, origin and repetition" (29).

BIBLIOGRAPHY

Ades, Dawn, Neil Cox and David Hopkins
      1999   *Marcel Duchamp.* London: Thames and Hudson.

Adorno, Theodor
      1997   *Aesthetic Theory,* ed. Gretel Adorno and Rolf Tiedemann, trans. Robert Hullot-Kentor. London: Athlone Press.

Bastian, Heiner (ed.)
      2000   *Andy Warhol: Retrospective.* London: Tate Publishing.

Buchloh, Benjamin
      1984   "Theorizing the Avant Garde". In: *Art in America.* November 1984, 19-21.

      1986   "The Primary Colors for the Second Time: A Paradigm Repetition of the Neo-Avant-Garde". In: *October*, no. 37.

Bürger, Peter
      1984   *Theory of the Avant Garde*, trans. Michael Shaw. Minneapolis: University of Minnesota Press.

Duchamp, Marcel
 1983   *Marcel Duchamp, Notes*, arranged and translated by Paul
             Matisse. Boston: G.K. Hall.

Foster, Hal
 1996   "Who's Afraid of the Neo-Avant-Garde". In: *The Return
             of the Real*. Cambridge, Mass: MIT Press, 1-32 .

Klein, Yves
 1983   "Mon Livre". Section reprinted in: *Yves Klein*. Paris:
             Musee National d'Art Moderne, Centre Georges
             Pompidou.

Lebel, Robert
 1967   "Marcel Duchamp maintenant et ici". In: *L'oeil*, no. 149.

Naumann, Francis
 1999   *Marcel Duchamp: The Art of Making Art in the Age of
             Mechanical Reproduction*. Amsterdam: Ludion Press.

Richter, Hans
 1965   *Dada: Art and Anti-Art*. London: Thames and Hudson.

Scheunemann, Dietrich (ed.)
 2000   *European Avant Garde: New Perspectives*. Amsterdam:
             Rodopi.

Schwarz, Arturo
 1997   *The Complete Works of Marcel Duchamp* (2 vols).
             London: Thames and Hudson.

Stich, Sidra
 1995   *Yves Klein*. London: Hayward Gallery.

Paint it Black: Ad Reinhardt's Paradoxical Avant-Gardism

BEN HIGHMORE

In the pages of *Art News* (March 1965) the painter Ad Reinhardt conducted an interview with himself; he claimed that no one else was interested in the job. In it he addresses the question of his relationship with a putative avant-garde:

> "You're the only painter who's been a member of every avant-garde movement in art of the last thirty years, aren't you?" I asked him in his Greenwich Village loft-studio where Lower Broadway meets Waverly Place.
> "Yes," he said.
> "You were a vanguard pre-abstract-expressionist in the late thirties, a vanguard abstract-impressionist in the middle forties and a vanguard post-abstract-expressionist in the early fifties, weren't you?" I asked.
> "Yes," he said.
> "You were the first painter to get rid of vanguardism, weren't you?" I asked.
> "Yes," he said.
> (Reinhardt 1991: 11)[1]

Leaving aside the implicit critique of the conventions of magazine interviewing performed by relentlessly foregrounding the directive content provided by the interviewer, this auto-interview stages a crucial paradox for the theorising of avant-gardism. How is it, we might want to ask, that someone who consistently identifies with avant-gardism ends up characterising themselves as anti-avant-garde or non-avant-garde? And more precisely: under what conditions might anti-avant-gardism be seen as a form of avant-gardism? The example of Ad Reinhardt will do nothing to make the job of theorising avant-gardism any easier. Yet to ignore awkward cases like Reinhardt's will only produce a theory incapable of dealing with some of the most intransigent contradictions within modern culture.

Ad Reinhardt at work in his studio in Greenwich Village (1966)

From 1960 until his death in 1967 Reinhardt painted only one type of picture. Five feet square and "black", these paintings were for Reinhardt "the last paintings which anyone can make" (1966: 13).[2] When displayed within group exhibitions in Paris (1963), New York (1963), and London (1964), the paintings had to be roped off from an angry viewing public.[3] If this was anti-avant-gardism, its success as an affront to bourgeois sensibility (*épater le bourgeois*) echoes with the memory of much earlier avant-garde events.

In a bid to defend these paintings from being absorbed within the interpretative frameworks for modern art at the time, Reinhardt surrounded them in a barrage of what he termed "Art-as-Art Dogma". Reinhardt worked hard to tell us exactly what these paintings were *not*. First of all they were not expressive: "no scumblebumpkinism, no personality-piturequeness, no texturing-gesturings […] no brushwork-bravura" (103). "It is not right" wrote Reinhardt in a text called "The Artist in Search of a Code of Ethics",

> for artists to encourage critics to think that sloppy impasto is Dionysian and that neat scumbling is Apollonian. Artists who peddle wiggly lines and colors as representing emotion should be run off the streets. (1960: 163)

Secondly, and partly as a consequence of their non-expressivity, Reinhardt's paintings did not possess subject matter: "no […] society-reflecting, universe insighting, zeit-geisting" (103). "It is not right", states his code of ethics,

> for artists to plug their paintings as a valuable report or record of world wars and peace, or pass themselves off as visionaries of cosmic orders or seismographs of universal disorders. (1960: 163)

Reinhardt's "art-as-art dogma" insisted on an absolute autonomy: "Art is art. Everything else is everything else" (1958: 51). Thirdly, and perhaps most problematically, they were not, or had to be constantly defended from being, marketable commodities: a black painting was a "useless, unmarketable, irreducible, unphotographable, unreproducible, inexplicable icon" (1955: 83).[4] Writing about a specific black painting, and with more than a hint of self-deprecating irony, Reinhardt wrote:

> this painting is unsalable and it is not for sale except to someone who wants to buy it. […] This painting is priceless, has no price tag, no markets, no buyers, no sellers, no dealers, no collectors, with few exceptions. (1963: 85)

We could go on like this for a while. Reinhardt's protectionism is vociferous, exhaustive, and exhausting. But it is also humorous, knowingly bombastic (as if, parodically, miming the posture of avant-gardism itself) and a vivid articulation of an avant-gardist problem: how to make avant-garde art at a moment when it seemed that anything could simply be recuperated as a commodity? This is no doubt oversimplifying Reinhardt's position, but the question of the commodity was a basic and central problem for anyone wanting to produce an art that could work adversarially at this time (pop art would find its own response to this quandary). After all to have the value of a work, avant-garde or not, returned as exchange value would emphatically blunt opposition to the kind of capitalism that dominated US culture in the early 1960s.

Theorising avant-gardism has as its all too silent problematic the artistic non-avant-garde, and the non-avant-gardism of the more general cultural field. After all something is only avant-garde in relation to other things which are not avant-garde but are mainstream, established, or otherwise part of a dominant and dominating culture. As Fred Orton and Griselda Pollock suggest:

> *Avant-garde* must [...] signify, as it did in its inception in the second half of the nineteenth century, a range of social postures and strategies for artists by which they could differentiate themselves from current social and cultural structures while also intervening in them. To be of the *avant-garde* was to participate in complex and contradictory tactics of involvement with, and evasion of, immediate forms of metropolitan social and economic life. (Orton and Pollock 1996: 142)

It is this involvement and evasion that is at the heart of it. Reinhardt's negativity, his ceaseless and at times paranoid dogma, is bound up with certain forms of evasion, and differentiation. The question that this poses for Reinhardt's work is *where* this involvement and evasion is taking place, or to be more precise, in relation to *what* exactly is the avant-garde work getting done? Is its avant-gardism in relation to a limited and local art-world to which it responds and differentiates itself? Is this art-world comprised of a conservative establishment (a beaux-arts tradition, or something more nationalist in flavour?) or of various avant-garde factions, including some which had become or were becoming the establishment? And if the work is aimed against a larger set of cultural and social structures, then which structure or bit of structure?

Post-war avant-gardism faced, and still faces, a cultural field against which the idea of some pure or absolute adversarial or contestatory role seems highly unlikely. After all can we expect any form of avant-gardism to find a coherent adversarial position against a cultural field characterised by contradiction, conflict, and fragmentation; literally an incoherent field? Does it make much sense to even talk about *the* mainstream, against which an avant-gardism might measure itself, in a culture where both avant-gardism and non-avant-gardism can function as blue-chip commodities, and where previous avant-garde works can decorate calendars and biscuit tin lids, and where the sheer promiscuity of cultural products seems to have reached unmanageable proportions? And looking to the wider cultural sphere; was there in the US in the early 1960s a position to be adopted that would emphatically mark an antipathy to *both* capitalist expansionism and isolationist nationalism? Faced with a culture where Pollock's drip paintings could be used as backdrops for *Vogue* models (see Clark 1990), and where leftist social realists like Ben Shahn could be used to smooth the way for US interests in Italy (see Pohl 1989), what would a pure and uncompromising avant-gardism have looked like? A theory of avant-gardism, then, would have to shrug off the seductions of pursuing heroic narratives, opting instead for something more defiled, something with impurity as its very essence. It would necessarily have as its task the delimiting of more particular and limited relationships between artworks and the more general cultural field.

In the next section I want to juxtapose Reinhardt's work with other some other cultural practices in order to make vivid his peculiar and recalcitrant negotiation of a more general cultural field. My choice of contexts is to some extent wilful and premised on what might be mere coincidence. My defence of this is that such contexts (car manufacturing, cold-war propaganda, and such like) can be read as synecdoches of much larger cultural phenomena.

Contexts and Connections

The first context juxtaposes a non-happening in New York with a multi-media propaganda presentation in Moscow. In October 1958 and again in January 1959 Reinhardt presented two non-happenings at the Artists Club. On each occasion Reinhardt's aim was to show about 2,000 of the 10,000 slides he has taken of "significant forms" of architectural and sculptural work in "The Moslem World and India". Reinhardt's collection was divided into repeated motifs and patterns from the material he had photographed while touring the world. The evening proceeded slowly with Reinhardt supplying little commentary and lingering on each image for about five minuets.

Most of his audience had left within the first half-hour. Had this non-happening been completed it would have lasted about 167 hours.

In 1959 the Ray and Charles Eames, working under the aegis of the United States Information Agency produced a display for the American Exhibition in Moscow (see Kirkham 1995). *Glimpses of the USA* was the result. It lasted 12-minutes and consisted of 2,200 rapidly changing images projected onto seven enormous screens, each 32-feet wide, attached to the inside of one of Buckminster Fuller's geodesic dome. Leaving aside the question of whether the

Charles and Ray Eames, *Glimpses of the USA* (1959)

work of the Eameses can be classified as avant-garde (and if not, why not?), it is worth noting the synchronicity between these two events. It is also worth noting the relative differences in terms of speed. The Eameses' display processed images at roughly 835 times the speed of Reinhardt's. Or more to my point, the speed of Reinhardt's non-happening was nearly one-thousandth the speed of the Moscow show.

The second context relies on juxtaposing two ways to paint it black. In 1914 in a bid to further standardise production of the Ford Model T car, Henry Ford did away with colour variation. In an oft-quoted remark he states that "any customer can have a car painted any color he wants as long as it is black" (Gartman 1994: 45–6). In 1960 Reinhardt also gets rid of colour variation. Reinhardt's practice had by 1960 become standardised in terms of colour, size, surface finish, and working process:

> No easel or palette. Low, flat, sturdy benches work well. Brushes should be new, clean, flat, even, one-inch wide, and strong. [...] The brush should pass over the surface lightly and smoothly and silently. No rubbing or scraping. Paint should be permanent, free of impurities, mixed into and stored in jars. [...] A picture is finished when all traces of the means used to bring about the end has disappeared. (1957: 206–7)

Such a practice seems to suggest something like a factory production and the limited variation in colour must have echoed with

Ad Reinhardt: A 'black' painting in production (1966)

Ford's famous refusal. Yet by 1960 much that we associate with early Ford production was simply redundant.

In 1923 Ford's domination of the automobile market in the US was a massive 50 percent of total sales. But by 1927 this had slipped to 15 percent. The model T it seems was just too well built and further demand for cheap cars could look to a burgeoning market in

116   Ben Highmore

second-hand automobiles. For those who wanted style, luxury and conspicuous consumption Ford held little promise. It was General Motors that heralded what could be seen as the major revolution in car design. From the middle of the 1920s on, the quality of cars was partly going to be measured by their distinctive look. It was Harley Earle, heading up General Motors' Art and Colour Section — or the "beauty parlor" as it was also known, along with GM president Alfred Sloan that devised a production based around variety and innovation. And if Ford had recognised the need for mass advertising for mass-production, GM recognised an even greater need to create desire through advertising for its stylised ever-changing products. The automobile industry, then, evidences a shift from being production lead to becoming consumption lead, and what becomes evident by the 1930s is that "marketing began to dominate the production process itself" (Wollen 1989: 27).

In 1966 the Jewish Museum in New York staged a major retrospective of Reinhardt's work. One room contained nothing but five-foot square black paintings. How would these pictures have looked: like dada provocation? Like Yves Klein's "blue" paintings? Like a factory line production of Model T paintings? Perhaps, but the important historical point is that they would not have looked like the kinds of mass production dominant at the time. If they do foreground a production aesthetic that shares similarities with early Fordism, they do not share the kind of consumer aesthetic that invested so much in style and innovation. As far as this goes both Pop art and most abstract expressionism would have fared worse. For instance Harold Rosenberg's classic essay of 1952 "The American Action Painters" sets out the value of abstraction in equivocal terms. While action painting (Rosenberg's name for abstract expressionism) might abhor the world of commerce as it existentially tries to find meaning in a world that has made it necessary to vacate social criticism, it is continually in danger of being overrun by commerce. So, for instance, while productive tensions might be generated in the drips and daubs of abstract art, the "style" of such endeavours can become simply a signature for a "commodity with a trademark" (Rosenberg 1952: 82). Seen alongside post 1930s auto styling, "abstract expressionist" practices might evidence a number of shared orientations. For instance, if Chrysler continually provide new models with distinct detailing and surface styling, while remaining recognisably consistent (always a Chrysler car), then does not this correspond with *something* in the practices of Pollock, Rothko, Newman, *et al*? Structural continuity, recognisable "style", yet with continual innovation at the level of surface and detail? The point here is not to suggest that Reinhardt's black paintings successfully avoided commodification, only that in attempting to avoid commodification they look back to a very specific mode of production that had become significantly outmoded: the invariable and standard product.

The third context works by juxtaposing the durational aspects of commodification with the durational condition of Reinhardt's black paintings. First let me have a go at describing a "black" painting. The surface is matt. The matt-ness is the result of a process that layers thin "washes" of paint within a square trisected pattern, like a naughts and crosses grid. Matt-ness is also a result of the peculiar mix of the paint dilution: Reinhardt mixed oil paint with both turpentine and "size" (a sloppy "glue" used for preparing canvases). The paint, or rather the pigment, thus adheres to the surface in a suspension where the oil of the oil paint is significantly de-saturated. Any contact of the surface with oily matter (fingers, noses, and such like) immediately leave oily residues that produce glossy pools on the surface. The blackness of the painting is actually a blackening of colour to the point where the colour pigment, green, red, blue in the main, only reveals itself when your eyes have accustomed themselves to the insistent darkness of the surface. The light, like oil, is sucked in and absorbed by the painting's surface; these are paintings that as Rosenberg once said "turn the lights out".

The black paintings take time to see. Not only do your eyes have to get used to the blackness; it will take time for the colours to find the light to emerge out of the darkness. And when the colours do emerge, they will have a dark luminosity that can literally pull you in, which resulted in damage being done to the paintings when oily noses touched the surface. This is not some strange mystic response, this is not aestheticism standing in for art criticism or history, and it is not about how sensitive your are. It is more physiological than that. The paintings are addressed to a sensorial consciousness and perception prepared to suspend visual gratification. As a result the black paintings demand phenomenological enquiry. This is not the place to pursue such an enquiry, but it is the place to note their specific duration; the time it takes to view these paintings, or at least to see them as something more than "black". Dore Ashton suggested in 1960 that the early black paintings took about 10 minutes to actually see the illumination of colour: "it takes a good ten minutes for the first impression to register" (Lippard 1981: 141). One of the things that made the black paintings worth repeating was that each one was different and each one deferred its moment of revelation for a different duration. If there was a developing practice here and not simply the semblance of standardisation, then it was partly to do with lengthening the duration of their showing. Some of the most successful later black paintings need to be timed at closer to 25 minutes.

The durational condition of the commodity is almost an exact reverse of this. Commodities require almost instantaneous gratification. They can not afford to be "stand-offish". Of course, then they let you down. Their sheen wears off. Their obsolescence has been guaranteed in advance. If the black paintings initially provide dissatisfaction which gets replaced by visual gratification; the commodity allows instant gratification followed by a slow release of dissatisfaction.

We could multiply these contexts indefinitely, and in doing so accentuate Reinhardt's paintings along several different lines. Multiplying the contexts would also alter the adversarial value of the work. Any account of Reinhardt's work that wanted to be adequate would need to explore some contexts for the following: Reinhardt's continued commitment to political activism (see Corris 1994); his continual promotion of the writing of Clive Bell, George Kubler, and Henri Focillon; and his relationship to various religious forms (Islam and Buddhism, for instance). The job here, though, is not to provide an adequate account of Reinhardt's work, but to use Reinhardt as an example for a more productively theoretical approach to the study of avant-gardism.

The Syntax and Rhythmanalysis of Avant-Gardism

In 1939 Roger Caillois published a book titled *Man and the Sacred* (*L'homme at le sacré*). Right at the start of his book, Caillois seeks to qualify his project of writing an account of the sacred: "being unable to attack the study of the inexhaustible morphology of the sacred, I have tried to write its syntax" (Caillois 2001: 13). The same qualification might stand for anyone attempting to write a theory of avant-gardism; it is the generalisations about the morphology of avant-gardist artworks that seem to scupper the project of theorising the avant-garde. Peter Bürger's *Theory of the Avant-Garde*, to take an obvious example, is convincing when his concern is with detailing the contradictory and dialectical relations between autonomous art and a more general life-world. It comes unstuck when he makes a claim to see the desire for repatriating autonomous art to the life-world as an essential ingredient *within* the artworks themselves. In other words, it works as syntactical description (avant-garde art and artists seeking to refashion the category art and trying to burst out of the bourgeois or establishment category of art); it flounders as morphological analysis (the form of avant-garde artworks as characterised by a desire to repatriate art and the life-world). The floundering is due to what we too might recognise as the seemingly "inexhaustible morphology" of avant-gardism. Nor should this floundering in the face of an unmanageable variety of forms come as much of a surprise if we judge avant-gardism by its more usual characterisation as a frenetic generator of new forms. After all it is something of a truism to see avant-gardism as premised on technical innovation and experimentation.[5]

Reading some of the literature written since Bürger's contribution it seems that much of the energy of theorising avant-gardism has been spent mapping the syntactical relationships between avant-gardism and the larger cultural sphere in which it is embedded, and within which its claim for avant-gardism would be measured. Take for instance T.J. Clark's short but valiant attempt to provide an overview of a general avant-gardist strategy. In an extended footnote to an essay discussing Clement Greenberg's early writing on modern art, Clark suggests a general orientation of modern art as avant-gardist challenge to the values and protocols of established artistic practice, and, more implicitly, to the social values they codify. Clark's term for describing and connecting the diverse range of forms and contents within avant-gardism is "practices of negation":

> By "practices of negation" I meant some form of decisive innovation, in method or materials or imagery, whereby a previously established set of skills or frame of reference — skills and references which up till then had been taken as essential to art-making

of any seriousness — are deliberately avoided or travestied, in such a way as to imply that only *by* such incompetence or obscurity will genuine picturing get done. (Clark 1985: 55)

Clark provides an extensive array of practices, from Manet to pop art, for exemplifying practices of negation. The following is representative of the kinds of characteristic negations that he sees avant-gardism performing:

Deliberate displays of painterly awkwardness, or facility in kinds of painting that were not supposed to be worth perfecting. Primitivisms of all shapes and sizes. The use of degenerate or trivial or "inartistic" materials. Denial of full conscious control over the artefact; automatic or aleatory ways of doing things. A taste for the margins and vestiges of social life; a wish to celebrate the "insignificant" or disreputable in modernity. (Clark 1985: 55)

Crucially, of course, such practices are only "negations" in relation to another set of practices that would demand, for instance, that art-making should be sophisticated, fully conscious, and portray subject matter of established worth, and so on. Clark's "practices of negation" convincingly manages to bring together a much wider spectrum of artists than Bürger's thesis, yet for all that it does not get at some of the paradoxes and awkwardness of avant-gardism.

Clark's essay provides another footnote, this time using the paintings of Ad Reinhardt as an exemplification of how such negation is necessarily bound up with the endgame of modernism that, for Clark, drives modernist avant-gardism. For Clark the endgame of negation is purism: "practices of negation […] seem to me the very form of the practices of purity" (Clark 1985: 55). I'd want to suggest that the limitations of "practices of negation" is precisely that it ca not see in Reinhardt's work anything more than negation, anything other than blank blackness. In seeing Reinhardt's paintings as pure negation it mistakes the task of the writing, which was negation, for the painting's task of establishing a temporal opposition to the durational logic of commodification.

Rhythmanalysis could, potentially, provide a more productive orientation for perceiving the syntax of avant-gardism. More than this though it might be able to perceive different morphological patterns as well. Unlike "practices of negation", or Bürger's thesis about the repatriation of art and life, rhythmanalysis would not require immediate assessment of the critical power of avant-gardism; its revolutionary power versus its conformist function, for instance. Rhythmanalysis would start by allowing for new forms of description for avant-garde work, or for any other kinds of work for that matter.

Rhythmanalysis, despite its name, is not a fixed methodology. Its most vivid practitioner, perhaps the only practitioner to self-consciously claim rhythmanalysis as their project, was Henri Lefebvre (see Lefebvre 1992). Lefebvre used it as a way of registering the polyrhythmic movements, circuits, exchanges, flows and so on, of city life. For him it was a way of phenomenologically registering the lived-ness of experience, while at the same time being able to grasp more structural imperatives; the circulation of money within the city, for instance. We should not make too much of the "analysis" of rhythmanalysis: Lefebvre treats it as an orientation, a loose approach that allows for complexity, vivid description and his own brand of philosophical speculation.

Rhythmanalysis is not merely concerned with speed. It is interested in durations, directions of circulation, flows, interruptions, tenacity, absorption, movement, stillness, historical rhythms and returns, and so on. Everything has rhythmicity, because everything circulates within a dynamic culture. Lefebvre writes about the rhythms of the body, the rhythms of seasonal time, while also being interested in the a-rhythmic movements of the state. I want to be clear here: there is no special reason why rhythmanalysis is suited to studying the avant-garde, at least there is no reason why it will be any more suited to studying avant-gardism than to studying anything else. My point is that rhythmanalysis is *generally* productive for attending to culture, partly because it immediately assumes that culture is dynamic and in flux, and partly because it overcomes the reification of either the synchronic or diachronic approaches to culture. In what follows I want to suggest ways that rhythmanalysis might be used for the study and theorisation of avant-gardism.

The durational experience of avant-garde art will be crucial. Reinhardt's work offers a vivid example of delayed duration, refusing the immediacy and gratification of perception. A number of other examples could be recruited here, most particularly work in the area of film, music and performance: Michael Snow and other filmmakers loosely grouped as "structural materialists", Andy Warhol's early film-works, Chantal Akerman's *Jeanne Dielman*, John Cage, and so on. Against this we would need to also register an avant-gardism of the instantaneous. Michael Fried is probably the most famous commentator on this. For Fried it is the "presentness" of the artwork that

> one experiences as a kind of *instantaneousness*: as though if only one were infinitely more acute, a single infinitely brief instant would be long enough to see everything, to experience the work in all its depth and fullness, to be ever convinced by it. (Fried 1967: 22)

Of course Fried is using the immediacy of the work as a lynchpin to support a system of value, but we could also include work here that he would certainly not value, for instance, pop art. Again, just to emphasise the point, the study of avant-gardism would always need to keep one eye on the more general cultural field, so the durational aspects of commodification would operate here as a general cultural marker for measuring the velocities of these avant-garde durations (too slow, too fast).

The theme of technological and material temporality would also need to be central to a rhythmanalysis of avant-gardism. It was Walter Benjamin who recognised in surrealism the insistent use of the recently outmoded, and claimed that Breton

> was the first to perceive the revolutionary energies that appear in the "outmoded", in the first iron constructions, the first factory buildings, the earliest photos, the objects that have begun to be extinct, grand pianos, the dresses of five years ago, fashionable restaurants when the vogue has begun to ebb from them. (Benjamin 1929: 229)

Here is not the place to fully discuss why such outmoded forms might be harbingers of revolutionary energies, merely to recognise what might be seen as a radical nostalgia in various forms of avant-gardism. Rhythmanalysis would need to be attuned to the rhythm of these historical returns, the recycling and re-circulation of forms, objects, techniques and materials.

Such nostalgia does not begin and end with surrealism. We have seen how Reinhardt operates with a practice built out of the production forms of early Fordism, as well as earlier craft-based practices, but other artists should also be included here. For example when Benjamin Buchloh discusses the work of Jacques de la Villeglé, Raymond Hains and François Dufrêne he points out that their interest in billboards coincides with a moment when the billboard had been superseded as a central weapon in the capitalist armoury. Writing more generally, he suggests a reason for avant-gardist interest in the recently outmoded:

> Once on the wane, they [billboards] would increasingly qualify as an artistic attraction, the same way that all evacuated locations (ruins) and obsolete technologies, appearing to be exempt from or abandoned by the logic of the commodity and the instrumentality of engineered desire, had so qualified. (Buchloh 2000: 445)

Avant-garde interest in technologies will also need to be measured in terms of the uses of technologies by other arms of the culture industry. For instance the use of photography might signal the embracing of technological modernity within the sphere of art, yet when pitted against the photographic practices of mass-circulation magazines, for instance, it might signal an earlier moment of technology. How up-to-date, for instance, was the peculiar use of technology by Fluxus? Here too we could look at the continual use of trash by avant-gardism; everything from Kurt Schwitters to Mike Kelley. Artistic recycling always suggests a precise historical rhythmicity: think, for instance, of the continual use of Victorian etchings in the work of Max Ernst and others.

Rhythmanalysis might be interested in the rhythmic content of artworks (futurism's interest in planes, trains and automobiles, for instance) but it would be *more* interested in those rhythms that are fundamental to the business of avant-gardism. One of the aspects of avant-gardism that suggests a close connection to the market economy, and suggests that avant-gardism might be treated as a symptom as much as a diagnosis of capitalist culture, is the relationship between fashion and avant-gardism. Avant-gardes seem to suffer from built-in obsolescence and from the incessant replacement by the latest "avant-garde gambit" (Pollock 1992). There is a rhythm here that needs studying. On the one hand the rhythm by which one avant-garde is replaced by another — "the avant-garde is dead, long live the avant-garde" (Mann 1991: 33) — on the other hand, the voracious capacity of the host culture to absorb critique. This is the rhythm of recuperation. As Paul Mann suggests in his excellent meta-critical study of theories of the avant-garde, "recuperation is the syntax of cultural discourse", with avant-gardism being "the most fully articulated discourse of the technology of recuperation" (Mann 1991: 15). It is not hard to find an awareness of this recuperative rhythm peppering the writing of Ad Reinhardt; it is a pressing and depressing issue for avant-gardism. As Mann suggests "death" haunts avant-gardism at its root:

> experimental techniques become codified, their results predictable; madness reveals its methods and the methods are distributed as aesthetic gadgets for general use; anarchists find their work installed in museums and themselves in university chairs. (Mann 1991: 37)

The question for the rhythmanalysis of avant-gardism is not whether this is inevitable or to search for work that has been untouched by such processes, but to attend to their rhythms. Is the perception that the rhythms of recuperation are speeding up correct? Or is there a different relationship between so-called "tradition" and the avant-garde which means that recuperation and its rhythmicity need to be rethought, re-registered?

As stated in the first section of this essay, to theorise avant-gardism is not to look for purity but to begin from the very ground of impurity. Rhythmanalysis is dedicated to the polyrhythmic fusion and confusion of modern life. It would be attuned to the varied connections and disconnections between the putative avant-garde work and the panoply of contexts that might make sense of it. It would need to be able to recognise how a work ticks with the tempos of structural patterns (commodification, increased technical specialisation, and so on) while at the same time hearing the beat of its utopian pulse. It would need to see how a work might be both affirmative and disaffirmative at the same time (but at different rhythms). Rhythmanalysis would rise to the challenge of trying to orchestrate such plural accounts.

I am left wondering, though, if it is really the *avant*-garde that is the object of study here or something that could be more vividly described as a derrière-garde; purposely slothful, tenaciously recycling abandoned materials and technologies, forcing a historical memory on the culture of amnesia? Reinhardt's paradoxical avant-gardism might suggest this, but so too would any number of other examples of avant-gardism. Any description of avant-gardism that foregrounds technical experimentation, anti-traditionalism, and continual innovation will have to content with the fact that such phenomena, rather than being marginal to modern culture, lies at its dynamic centre. This much at any rate is what Marx and Engels described in 1848 with their account of bourgeois society:

> Constant revolutionising of production, uninterrupted disturbance of all social conditions, everlasting uncertainty and agitation distinguish the bourgeois epoch from all earlier ones. All fixed, fast-frozen relations, with their train of ancient and venerable prejudices and opinions, are swept away, all new-formed ones become antiquated before they can ossify. (Marx and Engels 1848: 36–7)

Does not this read like a description of the avant-gardism of capitalism? And when faced with this would not it be logical that an adversarial culture would, more likely, resemble a derrière-garde, struggling to differentiate itself from the driving forces of capitalism without falling into the reactionary mire of bourgeois nostalgia? And might not this be a reason why an adversarial Reinhardt would like to think of himself as the first avant-garde painter to "to get rid of vanguardism"?

NOTES

[1] Ad Reinhardt's writings have been collected in Reinhardt (1991) *Art as Art* (see bibliography for details). Throughout this chapter unspecified quotations are references to this volume. I have included the dates of original publication (or date of writing) unless the text is not dated.

[2] There are a couple of exceptions to this, but the variation is only in size — they remain ostensibly "black". Information about Reinhardt's practice and output can be gathered from the following publications: Inboden and Kelle in 1985; Lippard 1981; and The Museum of Contemporary Art, Los Angeles and Museum of Modern Art, New York 1991. We will have something to say about this blackness later; for the moment it is enough to mention that the blackness is not the absence of colour, but its compound density. It is colour at its most absorptive.

[3] "Angry public" is how Reinhardt describes the "roping off" in an interview in 1966 (15). That same year he also claimed that the paintings were "roped off because too many of viewers were unable to resist touching the surface of the paintings and leaving their marks" (84). Of course an irresistible surface, which demands touching, is hardly the same as angry provocation. Perhaps part of the contradiction animated in, and by, these paintings is that responses to them range from fascination to angry frustration and both responses seem to result in damage (the surfaces of the paintings were peculiarly sensitive to touch). The one form of attention that would not "touch" these works was indifference. It should be noted that Reinhardt was fully prepared for the continual spoiling of the surface (either through too much interest or too much anger or through more practical handling) and would repaint them according to the paint recipes he had recorded.

[4] Actual examples of "black" paintings do not work as reproductions, nor were they meant to. For this reason I have only included production stills.

[5] For instance for Poggioli: "one of the primary characteristics of avant-garde art is, technically and formally, experimentalism" (1968: 131). Not only is innovation and experimentation a primary characteristic but "the experimental factor in avant-gardism is obvious to anyone having even a summary knowledge of the course of contemporary art" (131).

BIBLIOGRAPHY

Benjamin, Walter
    1929   "Surrealism: The Last Snapshot of the European Intelligentsia". In: *One Way Street and Other Writings*, trans. Edmund Jephcott and Kingsley Shorter. London: Verso, 225–39.

Buchloh, Benjamin H. D.
    2000   *Neo-Avantgarde and Culture Industry: Essays on European and American Art from 1955 to 1975*. Cambridge, Mass. : MIT Press.

Bürger, Peter
    1984   *Theory of the Avant-Garde*, trans. Michael Shaw. Manchester: Manchester University Press.

Caillois, Roger
    2001   *Man and the Sacred*, trans. Meyer Barash. Urbana and Chicago: University of Illinois Press.

Clark, T. J.
    1985   "Clement Greenberg's Theory of Art". In: Francis Frascina (ed.), *Pollock and After: The Critical Debate*. London: Harper and Row, 47–63.

    1990   "Jackson Pollock's Abstraction". In: Serge Guilbaut (ed.), *Reconstructing Modernism: Art in New York, Paris, and Montreal 1945–1964*. Cambridge, Mass. : MIT Press, 172–243.

Corris, Michael
    1994   "The Difficult Freedom of Ad Reinhardt". In: John Roberts (ed.), *Art Has No History! The Making and Unmaking of Modern Art*. London and New York: Verso, 63–110.

Fried, Michael
    1967   "Art and Objecthood". In: *Artforum*, vol. 5, no.10, 12–23.

Gartman, David
    1994   *Auto Opium: A Social History of American Automobile Design*. London and New York: Routledge.

Inboden, Gudrun and Thomas Kellein
    1985   *Ad Reinhardt*. Stuttgart: Staatsgalerie Stuttgart.

Kirkham, Pat
    1995   *Charles and Ray Eames: Designers of the Twentieth Century*. Cambridge, Mass.: MIT Press.

Lefebvre, Henri
    1992   *Éléments de rythmanalyse: Introduction à la connaissance des rythmes*. Paris: Éditions Syllepse.

Lippard, Lucy R.
    1981   *Ad Reinhardt*. New York: Harry N. Abrams.

Mann, Paul
    1991   *The Theory-Death of the Avant-Garde*. Bloomington and Indianapolis: Indiana University Press.

Marx, Karl and Frederick Engels
    1848   *Manifesto of the Communist Party*. Beijing: Foreign Language Press, 1973.

Orton, Fred, and Griselda Pollock
    1981   "Avant-Gardes and Partisans Reviewed". In: *Avant-Gardes and Partisans Reviewed*. Manchester: Manchester University Press, 1996, 141–64.

Poggioli, Renato
    1968   *The Theory of the Avant-Garde*, trans. Gerald Fitzgerald. Cambridge, Mass. : Harvard University Press.

Pohl, Frances K.
    1989   *Ben Shahn: New Deal Artist in a Cold War Climate 1947–1954*. Austin: University of Texas Press.

Pollock, Griselda
    1992   *Avant-Garde Gambits 1888–1893: Gender and the Colour of Art History*. London: Thames and Hudson.

Reinhardt, Ad
    1991   *Art as Art: The Selected Writings of Ad Reinhardt*, ed. Barbara Rose. Berkeley and Los Angeles: University of California Press.

Rosenberg, Harold
    1952   "The American Action Painters". Reprinted in: David and Cecile Shapiro (eds), *Abstract Expressionism: A Critical Record*. Cambridge: Cambridge University Press, 1990, 75–85.

The Museum of Contemporary Art, Los Angeles, and Museum of Modern Art, New York
    1991   *Ad Reinhardt*. New York: Rizzoli.

Wollen, Peter
    1989   "Cinema/Americanism/the Robot". In: *new formations*, vol. 8, 7–34.

III.

ON THE ALCHEMY OF THE WORD

VERBAL CHEMISTRY AND CONCRETE POETRY

KEITH ASPLEY

In his early essay "Les mots sans rides" (Words without wrinkles) which was first published in the seventh number of the new series of *Littérature* in December 1922 André Breton coined the idea of a "verbal chemistry" that arose out of Rimbaud's concept of "Alchimie du verbe", the subtitle of the second of the "Délires" texts in *Une saison en enfer*:

> The "alchemy of the verb" had been followed by a veritable chemistry which at first applied itself to releasing the properties of those words of which only one, their meaning, was specified by the dictionary. It was a question: 1) of considering the word in itself; 2) of studying as closely as possible the reactions of words to each other. (Breton 1988: 284)

According to Breton, verbal chemistry was exemplified first of all by Rimbaud's famous sonnet "Voyelles", but to illustrate the different forms of the process, he highlighted the experiments conducted by Jean Paulhan, Paul Eluard, Francis Picabia, Isidore Ducasse (the self-styled Comte de Lautréamont), together with Mallarmé's *Un coup de dés jamais n'abolira le hasard*, with its exploded layout, some of Apollinaire's "calligrammes" and "La Victoire", and the twin series of texts entitled *Rrose Sélavy* penned by Marcel Duchamp and Robert Desnos respectively.

A number of these examples immediately catch the eye because of their visual appearance. This essay sets out to examine the changing physical shape of poetry in the course of the twentieth century, with reference in particular to surrealism (representing the historical avant-garde) and concrete poetry (as a manifestation of the neo-avant-garde), even though it is more conventional to seek precursors of concrete poetry in other quarters: the origins of concrete poetry are often located in the Brazil of the 1950s and the *Noigrandes* group there: in their "pilot plan for concrete poetry" they acknowledged the influence of the Mallarmé-Pound-Joyce-e.e.cummings-Apollinaire nexus, together with futurism and dadaism (Solt 1970: 71-72). It is nonetheless interesting that in "Les mots sans rides" Breton actually talks in terms of the "concrete existence" that words had recently acquired.

Of course, one can go back at least as far as Rabelais's "Dive bouteille" in the sixteenth century and a number of texts by George Herbert (for instance, "The Altar") in the early seventeenth century to find antecedents for "calligrammes", poems whose visual form denotes their content; but however fascinating these two examples are, this is arguably not the place to subject them to detailed exegesis, but just to note their existence *en passant*:

The Altar

A broken ALTAR, Lord, thy servant reares,
Made of a heart, and cemented with teares;
Whose parts are as thy hand did frame;
No workmans tool hath touch'd the same.
A HEART alone
Is such a stone ,
As nothing but
Thy pow'r doth cut,
Wherefore each part
Of my hard heart
Meets in this frame,
To praise thy Name:
That, if I chance to hold my peace,
These stones to praise thee may not cease.
O let thy blessed SACRIFICE be mine
And sanctifie this ALTAR to be thine.
(Herbert 1964: 26)

Dive bouteille

O Bouteille
Pleine toute
De misteres,
D'une aureille
Je t'escoute :
Ne differes,
Et le mot proferes
Auquel pend mon cœur.
En la tant divine liqueur,
Qui est dedans tes flancs reclose,
Baccus, qui fut d'Inde vainqueur,
Tient   toute   verité   enclose.
Vin tant divin, loing de toy est forclose
Toute mensonge et toute tromperie.
En joye soit l'ame de Noach close,
Lequel de toy nous fit la temperie.
Sonne le beau mot, je t'en prie,
Qui me doit oster de misere.
Ainsi ne se perde une goutte.
De toy, soit blanche, ou soit vermeille.
O   Bouteille
Pleine   toute
De misteres,
D'une aureille
Je t'escoute :
Ne differes.[1]
(Rabelais 1994: 1509)

Such cases were, however, exceptional, whereas the twentieth century witnessed an exponential growth in the number and variety of rethinkings of the frontiers between words and images, signs and shapes, the ludic and the serious, the childlike and the sophisticated, so that crossovers between genres and media became the norm.

One might, of course, go so far as to claim that all poetry has shape and that some of its shapes are more distinctive than others: in the simple case of the sonnet, its fourteen lines have been disposed traditionally either in the form of the two quatrains and the two tercets of the Petrarchan or Italianate sonnet or in the form of the octet and the sestet of the Shakespearean sonnet, but in both cases, despite the physical difference on the page, a significant change of tone, direction or subject would normally occur after line 8.

Be that as it may, I propose now to concentrate on a handful of poems from the twentieth century in order to examine possible links between surrealism and concrete poetry, as far as the concept of "verbal chemistry" is concerned.

It would be inappropriate, indeed absurd, to pursue the chemistry metaphor beyond the barest essentials, to hope for even a reasonably fluid set of equivalents between atoms, molecules and compounds et cetera on the one hand, and letters, words, images of all kinds, numbers, equations et cetera on the other. Similarly I would doubtless be guilty of mixing metaphors if I used the cliché of "building bricks" with reference to concrete poetry. However, when my attention was drawn to the second *De Stijl* manifesto of 1920, I realized that its list of possible ways of giving new meaning to the word and new force to expression includes a number of items which are central to both surrealism and concrete poetry: syntax, prosody, typography, arithmetic and orthography. In their experiments with language and related codes, the different avant-garde movements were inevitably drawn towards similar or sometimes identical fields of study.

With reference to the experiments with numbers and mathematical symbols, I should like to juxtapose Julien Blaine's "3 + 3" and the surrealist Benjamin Péret's "26 points à préciser". The pattern of repetition in Blaine's text operates very clearly at the verbal level; the significance of the recurrence of the number 3 and its relationship with the number 12 is less obvious, or so it seems to me, so that it is not possible to replace the final question mark with a capital letter continuing the sequence X, Y, Z, which, in any case, comes to a natural stop:

$$3 + 3$$

3 + 3
et 12 + 3
3 + le vent suggéré par la nuit
et le vent suggéré par la nuit + la pluie inspirée d'une cythare,
la pluie inspirée d'une cythare + la mouette tissée de vagues ...
Et la mouette tissée de vagues + l'oiseau en sève de frêne ???

Rappel   : $3 + \text{vent} = X$
vent + pluie = Y
pluie + mouette − Z
mouette + oiseau = ? (Solt 1970: 166)[2]

Mary Ellen Solt responded to this poem in the following terms:

> Julien Blaine follows a course closer to traditional concepts of the poem. In "3 + 3" a high degree of lyricism is achieved with the concrete method of formula and repetition. The effectiveness of the poem results from the play of subjective tone and musical quality against a "mathematical pattern". [...] The use of italic type face as contrast in the poems of Julien Blaine, published by Furnival, seems entirely suitable to the play of lyric and fantastic content against mathematically defined formula. (Solt 1970: 36, 64)

Benjamin Péret's poem from the 1920s looks much more complicated. It begins with three lines which are straightforward as far as their layout is concerned:

Ma vie finira par *a*
Je suis *b − a*
Je demande *cb − a* (Péret 1969: 131)[3]

Although the verbal element remains relatively simple, consisting as it does of a single phrase or clause in all instances throughout the text, the algebraic formulae become increasingly complex. The latter are based on a pattern: from one "line" of the poem to the next Péret invariably adds one new element, as can be seen from the opening sequence. By the end of the text the formulae *look* very involved, whether or not they actually signify anything:

Ma fortune

$$\left(\frac{\frac{m}{n}\left(\sqrt[q]{\frac{de}{(cb-a)f}}+h-i\right)^{j}+kl+o}{\sqrt[t]{(pq+r)\,s}}-uv-w\right)^{x}-y$$

Ma date de naissance

$$\left(\frac{\frac{m}{n}\left(\sqrt[q]{\frac{de}{(cb-a)f}}+h-i\right)^{j}+kl+o}{\sqrt[t]{(pq+r)\,s}}-uv-w\right)^{x}-\frac{y}{z}$$

On the language side there are different kinds of groupings: the main sequence lists parts of the body and verbs that indicate actions associated with the body part in question, beginning with "Avec mon nez je sens" (With my nose I smell) and concluding with "Avec mon sexe je fais l'amour" (With my sex I make love). Shortly afterwards "Mon travail du matin" (My morning work) is followed by "Mon travail de l'après-midi" (My afternoon work) and then "Mon sommeil" (My sleep).

A much more transparent integration of numbers into words in a surrealist poem is found in "Art rythmé tic" by Robert Desnos, where the sound of the French word for the numbers in question approximates other words that fit semantically into the sentences. This poem from *L'Aumonyme* (Desnos 1999: 526) starts with the instruction, "Prenez vos 16", which has to be read as "Prenez vos aises" (Set yourself at ease); and a little later there are the lines "Par nos amours décuplés nous devenons vains/mais 10-20-2-20", where the numbers may be heard as the alliterative and rhyming words "divins devins" (divine soothsayers). Immediately afterwards Desnos changes direction, or rather changes key, so to speak, when he incorporates a few musical notes into the verbal matter but on a similar principle, that is to say, that the name of the notes, either in terms of their letters or the tonic sol-fa can be heard and understood as words. Thus at the end of the text we can see not only the marriage that the poet arranges between musical notation and words but also a further example of his personal shorthand in which the letters F M R F I J can be heard and comprehended as "Ephémères effigies" (ephemeral effigies); and indeed the last two lines are reminiscent of the utterances of *Rrose Sélavy*: in this particular case Desnos points up the paronomasia of "cow-boys" and "cobayes" (guinea-pigs), "l'Arizona" and "l'horizon", and "laboratoire" and "labyrinthe" — and this final example, by confronting the French words for "laboratory" and "labyrinth" respectively, associates science with myth, or viewed in another perspective, the dangers of losing oneself in experiments of this nature. Even the punning title, "Art rythmé tic",[4] seems to imply that the rhyming (or rhymed) art is just a tic, a spasmodic and involuntary muscular contraction.[5] Any attempt to envisage arithmetic in the same light clearly is a matter for the mathematician rather than the literary critic, but a generation or so ago Anna Balakian noted that Paul Vendryes, pursuing the physicist Jean Perrin's experiments with the Brownian movement of particles in terms of the aleatory movements of a fly and the chance patterns of a taxicab cruising in the streets of Paris, was "struck by the extraordinary parallel between his own studies of the applications of the laws of probability and the surrealist concept of objective chance" (Balakian 1971: 41).

Desnos pursued his musical theme in one of the compositions in his next collection, *Langage cuit*, the poem entitled "L'Asile ami" (The Friendly Asylum), which opens with a paragraph in which alliteration, assonance and a crazy clowning with words and sounds are prominent features:

> Là! L'Asie. Sol miré, phare d'haut, phalle ami docile à la femme, il l'adore, et dos ci dos là mille a mis! Phare effaré la femme y résolut d'odorer la cire et la fade eau. L'art est facile à dorer: fard raide aux mimis, domicile à lazzis. Dodo l'amie outrée. (Desnos 1999: 534)[6]

After this "prelude" or "overture", the musical notes, pronounced in the language of the tonic sol-fa, reproduce — more or less — the verbal text, the range of which is circumscribed by the limitations of the seven notes in an octave.

The interplay between words and musical notation was to be examined from the opposite direction by Alain Arias-Misson, a

Belgian by birth but educated in the United States and married to the Spanish painter Nela Arias. His "St. J de L.C." (St. Jean de la Croix) (Solt 1970: 202) replaces the normal musical clefs and notes with words that are disposed around the stave:

St. J de L.C.

The "melody" is created by a series of subtle modulations of the vowels that inevitably calls to mind the famous Rimbaud sonnet mentioned earlier, vowels that give the text its "golden sonority", despite the occasional spelling mistake. Whether or not this composition, with its near oxymoron of "sonorous solitude", not to mention the alliteration and assonance, captures either the "mystical doctor's" long night of the soul or his "cantique spirituel" is, however, a matter of opinion. Of course, both Desnos and Arias-Misson were possibly aware of the Apollinaire poem in *Calligrammes*, "Venu de Dieuze" (Apollinaire 1966: 106), in which three snatches of music are embedded in the manuscript.

Venu de Dieuze

The reader is left to speculate to what extent these poets set out to point up, doubtless ironically, the concepts of musicality and harmony, just as the integration of numbers and mathematical symbols may be seen as reminders of the role of rhythm, metre and metaphor. In 1942, in the postface that he wrote for his anthology *Fortunes*, Desnos, when contemplating possible future projects, presented the link between poetry and mathematics in the following general terms:

> What shall I do from now on? If all projects were measured only in terms of a lifetime, I should like to go back to my study of mathematics and physics, abandoned a quarter of a century ago, to learn once again that beautiful language. In that case I would have the ambition of making "Poetics" a chapter of mathematics. Admittedly it would be an enormous project, the success of which would not be detrimental to inspiration, to intuition or to sensuality. Is not Poetry too a science of numbers? (Desnos 1969: 162)

Sadly, he was unaware at that stage that his destiny was to die, exactly one month after the end of the war in Europe, of the typhus contracted in a concentration-camp. Of greater relevance for our purposes, however, is Desnos's readiness to regard mathematics as a language and to envisage poetics as a chapter or branch of mathematics.

Most forms of concrete poetry (the visual, the kinetic and the phonic varieties) have counterparts earlier in the twentieth century, but in the changing face of poetry the innovations tend to be in the form of variations in the mode of composition (techniques, working methods, the context and the shifting frontiers of poetry) rather than the introduction of something totally new. These variations include the use of colour or a computer program or sculpture. So I shall now proceed to consider a few examples of such developments.

Mary Ellen Solt's 'Forsythia' (Solt 1970: 243), from her 1966 volume *Flowers in Concrete*, clearly is a "calligramme" but one that begins the exploration of the potential of colour in poetry, in a much more direct way than Rimbaud's "Voyelles", thus taking it one step closer still to painting. The impression or illusion of the characteristic yellow blossom is conveyed by employing a yellow ground on which the text is printed.

Forsythia

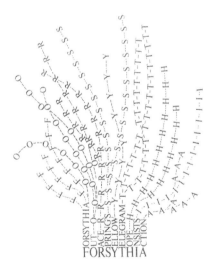

The trunk of the shrub is made up of words which begin with the letters of the eponymous word (FORSYTHIA OUT RACE SPRINGS YELLOW TELEGRAM HOPE INSISTS ACTION). The letters of the word "Forsythia", together with the appropriate dots and dashes of the Morse code, are then set out in more or less ascending shapes, in the correct order from left to right, to make up the branches, in a manner reminiscent of the creation of the verbal spray in the fountain element of Apollinaire's "La colombe poignardée et le jet d'eau" (The Stabbed Dove and the Fountain) (Apollinaire 1966: 1974):

La colombe poignardée et le jet d'eau

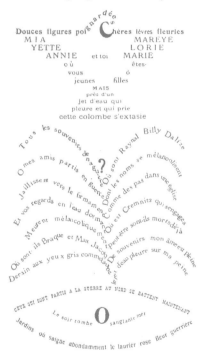

Solt has acknowledged her debt to William Carlos Williams and his much maligned sense of space in his poems, whether it was the space at the beginning of his lines as a structural measure or his awareness of the importance of the "spaces between the words".[7] André Breton likewise revealed that when he was composing some of the pre-surrealist poems of *Mont de piété*, he would pamper words "for the space they allow around them" (Breton 1988: 323).

In this very brief survey, given the location of the conference, I would be less than polite, were I to pass over in silence a couple of eminent Scottish poets, Edwin Morgan and Ian Hamilton Finlay. The potential of computers was explored by the former in "The Computer's First Christmas Card" (Solt 1970: 210). As has been pointed out (Solt 1970: 46), it is Morgan the poet rather than the computer itself who is responsible for this work, despite the implications of the title — the role of the computer seems to be limited to its word-processing function. Morgan rings the changes on the four rhyming opening words, all of which are traditionally associated with Christmas, "jolly", "holly", "merry" and "berry", by gradually substituting different letters. Before long he contrived to bring into the scenario a series of proper names (Molly, Jerry, Harry, Barry, and from there the author of the *Ubu* plays, Jarry), before eventually arriving, slightly arbitrarily, after the metaphorical gramophone needle seemed to stick briefly on "merry", at Chris, before the final variation on the theme, the joky modified Christmas greeting, "MERRY CHRYSANTHEMUM". The lyrics, with their neologistic coupling of two bisyllabic words — at least most of them are existing words — throughout the poem until the last four lines, sound vaguely like a jazzy Christmas carol:

The Computer's First Christmas Card

jollymerry
hollyberry
jollyberry
merryholly
happyjolly
jollyjelly
jellybelly
bellymerry
hollyhappy
jollyMolly
marryJerry
merryHarry
hoppyBarry
heppyJarry
boppyheppy

berryjorry
jorryjolly
moppyjelly
Mollymerry
Jerryjolly
bellyboppy
jorryhoppy
hollymoppy
Barrymerry
Jarryhappy
happyboppy
boppyjolly
jollymerry
merrymerry
merrymerry
merryChris
ammerryasa
Chrismerry
AsMERRYCHR
YSANTHEMUM

With Ian Hamilton Finlay poetry has been steered in the direction of sculpture and its various media: wood, stone, bronze etc. The verbal text is normally brief and serves to concentrate the mind and, sometimes literally, to throw into relief, or the opposite, the material on which it is inscribed and also the context or location. Thus the "Westward-facing sundial" from 1971 (Abrioux 1992: 234), made in wood with the aid of John R. Thorpe, simply juxtaposes the two statements, "Evening will come" and "They will sew the blue sail", linked visually and physically by the graceful image of a sail blowing in the wind. Despite the change of colour, there may well be echoes of the old standard "Red Sails in the Sunset".

"Umbra solis" (The Shadow of the Sun) (Abrioux 1992: 237), created in slate in 1975 with Michael Harvey for the Royal Botanic Garden in Edinburgh, confidently alludes to its *modus operandi*, and teasingly rejects the alternative, "Non aeris" (and not of the Bronze, which could also be read as "not of the air" or even "not of the cloud"), words which once more invite meditation and contemplation.

We have to remember that, at the time of its installation, the physical context of "Umbra solis" was even more pertinent than it is today, since in 1975 the Scottish Gallery of Modern Art was still located in the heart of the Botanic Garden, in Inverleith House, just a short distance away from Finlay's construct.

It is probably pointless to attempt to draw grandiose conclusions: it goes without saying that surrealism was already a very international movement, albeit with Paris as its initial hub before New York took over during the Second World War, when that city became the main refuge for artists and writers who felt compelled to leave Paris after the fall of France; but already during the interwar period surrealist groups had sprung up in many countries, Belgium, Czechoslovakia, Yugoslavia, even as far afield as Japan, to name just a few; and the surrealist group based in Paris itself attracted numerous adherents from all over the world. The process of globalization, however, which increasingly affects so many walks of life, together with the breathtaking acceleration in modes of communication, led to concrete poetry arguably becoming an international phenomenon even more quickly. This must be one of the features of the transition from the historical Avant-Garde movements to the Neo-Avant-Garde. Yet all kinds of echoes, resonances, cross-references, influences across time as well as space have been involved in the creation of an ongoing dialogue between the founder-members of the former (not to mention their precursors) and the various exponents or practitioners of the Neo-Avant-Garde: the process has tended to be one of evolution rather than revolution, despite the innovatory impact (at times the dramatic and very radical impact) of some of the latter's manifestations.[8] The symbiosis of verbal chemistry and concrete poetry may even be seen and understood in terms of the kind of chiasmus that is the trope that lies behind so many of the aphorisms of both series of *Rrose Sélavy*,[9] but whereas a degree of scepticism is called for in evaluations of the nature of the communication between Duchamp and Desnos — was it really a case of transatlantic telepathy? — the cross-fertilization between surrealism and other radical movements of the twentieth century seems to be a statement of fact.

NOTES

[1] "Bottle dear/Whence proceed/Things unknown/With one ear/You I heed;/Don't postpone,/But intone/my heart-awaited word./In the drink let it be heard,/Where Bacchus, who crushed the Indian herd,/Holds all truth concealed inside./Wine divine, by you denied/Are all things false and all deceit./Let joy through Noah's era still abide,/Who taught us how to make it, dry or sweet./pray speak that lovely word, I do repeat,/And end the woes from which I groan./No drop be wasted in my need,/Whether of white or claret clear./Bottle dear,/Whence proceed/Things unknown,/With one ear/You I heed;/Don't postpone." (Rabelais 1991: 707)

[2] $3 + 3$
and $12 + 3$
$3 +$ the wind suggested by the night
and the wind suggested by the night $+$ the rain inspired by a cither
the rain inspired by a cither $+$ the seagull woven of the waves...
and the seagull woven of the waves $+$ the bird in the sap of the ash tree
???
Recall: $3 + \text{wind} = X$
        $\text{wind} + \text{rain} = Y$
        $\text{rain} + \text{seagull} = Z$

seagull + bird = ?
(Solt 1970: 167, trans Ann McGarrell)

[3] "My life will end in a/I am $b - a$/I am asking for $cb - a$" (trans K.A.)

[4] In fact "Art rythmé tic" is really only one half of the title since this phrase is accompanied by another, "Lit temps nie", above which it is placed, separated by the conventional dividing line.

[5] Many years later Breton was to elucidate the phenomenon of lyricism that the nascent surrealists investigated at the end of the First World War in terms of "some kind of spasmodic outstripping of controlled expression" (Breton 1999: 451).

[6] It is impossible to translate this poem adequately since everything depends on the identity between the sound of every syllable and a note in the tonic sol-fa.

[7] William Carlos Williams, "Measure". In: *Spectrum*, vol. III, no. 3, Fall 1959, 149.

[8] The theme of revolution, especially the French Revolution, has been one of the great watchwords of Ian Hamilton Finlay's work, especially during the so-called "Little Spartan War", when his more militant supporters were known as the Saint-Just Vigilantes.

[9] See, for example, number 61 in Desnos's definitive series: "Apprenez que la geste célèbre de Rrose Sélavy est inscrite dans l'algèbre céleste" (Desnos 1999: 506).

BIBLIOGRAPHY

Abrioux, Yves
    1992   *Ian Hamilton Finlay: A Visual Primer*. London: Reaktion Books Ltd.

Apollinaire, Guillaume
    1966   *Calligrammes*. Paris: Gallimard.

Balakian, Anna
    1971   *André Breton: Magus of Surrealism*. New York: Oxford University Press.

Breton, André
    1988   *Œuvres complètes* I. Paris: Gallimard.

    1999   *Œuvres complètes* III. Paris: Gallimard.

Desnos, Robert
    1999   *Œuvres*. Paris: Gallimard.

Herbert, George
    1964   *The Works of George Herbert*, ed. F.E.Hutchinson.
                Oxford: The Clarendon Press.

Péret, Benjamin
    1969   *Œuvres complètes* I. Paris: Le Terrain vague.

Rabelais, François,
    1991   *The Complete Works of François Rabelais*. Translated by
                Donald Frame. Berkeley: University of California Press.

    1994   *Les Cinq Livres* (Gargantua/Pantagruel/Le Tiers Livre/Le
                Quart Livre/Le Cinquième Livre). Paris: Le Livre de
                Poche.

Solt, Mary Ellen (ed.)
    1970   *Concrete Poetry*. Bloomington and London: Indiana
                University Press.

How the Letters Learnt to Dance: On Language Dissection in Dadaist, Concrete and Digital Poetry

ANNA KATHARINA SCHAFFNER

I. Introduction

Poetry is not only made of language, but also essentially *about* language. By implication, poetic language is both vessel and content, vehicle and subject matter, transmitter of information and aesthetic message. At times, however, language stops to be vessel and communicates its own structure and physical features instead. At times, language is not considered as transparent tool for the analysis and representation of reality, but perceived as an arbitrary, convention-based system epitomising failed or deficient human interaction. Then, the very validity of the most elemental cultural system is questioned — and it is taken apart. Language is dissected and linguistic laws are dismantled and violated on all levels. The physical, material features and the underlying codes of the sign system become subject of poetic investigations; language then serves not as vehicle for facts outside of language anymore but thematises itself.

By virtue of dissecting the smallest atoms of language, poets venture into the very heart of communication and culture, for language is both product and prerequisite of human interaction. It not only provides the conceptual framework for the analysis of reality and the verbal equipment for its description, but structures the very configuration of human cognition. Moreover, as Saussure has pointed out, language is a form of contract, a body of conventions adopted to enable more or less precise and standardised exchange of ideas and experiences, which is the fundamental premise all culture is based on. Sometimes, however, poets set out to break that contract. Culture is to be shaken and reformed at its very basis: it is to be taken at its words. "The rupture with the continuum of domination must also be a rupture with the vocabulary of domination", proclaims Marcuse (1969: 33). The poets of the avant-garde embrace this assertion literally, abandoning not only a certain style or discourse, but often vocabulary itself, thereby challenging the very pillar all culture is based on. And the war of signs fought by poets of the avant-gardes has triggered eruptions indeed — at least in the language-landscapes of the 20th and 21st century.

Language dissection sweeps through the century in phases that are intricately interwoven with each other. An initial wave takes place in the first decades of the 20th century. The taking apart of linguistic units from text to word, the discovery of the visual and acoustic dimension of the linguistic sign, the instrumentation of typography, the reduction of the word material and the conceptual use of space by means of non-linear arrangement of letters on the page are vital innovations of the movements of the historical avant-garde. Of particular interest here is their distinct method of operating with language: the foregrounding and scrutiny of the linguistic material, the poetic act of cutting open and laying bare structures and properties of language at different levels of organisation — be it at the level of text, sentence, word or letter, at the level of semantic compatibility, syntax, lexicology or phonetics. Particularly in the context of dadaism, signifiers are frequently manipulated without or with only little regard to their potential semantic charge, and the acoustic and visual qualities of linguistic signs, sound and shape, are foregrounded instead.

A similar concentration upon the material features of language and profound language scepticism can be found in concrete poetry. In the fifties and sixties, the language material is thematised, reduced and thoroughly explored as well, the visual gestalt and the position of words and letters on the page determine meaning and are important elements of structure. Space is utilised as semantic element. Here also the poets refrain from anecdote and narrative and exemplify the rules of the language system instead.

In digital poetry, the very notion of text is thoroughly re-defined: not only are production, distribution and reception fundamentally changed, but sound, shape and meaning can co-exist simultaneously. Signs are not analogue and material but digital and immaterial, not fixed and stable but transient and in flux. Movement and interactivity are introduced, fluid space and hybrid architectures between word and image are explored, the computer screen functions as playhouse for visual and phonetic experiments and the codes not only of language but also of the computer itself are unmasked and exemplified. Language is dissected on a new level, it is aesthetically staged: letters, like actors, are met on scene and perform.

Lines of continuities between the historical avant-garde, concrete poetry and digital poetry become manifest in their dedication to language dissection above all, but also in manifold other categories and parameters. Predecessors and descendents are not only related to each other because of similar aesthetic strategies and techniques, the fact that they are all trans-national phenomena marked by an "avant-garde consciousness", as Friedrich W. Block has pointed out (2000: 1–10), and because digital poetry emerged in the orbit of the neo-avant-garde, but numerous other analogies exist.

The reflection upon and creative analysis of the material properties of the media of usage is a general characteristic of avant-garde art — be it colour, space, perspective and line in painting, or sound and shape of language and the conditions of meaning in literature. A concentration upon the physical qualities of linguistic signs and a highly self-reflective contemplation of the media-specific qualities are thus dominant features of all three stages. The unifying leitmotif and key concern of the poetic works of the historical avant-garde, concrete and digital poets is the problematisation and exploration of language and the impacts of new media. Moreover, they all try to tackle the specific needs and concerns of their time: "dada is the international expression of our times" the Berlin dadaists proclaim programmatically in the *Collective Dada Manifesto* of 1920:

> Art in its execution and direction is dependent on the time in
> which it lives, and artists are creatures of their epoch. The highest

> art will be that which in its conscious content presents the thou-
> sandfold problems of the day, the art which has been visibly
> shattered by the explosions of last week, which is forever trying
> to collect its limbs after yesterday's crash. (Motherwell 1981:
> 242–43)

Raoul Hausmann additionally explains the international and often independent simultaneous developments of similar aesthetic
strategies, that are characteristic for concrete and digital poetry as
well, in terms of a Zeitgeist necessity:

> The necessities of an epoch automatically lead to similar results,
> just as technological innovations also emerge from the needs of
> their particular time. (Hausmann 1972: 12, trans. AKS)

Hausmann suggests: "All innovations are made when they become
necessary. For them, there is always a climate" (1972: 155, trans.
AKS). Eugen Gomringer too names a "demand for representation of
contemporary language usage and zeitgeist" (1997: 13, trans. AKS),
the international character and the independent simultaneous emergence of various groups developing similar strategies at the same
time as important parameters of concrete poetry.

Intermediality is an other key concern: the poets in the lineage
under discussion co-operate closely with artists from other disci-
plines, they operate at the interface of visual, verbal and acoustic
arts, undermining genre limits and violating habits of reception.
Gerhard Rühm recalls:

> The close contacts that were held between the progressive repre-
> sentatives of the various arts were typical of our Viennese group
> and had a most fruitful effect. (Weibel 1997: 20)

In addition, an engagement with the creative utilisation of space as a
means of expression for thought, with multi-linear and topographical
writing can be detected. But particularly technology and the emergence of new media constitute a vital trigger for the creative
endeavours of the avant-garde poets: all of them react, directly or
indirectly, to technological changes, creatively instrumentalise new
media or reflect their impacts upon artistic production. Interestingly,
both the theoretical assessment and the circulation of their works
remains to a large degree their own responsibility: Not only do they

formulate a considerable body of theoretical positions on their works themselves, but they are also forced to develop strategies to publish them, depending predominantly on their own means of distribution. Gerhard Rühm recalls the situation in Vienna 1958:

> save for a few texts printed in magazines and anthologies, our manuscripts kept filling our drawers. we hardly had a chance here. arrogant provincialism prevailed in radio and television stations as well as in publishing. we had applied repeatedly in vain to the ministry of education for support to publish a small series of progressive poetry. in those days official subsidies were channelled to conservative camps exclusively. (Weibel 1997: 28)

Even though various techniques, strategies and aesthetic quests of the historical avant-garde are taken up again and re-elaborated, the activities of neo-avant-gardists and digital poets are not at all a mere reprise. There is a substantial body of innovation, development and change which is closely interrelated with the creative instrumentation of new communication technologies. This essay aims to give an account of the continuities and discontinuities of language dissection in avant-garde poetry and the intricate entanglements of the predecessors and descendants, outlining profiles of the distinct stages and proceeding towards a close reading of exemplary texts from each phase of experimentation.

II. Phase One: Raoul Hausmann's "fmsbw"

The impetuses for language dissection in the first decades of the 20th century are manifold: radical language scepticism that was at its preliminary peak at the fin de siècle and epitomised by Hofmannsthal's Lord Chandos letter, is one facet of the intricate network of motivations. Trust in words and their capacity to represent reality has withered. The idea of language as a transparent medium through which reality can be described and represented is radically challenged by theoretical and philosophical discourses, crumbling certainties in science and technological changes that profoundly effect everyday life. Man is confronted with speed, relativity and the atrocities of the first war fought with technological warfare. Numerous simultaneous sensations in urban settings severely affect perception. New technologies upset old patterns of communication and have vital impacts upon artistic production. Photography urges the painters into new niches, cars, trains and airplanes make speed in urban life visible, advertisements begin to invade public spaces, the phonograph is invented, transmitting acoustic signals independently from real-time performance, telephone and telegraph introduce body-less communication — and the artists try to depict these changes.

The avant-garde poets withdraw to the scrutiny of the linguistic core material and the very conditions of communication. Hugo Ball mentions the "special conditions of this age, which does neither let a standing talent rest nor mature, but pushes it to scrutinize the means" (Ball 1992: 101, trans. AKS). Moreover, the act of language dissection is often motivated by utopian efforts to restructure society from the basis of language. By means of revolutionizing and assaulting the dominant mode of communication, particularly the dadaists hope to revolutionize society itself. They programmatically subvert and disrupt linguistic and semiotic orders to provoke changes in thinking — changes outside of language. They fight their age by means of "semiologic warfare" (John Piccione in: Jackson/Vos/Drucker 1996: 101–109). It takes little wonder that the poets have to finance their war of signs mostly themselves. They are excluded from the official literary discourse and forced to withdraw to alternative publishing strategies: own (often short-lived) literary magazines, cabaret stages, newspapers, flyers and advertising columns serve as vehicles for poetic emanations.

In the early decades of the 20th century, verbal and fine artists co-operate as closely as never before. "We want the word to follow boldly after painting", demands the Russian cubo-futurist Velimir Khlebnikov. Both painters and poets are preoccupied with the aesthetic analysis of the auto-referential and self-sufficient qualities of painted or written signs, with the investigation into the potential of the media-specific means. A reciprocal merging of techniques and methods, of theoretical approaches and concepts takes place, and this alliance will have crucial impacts upon numerous artworks throughout the century. Fragmentation, collage, multi-linearity, multi-perspectivity and abstraction are techniques that dominate both the literary and the pictorial discourse of the early avant-gardes. But word and image interact not only theoretically, but are also fused together directly. Disparate semiotic codes are blended, dis-

crete media are brought into a conceptual fusion. Letters invade pictures, and language discovers its graphic and pictorial features. The insertion of linguistic signs into pictures or the pictorial arrangement of letters on the page radically undermine genre limits. Lessing's dichotomy of spatial and temporal media is ultimately invalidated: the futurists introduce the fourth dimension, time, into the spatial medium by developing pictorial strategies to depict movement and simultaneity (consider Marcel Duchamp's "Nude descending a staircase"), and Stephan Mallarmé is the first to let space intervene into the time-art.

Stephan Mallarmé abandons linearity in "Un Coup de Dés" as early as 1897: he pioneers the deployment of graphic space as structural agent.[1] The left-aligned line is omitted in favour of multi-linearity, a spatial abstract arrangement of words. Words are now brought into relation by means of their position on the page, not by hierarchic syntactical arrangements. The abandonment of line results inevitably in the reduction of the word material, because adjectives, conjunctions and prepositions become superfluous. Walter Benjamin attributes Mallarmé's innovation to the invasion of advertisements into public space, claiming that Mallarmé reacts to and assimilates the change in contemporary language that film, newspaper and the typography of commercials have brought about:

> Mallarmé […] was in the *Coup de dés* the first to incorporate the graphic tensions of the advertisement in the printed page. … Printing, having found in the book a refuge in which to lead an autonomous existence, is pitilessly dragged out onto the streets by advertisements and subjected to the brutal heteronomies of economic chaos. This is the hard schooling of its new form. If centuries ago it began gradually to lie down, passing from the upright inscription to the manuscript resting on sloping desks before finally taking to bed in the printed book, it now begins just as slowly to rise again from the ground. The newspaper is read more in the vertical than in the horizontal plane, while film and advertisement force the printed word entirely into the dictatorial perpendicular. (Benjamin 1986: 77–78)

The movements of the historical avant-garde have dispensed with various established poetic principles: linearity is among the first to be omitted; syntax, punctuation, narrative, context, semantic compatibility, lexicological laws, intentionality and even words are to follow. The futurists, in their call for "words in freedom", demand the abandonment of syntax, and moreover of punctuation, conjunctions and adjectives. They too want words to be brought into a relationship of correlation by means of their position on the page only, not by syntactical arrangements. They discover and explore the potential of typography. Semantic compatibility is discarded by various dadaists and Guillaume Apolliniare: the latter composes a text out of disparate conversation fragments that are torn from their respective context. Velimir Khlebnikov extends the principles of lexicology: he cuts words apart and recombines affixes and suffixes, feeling that existing concepts are limited and insufficient for the communication of experience. Frequently, the dadaists organise language material without or only little attention to semantic concerns. Tristan Tzara writes a recipe for creating a poem by means of cutting words out of a newspaper and arranging them randomly on the paper, thus dethroning author and intentionality. Aleatoric strategies for the composition of texts are discovered. Hugo Ball renounces the denotative function of language almost completely in his "verses without words" and composes poems that are euphonic architectures of sound; phoneme sequences that do not obey lexicological laws anymore but are arranged mainly according to aesthetic considerations. However, he plays with remnants of semantic properties, with analogies to existing words and with association. One poet went even further.

*

Raoul Hausmann's "fmsbw" can be considered as the most radical piece in this lineage. In "Zur Geschichte des Lautgedichtes" (On the History of Sound Poems) he recalls his motivation for exchanging the conventional medium of poetry, the page, against one of the visual arts, the poster:

> Last but not least, letter-poems may well be there to be seen, but also to be *perceived* — then why not make posters from them? On diversely coloured papers and in huge printed types? (Hausmann 1972: 35, trans. AKS)

The typesetter confronted with the task to arrange the fist "opto-phonetical" poster poems in 1918 chose the letters entirely at random; chance determined the sequence of the letters — an écriture automatique with solid wooden signs taken arbitrarily out of the typecase. "It was the first ‚readymade' of literature, realised according to the laws of chance" (1972: 156, trans. AKS). Hausmann claims. Characteristic avant-garde principles culminate: the poster poem is generated aleatorically with "ready made" materials and marks a point of utmost reduction and concentration upon the physical language material. Hausmann finally dispenses even with the word, and arrives at the smallest linguistic sign, the singular letter. Here, language is dissected into its smallest atoms, the letters do not fuse into word-like units anymore. The act of reading is impeded: the textual elements can not be connected into a coherent whole, they do not synthesize into words or even syllables and remain fragments. The text plays with reading expectations, habits of reception are irritated. Despite the fact that it consists of linguistic elements, it must be perceived like a picture.

fmsbwtözäu

pggiv-_?mü

Language is atomised into individual signs that have gained an aesthetic validity of their own. Their referential and semantic function is subverted. The letters are stripped of their linguistic duties and presented as abstract signs with a visual and an acoustic dimension only, illustrating poignantly Saussure's assertion that signs function only in a system of difference and relations, lacking any positive values of their own. Identities do not refer to essences but are constituted only in meaningful differential relations based on arbitrary convention. Hausmann too proclaims:

> Words have no meaning at all apart from the one established by convention — everything else, all other signification is futile, in vain! (1972: 35, trans. AKS)

The representational function of script is abandoned, and the other signs of the type case are equally a-referential, the hand pointing nowhere seems almost programmatic. The attention is drawn to the material signifier: to texture, plasticity, sound and shape. Grapheme and phoneme remain and refer to nothing but themselves. They do not point to anything outside of language anymore; all that is left are curves and lines on the paper and waves of sound in the air.

While Hugo Ball in his sound poem "Karawane" has created a smooth, euphonious sound composition that plays with remnants of semantic properties, Hausmann has produced something entirely abstract. He maintains that

> the poem makes itself from sounds emerging from the larynx and the vocal cords, and it knows no syntax, only flow and obstruction. (1972: 13, trans. AKS)

Inhibition and impediment are vital principles here: Not only is the act of reading impeded, but also that of articulation — the enunciation of the poem is thwarted and obstructed. The frequency of consonants with no vowels in between renders verbalization almost impossible. Irritation, boycott and de-automatisation of all strategies of reception is thus complete. The impediment of mechanisms of articulation serves once more to direct the attention towards the physical features of the letters, and not only their visual shape on paper but also towards the very process of their verbal formation: the movements of the tongue, the flow of air, the closing and opening of the glottis, the vibrations of the vocal cords. Awareness of the most basic bundles of phonetic features of human speech sounds is thus enforced.

III. Phase Two: Eugen Gomringer's "wind" and Gerhard Rühm's "zerbrechen"

The gesture of unmasking the relativity of established rules and norms and the scrutiny of the core material of language in times of cultural crisis is also characteristic for the neo-avant-garde. An even more profound mistrust in communication prevails in the fifties, particularly among writers in Germany and Austria: "along with history i reject its compromised language", writes Oswald Wiener of the Wiener Gruppe (Weibel 1997: 663), echoing Hugo Ball who also refused to utilise a language that he perceived as insufferable, debased and corrupted by war propaganda and journalism. After the experience of the Nazi regime and the holocaust, many experimental poets feel it is impossible to utilise the stained language in a discursive, message orientated fashion. They too refrain from telling stories, from anecdote and narrative, and withdraw to the scrutiny of the material instead. However, there are various other modules in the set of causes for the emergence of concrete poetry. Again, the movement is characterised by an independent and simultaneous appearance in various places and a concern with Zeitgeist representation. Gerhard Rühm recalls

> the fact that such creations emerged independently of each other at different places only confirmed their compelling up-to-datedness. transnationality, a new phenomenon in literature, is an important aspect of 'concrete poetry', which caters the need for a simplified world language, albeit limited to the realm of estheticism. its model-like clarity complies with the contemporary demand for condensed information. (Weibel 1997: 20)

In concrete poetry, various techniques and strategies of the historical avant-garde are re-discovered and elaborated. Aware or unaware of forerunners, the concrete poets continue the quest of the historical avant-garde after World War II. Rühm remarks that

> for us they [among others Gertrude Stein, Arno Holz, August Stramm, Kurt Schwitters, Hans Arp and Benjamin Péret, AKS] represented the rediscovered, true traditions with which our poetic work linked up organically. from where else should we proceed if not from the so-called 'end points'. (Weibel 1997: 16; 18)

Techniques and concerns taken up again include multi-linearity, fragmentation, permutation, aleatoric and combinatoric procedures, play, emphasise of the physiognomy and acoustic dimension of language etc. Manifestos have been issued and cabarets organized. Topographical writing and the use of the semantic implications of structured space are vital moments here as well. Mary Ellen Solt defines as fundamental requirement of the concrete poem a "concentration upon the physical material from which the poem or text is made":

> the concrete poet is concerned with establishing his linguistic material in a new relationship to space (the page or its equivalent) and/or to time (abandoning the old linear measure). Put another way this means the concrete poet is concerned with making an object to be perceived rather than read. (Solt 1970: 7–8)

Reduction of the word material is yet another key concern, resulting from the abandonment of line. Often, concrete poems consist of one or two words only. Utmost precision and restraint are just one consequence of the preoccupation with reduction, and Gomringer points out that concrete poetry is but a consequential continuation of the essential qualities of the poetic statement, namely "concentration and simplification".

As Benjamin has exemplified with Mallarmé's "Un Coup de Dés" thirty years earlier, advertisement and new media change the appearance of language, and these changes are reflected and assimilated by the poets. Gomringer too maintains that the brevity and precision of concrete manifestations is mirroring and taking up developments in contemporary language that are influenced by new media — television, technological commands, and advertisements among others. These formats require short and capturing statements; the time span granted for the communication of messages is shrinking, communication is speeded up and needs to be extremely precise:

> in order to preserve his share of the world, a poet may chose to study and scrutinise functions and forms of the non-aesthetic communication sphere, and he can express himself adequately, that means in the same language. (1997: 44–45, trans. AKS)

Even more to the point, Gomringer states: "i somehow wanted to establish an analogy between the shortened message the fast reader of today appreciates and precise poetic information that is freed from all circumstantialities" (1997: 46, trans. AKS). Language grows to become more and more visual, typography and design dominate its effect in advertisements, and poets call both for a change in language usage analogous to the changes of modes of perception and reception caused by new media and for a utilisation of their non-linear strategies of communication.

However, not only the reaction to technological changes, but particularly the creative instrumentation of new media leads to further elaborations of the scrutiny of the language material. The tape-recorder for instance, which becomes available for general use in 1951, allows for a technical manipulation of the human voice: speech now, detached from the body of the author and real-time performance, can be edited and manipulated; cut, pasted, slowed down, speeded up and blended, past sound can be mixed with present sound, pitch, volume and texture of the voice can be altered. The experiments of sound poetry enter a technologically expanded phase. Typewriter poetry emerges, the structural capacities of the typewriter are exploited and free writers from the often too expensive dependence on the services of the typesetter. The availability of colour and more elaborate printing techniques are also vital for the production of various concrete works, and, possible through the merits of cheaper printing technologies such as mimeography, the "small press" arises, numerous low-budget literary magazines are founded. Writers set up their own magazines and presses (consider Eugen Gomringer's art magazine "Spirale" from 1952/53–64 and the *eugen gomringer press,* founded in 1959 or the magazine "MATERIAL" of the Darmstadt circle, 1957–59) or publish anthologies (both Mary Ellen Solt and Emmett Williams for instance, who edited two seminal anthologies of concrete poetry in 1968, are concrete poets themselves). These alternative publishing strategies are, as in the historical avant-garde, essential for the circulation of concrete poetry.

*

The direct structural influence that art may exercise on poetry is particularly evident in the case of Eugen Gomringer and concrete art. The term concrete art is defined by Theo van Doesburg in the manifesto "The Basis of Concrete Art" launched in 1930 as follows: "A pictorial element has no other significance than itself and consequently the painting possesses no other significance than itself" (Turner 1996, Vol. 7: 689). The German poet Max Bense defines concrete poetry quite similarly: "everything concrete is nothing but itself" (Solt 1970: 74). Predominantly the deployment of the material in a functional, not a symbolical way can be considered as a common denominator. The letters are now the autonomous building material, just as in concrete art colour and form are self-sufficient modules of creation. Having worked as secretary to Max Bill on the Hochschule of Gestaltung in Ulm, Gomringer repeatedly emphasises the influence concrete art has exercised upon his poetic work, and characterises concrete poetry as "conscious study of the material and its structure [...]: material means the sum of all the signs with which we make poems" (Solt 1970: 69). Max Bense describes concrete poetry as "material poetry", a poetry that is less concerned with external representation but focuses on creation with linguistic means:

> Concrete poetry is a style of material poetry if it is understood as a kind of literature which considers its linguistic means (such as sounds, syllables, words, word sequences and the interdependence of words of all kinds) primarily as representation of a linguistic world which is independent of and not representative of an object extrinsic to language or of a world of events. (Solt 1970: 74)

Bense also delineates, following the coinage "verbivocovisual" of the Brazilian Noigandres group, the three dimensions of the communication sphere: "Seen as material the communication sphere is three-dimensional. The word has simultaneously a verbal, a vocal and a visual positional value", he writes (Solt 1970: 74). Here, a difference to dadaist works becomes apparent: Raoul Hausmann's optophonetical poem lacks the verbal dimension. It could be described, in Benses terminology, as a two-dimensional language object, since Hausmann entirely omits the sphere of semantics. The concrete poets, in contrast, consider meaning and semantic charge as functional material of equal value. Like the acoustic and the visual dimension, semantic components of words are likewise elements of construction. Bense writes:

> meaning and structure reciprocally express and determine each other. Simultaneity of the semantic and aesthetic function of words occur on the basis of simultaneous exploitation of all the material dimensions of the linguistic elements. (Solt 1970: 74)

The re-introduction of the semantic dimension constitutes thus an important moment of change.

Gomringer's ideogram "wind" exemplifies many of the above-mentioned principles. The reduced verbal material is arranged spatially on the page; line and syntax is omitted as well as consecutive reading structures. The structure is multi-linear and dynamic.

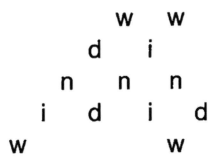

Multiple possible paths between the text segments exist. In the process of reception, reading and perceiving alternate, the eye has to travel. The word "wind" can be read in four directions, pairs each running the reverse course. If one follows the constellation crosswise, diagonally and reverse, "wind" can be composed out of at least eleven different letter constellations. Four "w" and three versions each of the other letters are structurally juxtaposed, and their combination and synthesis constitutes the poetic subject. Here, structure and meaning determine each other. Movement is evoked. Mary Ellen Solt states that the multi-linear arrangement captures the nature of wind far more truly than a longer poetic statement would be able to: "The letters actually seem to float as if the wind were acting upon them", she writes. Gomringer defines the poem as an ideogram depicting a compass card. In an ideogram, the elements of a mostly abstract word are spatially arranged and provide the term with a poignant visual gestalt. Particularly shape and meaning are significant here, in contrast to Hausmann's poem, where shape and sound were decisive.

The Wiener Gruppe concentrates predominantly on the exemplification of linguistic rules and structures, as Michael Backes has emphasised (2001: 16). Rühm states that "in a phase of radical reduction of the artistic means and contemplation of the basic elements, i arrived eventually in 1952 at the single word ("one-word-tablet") through poetry" (Weibel 1997: 614). The poem "zerbrechen", however, is composed of two words. Part of a series of typewriter ideograms written between 1954–57, it consists of ten identical lines with seven sound clusters each, and the decomposed word "zerbrechen" in line eleven.

```
un dun dun dun dun dun d
un dun dun dun dun dun d
un du n dun dun dun dun d
u ndun dun dun dun dun d
un dun dun dun dun dun d
un dun dun dun dun dun d
u ndu n dun dun dun dun d
un du n dundun dun dun d
un dun dundun dun dun d
un dun dun dun dun dun d
zer br eche     n
```

The German word "und", which appears six times per line, is torn apart; only fragments remain: one "un", five "dun" and a singular "d". Line eleven features the word "zerbrechen", to break into pieces, which is also fragmented into four random units. The title is programmatic: both the words "und" and "zerbrechen" are broken into pieces; they are segmented into non-semantic units. "To break into pieces" is exemplified literally: the "zerbrechen" both signifies its meaning and at the same time performs it. "Und" also, frequently repeated as in a litany, dramatizes its semantic charge, that is to announce that something follows and to connect words, which is carried out in the literal sense: even the signifiers of the conjunctions are joined together, by means of not leaving a space where one is required. Form and meaning are one, the letters perform the semantic charge they carry. Saussure seems to be proven right here again: language, it becomes obvious, is but a combination of graphemes or phonemes into segments that are significant only in certain sequences. Signs and concepts are arbitrary, the value of a phoneme is not absolute, but relative; ultimately it is their position and the way in which they pattern that decides if they are meaningful or not (compare Backes 2000: 47). A blank space serves already as distinctive feature that upsets the semiotic order. The border between meaningful and not is minimal. Again, both form and content are of major importance, structure and meaning determine each other. Rühm operates with space, and yet quite different from Mallarmé or the futurists. Here space is used functionally to reveal both the arbitrariness and the delicacy of linguistic conventions. Saussure has postulated that concepts cut up the world — Gerhard Rühm cuts up the concepts.

IV. Phase Three: Miekal And's "After Emmett" and Takaumi Furuhashi's "Kotoba Asobi"

The most radical technological transformation of the avant-garde quest, however, occurs on the computer screen: in cyberspace, the very notion of texts, of their production, distribution and reception, is fundamentally changed. Multimedia applications — the fusion of video, graphics, sound, text and interactive programs — make entirely new arrangements and experiments with verbal material possible. The poetic space of the computer screen is dynamic, transient and in flux, letters and words are not static and bound but wander and slip. The fusion of text, image and sound reaches its temporary climax: digital poetry is hyper-medial and all dimensions of the linguistic sign can co-exist simultaneously. "Thus, within a single 'page' ", writes Loss Pequeno Glazier, "sound, video, graphics, writing — a composition of media marked by a distinct style, form or content — converge". He concludes: "the electronic page crosses media by definition" (Glazier 2002: 79). The visual and auditory senses are thus fully re-integrated into the experience of text, and the concern with intermediality that has marked both the discourse of the historical and the neo-avant-garde finds it natural home in cyberspace.

Own means of distribution, of such major importance for the historical avant-garde and concrete poetry, are a vital necessity for the existence of digital poetry as well. The World Wide Web is perhaps the most democratic and accessible medium ever. The circulation of poetry in the Web allows for the creation of a secondary net of production and distribution, independent of any financial, political or canonical impediments. The regulation through the market can thus entirely be avoided. "Poets [have] taken over the means of poetry production" observes Loss Pequeno Galzier (2002: 29), and this applies to all three stages.

Of interest here is computer poetry that works creatively with the specific qualities of the medium, not just in it, that tests and questions its codes, possibilities and limitations, that applies multimedia effects to verbal artistry. In short: poetry that exploits the dynamics of the new media. Glazier remarks:

> Indeed, it is important to note that digital poetries are not merely
> print repositioned in the new medium. Instead, e-poetries extend
> the investigations of innovative practice as it occurred in print
> media, making possible the continuation of lines of inquiry that
> could not be fulfilled in that medium. (2002: 26)

Particularly Glazier and Friedrich W. Block have repeatedly emphasised the affinities of key strategies of digital poetry with "innovative" or "experimental" programs, which is further accentuated by the fact that the first experiments with machine generated stochastic texts were produced in 1959 by Theo Lutz, a member of the Stuttgart group surrounding Max Bense. Other neo-avant-gardists came gradually to the experimentation with the poetic potential of computer-bred texts, such as Oswald Wiener, Paul Fournel, Italo Calvino and Jaques Roubaud in the context of OULIPO, or Reinhard Döhl and Augusto de Campos, one of the founding fathers of the Noigandres group (compare Block 2000: 4–5). Thus digital poetry is not only sharing numerous strategies and principles with neo-avant-garde poetry, but it factually emerged from its orbit as well.

The scrutiny of the media of usage, of the means of communication, is just one of many returning analogies to the predecessors. Language dissection is performed on a new level: various avant-garde principles can be dramatized literally in cyberspace, such as movement, intermediality and interactivity. The invocation of movement and dynamics has been a concern of the historical avant-garde and concrete poetry also (consider Gomringer's "wind"), but was limited to static representation in print. Now, it can be put into effect. The fusion of sign systems is at its climax on the computer screen: text, image and sound have synthesised into a truly "verbivocovisual" spectacle. The active recipient, who has been so crucial for both avant-garde and neo-avant-garde, is now allowed a whole new sphere of influence. Interactivity is one of the major new possibilities of digital poetry, and never before could the recipient interfere on such a wide scope. In cyberspace, the recipient's active participation in the production of meaning finds its literal and physical equivalent. Digital poetry, however, does not only celebrate the new technologies, but various works problematise impacts of the massive proliferation of the World Wide Web and computers as well. Computer codes are made visible, media-specific qualities are brought back to the attention of the user. Source codes and binary codes, interfaces and formats, data processing and error messages are aesthetically staged. The attention of the user is sharpened; the medium and its impacts are examined. Poetry on the computer screen challenges the very notion of text, its material and definite qualities: static becomes kinetic, letters and images migrate over the screen; stable turns into transient, signs float and change while reading. What has been material is now immaterial, printed signs are now digital codes; two-dimensional becomes three-dimensional; final and definite is now open to continual change, variability and the sphere of influence of the recipient.

*

Miekal And's "After Emmett. A Voyage in ninetiles" does not exploit the various possibilities of multimedia applications in the Web at all. However, it is interesting nevertheless: as the name suggests, it is a tribute to the concrete poet Emmett Williams. It is a reflection upon the ancestry of the concrete poets and the position of digital poets in this lineage. It pays homage to William's poem "The Voy Age" from 1975 that consists of 100 word squares decreasing in size as the poem advances, until only a grid of the size of a semicolon remains. Miekal And's digital poem displays 53 consecutive screens featuring a three-by-three grid of nine letters or punctuation marks each. Each single character in those word squares changes typeface continually, switching through a sequence of five to eight different fonts. As a result, the letters dance: they swell and shrink, shimmer and flicker, bloat and shrivel, twitch and shake. They seem to move, to pulsate, palpitate, and a sense of motion and dynamics is evoked. Miekal And creates the "typofantastic epic voyage" in 1998, employing 43 different fonts, adobe photoshop and a simple animation technique. Thematically, most words in the poem refer to voyage — water is evoked, the sun, heat, past memories, a woman, love and a boat trip: "waterswho, sunhotday, forgotten, sheloving, heroneman, rowandrow, followmud." "Eyevoyage", the first trio of syllables, emphasises that this is a piece meant to appeal to the sense of vision. Here, the concern of concrete poetry with visual gestalt, structural space, typography, geometrical word patterns and movement is transferred into an other medium and enriched through a new feature: movement, characters in flux, changing size and typeface — dynamic signs in constant metamorphosis. The sign is not stable and static anymore but changes its appearance while it is read. Other pieces of concrete poets have been "transmediated", transferred from one medium to the other as well, for example Reinhard Döhl's poem "Apfel". The German word for apple is arranged in the shape of one, and in the midst of it stands "Wurm". In the Web, this apple is animated: the word worm wolfs its way through the apple, swallows the verbal material, growing bigger and bigger until only a red worm word fills the screen in the end. However, other poets exploit the dynamics and possibilities of the World Wide Web much more innovatively.

For instance Giselle Beiguelman, who takes up yet an other moment of avant-garde art, that of "ready-made" materials. In "recycled" she uses existing pages, "found material", takes them apart and attributes new values to their parameters and new functions to their performances, thus echoing aesthetic strategies with "objects trouvé". Consider also the Japanese poet Takaumi Furuhashi. In his shockwave application "Kotoba Asobi", the words of a sentence or proverb float randomly over the black screen, in different colours, sometimes alone, sometimes all at once, sometimes overlapping, sometimes fast and sometimes slow, from different directions. To a certain degree, the user can determine the speed and direction of the verbal material with the help of the mouse. Two balls drift across the screen as well. Whenever a word and a ball collide, the word changes size and colour and is audibly distorted from either a male or a female voice. The balls are out of the sphere of influence of the recipient, however, it is to some degree possible to influence which words are to hit the balls. Apart from the concern with machine-determined randomness that echoes chance-procedures for the generation of poetry employed by the dadaists, other parallels to the predecessors become evident. The words of eight different sentences, rather trivial in content and without much poetic potential, migrate over the screen independently from their position in the hierarchy of the sentence. The effect of this is to render the relation between the component parts fluid, language is dissected at the level of sentence: through a change of position, a semantic change occurs, syntax becomes instable and the words pair and combine in different constellations. The instability of meaning is dramatized: meaning, it becomes clear, depends on the position of the parts. If these are on the loose and float through space, meaning as well is rendered indeterminable. Words migrate through space and are not tied down to linguistic hierarchies anymore. Space here is used dynamically, multilinearity is put into effect. It takes the user a while to figure out the proper constellation of words — which is determined through gender, case and number of the subjects, adjectives, prepositions and adverbs. The proverb of screen six "Zwei Fliegen mit einer Klappe schlagen", to resolve two things with one effort (literally: to hit two flies with one fly swat), seems programmatic: here, the visual and acoustic dimension of words coexist simultaneously, language is finally dramatized in both possible manifestations, image and sound, at once.

V.   Conclusion

The dialectic of old and new, traditional quests and innovation made possible by new media results in a complex entanglement of the historical avant-garde with its descendants. The very method of operating with language, language dissection and the dedication to the exemplification of linguistic properties and rules is the dominant line of inquiry that weaves through all stages. And so are language scepticism, critique of culture, affinities to discourses in the fine arts and the impacts or instrumentation of new technologies as vital trigger for experimentation. In Takaumi Furuhashi's shockwave application, various key principles culminate: intermediality, the fusion of sound, image and text, interactivity, movement, chance as poetic principle, the exploitation of space, multilinearity, the dramatization of the combinatorial possibilities of instable syntax and the transience of fluid signs. Here, "words in freedom", as the futurists demanded, float through space, and are neither tied down by static fixation on paper, nor by syntax or other linguistic laws. Words are finally on the loose. "Fluid architectures of liquid textuality", as Giselle Beiguelman formulated, thus continue and refine literary practises that have been initiated in the first decades of the 20th century.

NOTES

[1] An important contrast to the age-old tradition of pattern or figure poems (cf. Jeremy Adler's "Text als Figur" or Dick Higgins' "Pattern Poetry" for examples) is that Mallarmé has, for the first time ever, created an *abstract* pattern poem, composed obeying structural and functional considerations only. Traditionally, pattern poems are mimetic, imitating concrete shapes and objects. Also, those poems have usually very conventional content, rhyme and meter, and do not challenge or problematise language as the avant-gardists do.

BIBLIOGRAPHY

And, Miekal
    1998   "After Emmett. A Voyage in Ninetiles". At: http://www. cla.umn.edu/joglars/afteremmett/bonvoyage.html

Arnold, Heinz Ludwig (ed.)
    1997   "Visuelle Poesie". Text und Kritik. Zeitschrift für Literatur, no. 9. Munich: edition text und kritik.

    2001   "Digitale Literatur". Munich: edition text und kritik, no. 132. Text und Kritik. Zeitschrift für Literatur.

Backes, Michael
  2001   *Experimentelle Semiotik in Literaturavantgarden. Über die Wiener Gruppe mit Bezug auf die Konkrete Poesie.* Munich: Wilhelm Fink Verlag.

Ball, Hugo
  1992   *Die Flucht aus der Zeit.* Zürich: Limmat Verlag

Beiguelman, Giselle
            "recycled". At: http://www.desvirtual.com/recycled.html

Benjamin, Walter
  1986   "One-Way Street". In: *Reflections. Essays, Aphorims, Autobiographical Writings.* New York: Schocken Books, 61 – 97.

Bense, Max
  1968   "Concrete Poetry". In: *Concrete Poetry. A World View.* Solt, 73–74.

Bloch, Friedrich W.
  2001   "Website: Zum Ort digitaler Literatur im Netz der Literaturen". In: "Digitale Poesie" (Arnold: 99–112). English translation: "Digital Poetics or On the evolution of experimental media poetry." At: http://www.brueckner-huehner.de/block/p0et1cs.html

  1997   Auf hoher Seh in der Turing-Galaxis". In: Visuelle Poesie. TEXT+KRITIK. Zeitschrift für Literatur. Sonderband. (Arnold 1997, 185–203).

de Campos, Augusto, Decio Pignatari and Haroldo de Campos
  1968   "Pilot Plan for Concrete Poetry". In: *Concrete Poetry. A World View.* Solt, 71–72.

Glazier, Loss Pequeno
            Digital Poetics: The Making of E-Poetries. Tuscaloosa, Alabama: University of Alabama Press.

Gomringer, Eugen
  1968   "From Line to Constellation". In: *Concrete poetry. A World View.* Solt, 67.

  1968   "Max Bill and Concrete Poetry". In: *Concrete poetry. A World View.* Solt, 68–69.

            theorie der konkreten poesie. texte und manifeste 1954 – 1997. Vienna: Edition Splitter.

Hausmann, Raoul
   1972   *Am Anfang war Dada.* Ed. Karl Riha and Günter Kämpf.
           Steinbach/Gießen: Anabas Verlag Günther Kämpf.

Jackson, K. David, Eric Vos and Johanna Drucker
   1996   *Experimental – Visual — Concrete: Avant-garde poetry
           since the 1960s.* Amsterdam, Atlanta: Rodopi.

Lentz, Michael
   2000   *Lautpoesie/-musik nach 1945. Eine kritisch-dokumen-
           tarische Bestandsaufnahme.* Vienna: Edition Selene.

Marcuse, Herbert
           An Essay on Liberation. Boston: Beacon, 33.

Motherwell, Robert (ed.)
   1981   *The Dada Painters and Poets: An Anthology.* Boston,
           Massachusetts: G.K. Hall & Co.

Riha, Klaus and Joergen Schaefer (ed.)
           Dada total. Manifeste, Aktionen, Texte, Bilder. Stuttgart:
           Phillip Reclam Junior.

Solt, Mary Ellen (ed.)
   1970   *Concrete Poetry. A World View.* Bloomington, London:
           Indiana University Press.

Weibel, Peter (ed.)
   1997   die wiener gruppe/ the vienna group. ein moment der
           moderne 1954–1960/ die visuellen arbeiten und die
           aktionen. a moment of modernity 1954–1960/ the visual
           works and the actions. Vienna: Springer-Verlag.

Williams, Emmett (ed.)
   1967   *An anthology of concrete poetry.* New York,
           Villefranche, Frankfurt, Stuttgart: Something Else Press,
           Inc.

American Language Poetry and the Definition of the Avant-Garde

JACOB EDMOND

A number of papers in the Edinburgh Conference on the Avant-Garde and Neo-Avant-Garde raised questions about the authenticity or otherwise of the so-called neo-avant-garde. In the case of Oulipo, for example, David Bellos claimed that the group is not avant-garde because of its lack of manifestos and its institutional organization, which resembles a "gentlemen's dining club". According to Bellos's description, "the term 'avant-garde' is inapplicable to the Oulipo, whilst remaining just about the only term we have for describing its position with respect to the field of literature" (2002). This comment raises the issue of the use of the term "avant-garde". On the one hand, it might be used for a narrow range of work produced prior to the Second World War in Europe. On the other hand, there is a range of work produced after this period in response to this work, or otherwise exhibiting striking similarities in practice and rhetoric, which in this sense might also be termed "avant-garde".

As Richard Sheppard notes in his book *Modernism — Dada — Postmodernism*, the distinction, made by Peter Bürger, and others such as Raymond Williams (see, for example, the chapters "The Language of the Avant-Garde", and "The Politics of the Avant-Garde" in Williams 1989: 49–80), between "high modernism" and the avant-garde "was a necessary corrective to the tendency of critics, especially in North America, to use the terms avant-garde and modernism interchangeably and represented a key move in the offensive against New Criticism with its central doctrine of artistic autotelicity" (2000: 6). In the same breath, Sheppard also notes that the distinction is flawed. What I want to examine here is the way in which the American language poets, a group active in the 1970s and 1980s, inherited the North American tendency to lump modernism and the avant-garde together, while also being part of a reaction against New Criticism. "Language poetry" demonstrates many of the difficulties in separating the two legacies and, contrary to Bürger's view in his *Theory of the Avant-Garde*, the ongoing relevance of modernism and the avant-garde in contemporary art. By examining the insights and shortcomings of Bürger's theory in the light of language poetry, I do not want so much to argue for or against the authenticity of the language poetry as an avant-garde movement, but rather to look at ways in which the movement both does and does not fit Bürger's characterization of the avant-garde.

The difficulty of categorizing language poetry as either avant-garde or otherwise is partly due to the difference between the "the field of literature" in North America and Europe. In the former, as Sheppard and many others have pointed out, the use of avant-garde and modernism as synonyms reflected an environment in which high modernist approaches could be combined in a new way with avant-garde attitudes and rhetoric. In poetry, in particular, the widespread conservatism toward modernist innovation in poetry has meant that there has been a constant battle for a more full-blooded modernist legacy, which has often been automatically considered "avant-garde". Consistent with this North American approach, a group like the "language poets" has significant points of contact with both high modernist and avant-garde literature from the first half of the twentieth century.

The work of the philosopher and art historian Arthur Danto has also been concerned with the continuities and oppositions between the avant-garde and high modernism. Danto's view of art history associates the term "avant-garde" with exactly the art with which Bürger contrasts the avant-garde. Danto, for example, picks up on Clement Greenberg's theory of modern art *and* the avant-garde. But while for Greenberg, avant-garde and modernist art aims "to collapse the distinction between reality and art," to make art "not *mean* but *be*", for Danto modernist art eventually proved this goal to be impossible:

> It is indeed as if the goal of the avant-garde was to collapse the distinction between reality and art by making an adjunct reality, with no more meaning than reality itself possesses, and the aesthetic qualities of which are analogous to those of sunsets and surf, mountains and woods, actual flowers and beautiful bodies. A work of art, to paraphrase the famous line, must not *mean* but *be*. In philosophical truth, this is an impossible theory, and its impossibility became manifest in the 1960s when artists produced objects so like real objects — I am thinking of the *Brillo Box* once again — that it became clear that the real philosophical question was how to prevent them from simply collapsing into reality. One small step toward a solution was to recognize, just as Greenberg says, reality has no meaning, but that, contrary to his posture, art does. At the most one can say that reality defines a limit art can be said to approach — but which it cannot reach on penalty of no longer being art. In a discussion of Picasso, in 1957, Greenberg wrote, "Like any other kind of picture, a modernist one succeeds when its identity as a picture, and as a pictorial experience, shuts out the awareness of it as a physical object. But this is just a leap of faith: how would a monochrome red painting show its difference from a flat surface just covered with red paint? Greenberg believed that art alone and unaided presents itself to the eye as art, when one of the great lessons of art in recent times is that this cannot be so, that artworks and real things cannot be told apart by visual inspection alone. (1997: 71)

To simplify Danto's view, the indiscernible art of Warhol marks the end of high modernism, with the realization that "artworks and real things cannot be told apart by visual inspection alone". Danto copes with "indiscernible" cases by suggesting that art must be about something. In this way, he tries to draw together some high modernist art, such as a monochrome painting, with some art that is more clearly intended to be "anti-aesthetic". While this is a good way of coping with some modern art, including some avant-garde art in Bürger's sense, it is not true of art in general (see Carroll 2001: 98). Bürger's division between aestheticism and the avant-garde while not perfect is a useful corrective to the conflation that sometimes appears in Danto's work. The creation of an "adjunct reality", according to this view, would be the modernist-Aestheticist line, subject to Bürger's criticism of lack of content, while the revelation of the indiscernible nature of some modern art, is an avant-garde attack on this self-sufficiency. But the two are, of course, often either indistinguishable and/or mixed in modern and avant-garde art, as Danto illustrates offering a continuous theory from abstract expressionism to Warhol. Both Danto's continuous theory of modern art and Bürger's sharp division of the avant-garde from modernism/aestheticism capture part of the nature of Western art in the twentieth century.

In the same essay, Danto also makes an important comment about the 1970s, which is of interest here as this was the time at which language poetry was developing. The comment also helps to emphasize the difference between Bürger's largely negative and Danto's largely positive view of postmodernism. Danto finds at this point in the visual arts a renewal of the avant-garde tradition:

> I think the ending of modernism did not happen a moment too soon. For the art world of the seventies was filled with artists bent on agendas having nothing much to do with pressing the limits of art or extending the history of art, but with putting art at the service of this or that personal or political goal. And artists had the whole inheritance of art history to work with, including the history of the avant-garde, which placed at the disposition of the artist all those marvellous possibilities the avant-garde had worked out and which modernism did its utmost to repress. (1997: 15)

As Danto sees it, with Warhol in the sixties, modernism came to an end. Modernism "was over because modernism was too local and too materialist, concerned as it was with shape, surface, pigment, and the like as defining painting in its purity" (1997: 14).

This new direction, which Danto sees as the end of modernism and which is often called postmodernism, has come to be associated most closely in the history of American poetry with language poetry, which began in the early to mid 1970s. Indeed Arthur Marwick's new survey of the arts in the West since World War Two gives over most space to language poetry in the poetry section of the chapter on postmodernism (2002: 285–289). Similarly, the new *Oxford Companion to Twentieth-Century Poetry* gives over a whole essay to language poetry, prompting Glyn Maxwell to devote most of his review in the *TLS* to the group (2002: 5–6). In *Manifesto: A Century of Isms* language poetry texts appear as the major examples of American literary manifesto since Frank O'Hara and Charles Olson in the 1950s (Caws 2001). Language poetry, then, has become somewhat paradigmatic of a shift to postmodern poetry in the 1970s. Since the 1980s, literary critics have viewed it as the major contemporary representative of English-language avant-garde poetry.

While in art history, the seventies brought, according to Danto, a reaction against materialist concerns with "shape, surface, pigment and the like", in poetry the situation was not analogous. Rather than rejecting formalism, language poetry tended to increase the focus on form. In language poetry poems are often constructed according to strict formal orders imposed prior to creation. For example, Lyn Hejinian's work *My Life* contains a section for each year of the poet's life with each section containing exactly the same number of sentences (1987 [1980]). The work has been published twice and is updated every year. Ron Silliman's *Tjanting* is based on the Fibonacci mathematical series, with the first paragraph of the poem containing one sentence and each subsequent paragraph containing as many sentences as appeared in the two preceding paragraphs (1981).

This renewed focus on form shows at least some move towards the position of those post-war advocates of high modernism, the New Critics, and other structuralist critics. The extent to which there was similarity between the two positions is illustrated by the fact that Marjorie Perloff, a critic with a background in New Criticism, became a major advocate for this new kind of poetry. While in 1970 she was making rhyme and meaning tables of semantic congruity and incongruity in "Sailing to Byzantium" (1970: 131), by the middle of the 1980s she was analysing language poetry (1985: 215–238).

One of the reasons why the situation in the fine arts and American poetry was different is that what might be termed the "first post-war American avant-garde" produced different results in the fine arts and poetry. This "avant-garde" came after the Second World War spearheaded by European émigrés (de Kooning et al) and flowered in abstract expressionism, new dance (e.g. Merce

Cunningham), but also included the poets Charles Olson, Robert Creeley, Alan Ginsberg, John Cage, the New York School poets John Ashbery and Frank O'Hara and on the West Coast Robert Duncan and others. The work of all these poets appeared in Donald M. Allen's famous 1960 anthology *The New American Poetry*. While all these poets experimented in a variety of formal techniques, there was no obvious analogy between these poets and high modernist art, which Danto sees as "too materialist". Such techniques as found poems, cutups, parodies and pastiches were all already available and widely used prior to language poetry.

There has been a tendency in recent criticism of American poetry to divide it into branching lines emerging from modernism: a mainstream modernism of T. S. Eliot, W. B. Yeats and, sometimes, Ezra Pound, with "transcendental" symbolic poetics; and an alternative or "true" modernism that includes Gertrude Stein, William Carlos Williams and Louis Zukofsky, which is generally seen as more "materialist", more focused on the process of language making and experiencing, rather than symbolic power of language. It is this "alternative modernism" that has been seen as providing the basis of the experimental developments in American poetry since World War Two and that is sometimes called "avant-garde." For critics arguing in this vein, language poetry has been seen as exemplary and corrective in its renewed "materialist" focus on language and form. Peter Nicholls, for example, argues in "Difference Spreading" that there is continuity in the focus on the material process of writing from Stein to language poetry, as opposed to the view of the poem as an "equation" for a thought or emotion in the Anglo-American mainstream modernist poetics of Eliot and Pound (1991: 116–118). On the other hand, Marjorie Perloff has long argued for language poetry being avant-garde by virtue of its being the true heir to the entire Anglo-American modernist poetry tradition. In *Dance of Intellect* (1985), she places Pound at the beginning of the alternate path, while in her most recent book *21st-Century Modernism* (2002), she argues for an avant-garde modernism that also includes the early T. S. Eliot. Since *Dance of Intellect*, Perloff has written of language poetry as exemplary of a renewed focus on material form in poetry, which she sees as "modernist" and "avant-garde". While, according to Danto, the fine arts were escaping the materialist concerns in the

1970s, literary postmodernism in American poetry brought just the opposite effect.

This highlights the way in which the pressure on theorists to accommodate different art forms has created difficulties for theories of the avant-garde, and for definitions of art generally (on the problems for definitions of art generally see Kivy 1997). In theoretical work on the avant-garde, the fine arts have often been regarded as paradigmatic, with Duchamp's anti-aesthetic as the exemplar of the avant-garde. It is much more difficult, however, to find the same kind of anti-aesthetic in poetry, in which mainstream modernist and avant-garde practice alike fluctuate, as Raymond Williams argued, between an emphasis on "language as a material in a social process, and attacking language in art and life as blocking 'authentic consciousness'" (1989: 77). And it is often difficult to see whether an anti-aesthetic or a kind of solipsistic tendency prevails. As Bürger writes:

> It is no accident that both Tzara's instructions for making a Dadaist poem and Breton's for the writing of automatic texts have the character of recipes. This represents not only a polemical attack on the individual creativity of the artist; the recipe is to be taken quite literally as suggesting a possible activity on the part of the recipient. The automatic texts also should be read as guides to individual production. But such production is not to be understood as artistic production, but as part of liberating life praxis. This is what is meant by Breton's demand that poetry be practiced (*pratiquer la poesie*). Beyond the coincidence of producer and recipient that this demand implies there is the fact that these concepts lose their meaning: producers and recipients no longer exist. All that remains is the individual who uses poetry as an instrument for living one's life as best one can. There is also a danger here to which Surrealism at least partly succumbed, and that is solipsism, the retreat to the problems of the isolated subject. (1984: 53)

Peter Bürger in part explains the fluctuation between the anti-institutionalism and solipsism in his theory, by seeing the avant-garde as a movement responding to aestheticism, which, according to Bürger, "is achieved first in aestheticist poetry: the striving for purity of form, which has characterized the idealist conception of art since its earliest formulations, threatens to annihilate that which makes producing a work worthwhile, i.e. the content". Bürger describes this response as follows:

> The earliest answer — unmatched to this day despite all contradictions — to the developmental tendencies of art in bourgeois society is given by the historical avant-garde movements. The demand for a return of art to life, the abolition of the autonomy of art, marks the counterpole to that tendency which extrapolated the status of autonomy right into the work. The aestheticizing primacy of form is now replaced by the primacy of expression. The artist-subject revolts against form, which now confronts him as something alien. What should master the facticity of the given, proves to be a coercion which the subject inflicts on himself. He rebels against it. (1992: 45–46)

This is difficult to understand, but it seems to me that Bürger is contrasting the championing of "purity of form" in BB with a view of form as a constriction on "the subject". What is interesting in language poetry is the way in which the poets rebel against form, understood as language as such, including grammatical forms, by using formal methods to highlight this necessary "coercion". This is an interesting combination of what Bürger describes as aestheticism and avant-gardism.

Peter Bürger acknowledges that the avant-garde "adopted an essential element of aestheticism", namely, the way in which aestheticism negated "the means-ends rationality of the bourgeois everyday", by making "the distance from the praxis of life the contents of works" (1984: 49). Language poetry exhibits a similar combination of aesthetic and anti-aesthetic tendencies.

Bürger's view of the relationship of aestheticism to the avant-garde leads him to see the "intended purpose or function" of avant-garde art as difficult to define. In Bürger's view it is only with aestheticism that "the work of art becomes its own end in the full meaning of the term". Bürger's view seems to be that the avant-gardistes aimed to extend the lack of means-ends rationality in aestheticism to all aspects of social life, thus destroying the very concept of "purpose" or "function": "art's purpose can no longer be discovered, because the existence of two distinct spheres (art and the praxis of life) that is constitutive of purpose or intended use has come to an end" (1984: 51).

Bürger's understanding of art history relates to his Marxist historicism. As he sees it, there are three major stages in the development of art: Sacral Art, Courtly Art, and Bourgeois Art. For Bürger, for art to be integral to the practice of life it must be "collective," or "social"; it also seems to require that art relate to a specific use or function (1984: 48). In bourgeois art, on the other hand, there is no specific use or function beyond "bourgeois self-understanding", which "occurs in a sphere outside the praxis of life". This seems to imply that bourgeois art is without any relation to collectives, social groups or specific functions. Television and film are, however, major, if not the major, art forms in bourgeois society and they do seem to be collective experiences.

This may not be a proper objection to Bürger's theory. Bürger writes specifically about "high art" in aestheticism, in which, according to him, "art becomes the contents of art" (this is similar to Danto's assertion of modern art history as a process of striving for "self-definition"). From this historical situation, according to Bürger, the avant-garde emerged:

> Aestheticism had made the distance from the praxis of life the content of works. The praxis of life to which aestheticism refers and which it negates is the means-end rationality of the bourgeois everyday. Now, it is not the aim of the avant-gardistes to integrate art into *this* praxis. On the contrary, they assent to the aestheticists' rejection of the world and its means-ends rationality. What distinguishes them from the latter is the attempt to organize a new life praxis from a basis in art. (1984: 49)

As Bürger sees it, the avant-garde attacked "autonomy" on three levels. Firstly, avant-garde art's "purpose" is somehow intended to remove the possibility of purpose: "art's purpose can no longer be discovered, because the existence of two distinct spheres (art and the praxis of life) that is constitutive of purpose or intended use has come to an end" (1984: 51). "Purpose" is antithetical because it involves rationalism, which the avant-garde rejects. The avant-garde also aims to negate individual "production" and "reception", and to "eliminate the antithesis between producer and recipient" (1984: 51–53). It is in this sense that some of the language poets experiments may be seen as avant-garde, according to Bürger's theory.

Bürger, however, would be unlikely to agree with this assessment. In relation to production, Bürger makes an interesting comment on what he sees as the effect of Duchamp's readymades in the world today: "Since now the protest of the historical avant-garde against art as institution is accepted as *art*, the gesture of protest of the neo-avant-garde becomes inauthentic" (1984: 53).

Given the difficulties that Bürger experiences in differentiating between Aestheticist-modernist approaches to poetry and "authentic" avant-garde practices, it seems worthwhile here to examine the points of continuity between the function, production, and reception of language poetry and what Bürger identifies in the function, production, and reception of dadaist and surrealist art.

Bürger's stress on the importance of modernist aesthetic theories and practices to the avant-garde is, I think, quite compatible with considering language poetry avant-garde. Language poetry often exploits the "high modernist" emphasis on "pure form" with a rhetorical avant-garde posture of opposition to any isolated or extra-social aesthetic, but rather for this pure form to play an important political function in society. In this regard, for the San Francisco poets Barrett Watten, Ron Silliman and Lyn Hejinian at least, Russian futurism, formalism, OPOYAZ and OBERIU were significant inspirations, because the Russian avant-garde and Russian formalism together offered perhaps the most coherent argument for linking modernist formalism with avant-garde social action. Specifically, Shklovsky's concept of *ostranenie*, or "de-familiarization", provided a reason to believe that formal innovations might have the positive consequence of revealing "false consciousness". Because of the language poets interest in Marxism, their conception of "de-familiarization" quite closely resembles Brecht's concept of Verfremdungseffekt, or "alienation effect."

The major art historical preconditions for language poetry seem to have been Anglo-American modernist poetry, particularly Pound and Stein, the Objectivists, especially Zukofsky, and Black Mountain, Beat and New York School poetry, and the European alternatives, in Bürger's view the "real avant-garde", surrealism, dadaism, and also the combination of poetic innovation and criticism in Russian futurism and formalism as seen through the somewhat idealizing lens of the American literary left.

The idea that some sort of modernist aesthetic might be mobilized to change the world is important to language poetry, or at least to several poets associated with it. If we accept Bürger's distinction between modernism and the avant-garde for the moment, we can see how language poets drew on the innovations of modernists such as Stein, but combined this sometimes with avant-garde experiments in production and reception. For example, the Language poet Bob Perelman notes the language poets' experimentations with collective creation of poetic works by simultaneous readings of various texts to a single typist, who would type while listening (32). This kind of approach to production-reception, in which the reader/listener is writer and the activity is communal coincides closely with Bürger's description of avant-garde production and reception (1984: 51–53).

The reception of language poetry also appears to challenge Bürger's claim for the end of the avant-garde. Bürger bases this claim on the apparently empirical observation that groups that seek to attack the boundaries of art no longer raise the ire of the bourgeoisie, and that this is a result of the "false sublimation of art and life", or the "aestheticization of everyday life", that resulted from the "failure" of the classical European avant-garde of the first half of the twentieth century. Contrary to Bürger's theory, however, language poetry did raise considerable heated opposition to its claim to art status, because of the way in which acceptance of this claim was seen to imply acceptance that the status of art, individual expression, or even the individual self is purely contingent, or constructed.

Apart from Russian formalism and futurism, language poetry found theoretical support for their experimentations in the writings of the Frankfurt school and French post-structuralists. The concept of and attack on the "centred" or "Cartesian subject" provided not only the major justification for the formal experiments of language poetry, but also provided a convenient way to differentiate the new work from previous generations of experimental poets in the United States. From Shklovsky to Adorno, language writers drew on many sources to emphasize the importance of language in the construction of social reality and their claim that: "new ways of thinking [...] make new ways of being possible". While acknowledging the influence of the previous generation, rather than the lighter playful touch of O'Hara or the bohemian exuberance of Ginsberg, language poets tended to take a more aggressive and utopian approach to their

work. Language poets questioned the idea of a singular voice in poetry and of an authentic self in society, taking their cue partly from
the rise of Theory in the academy. Language poets saw the dominant
concept of poetic voice as reflecting in Lee Bartlett's words, "a reductive approach, and one with political consequences" (1986: 745).
In an environment in which politics and poetry were widely assumed to belong to unconnected or at least only indirectly connected
realms, the language poets in their theoretical writings and
manifestos challenged the status quo by attacking what they
perceived as the political conservatism of mainstream poetry. For
some in the United States in the 1970s and 1980s, it seems that to
assert the interrelationship between poetry and politics was to bring
into question the status of a work as poetry, and was seen as
challenging the role of lyric poetry as expressing "bourgeois
subjectivity".

In the early to mid 1980s language poetry began to gain more
public exposure, provoking criticism of their linking of politics and
aesthetics, as well as their unorthodox poetic methods. In 1984 a
debate that took place amongst poets with competing poetics in
1984 in San Francisco illustrates the issues at stake. The group of
language poets based in the San Francisco Bay area were one side in
this "poetry war".

This "war" began in June and, as De Villo Sloan describes it,
centred around two terms of abuse that related to aesthetic position:
"crude mechanical access" and "crude personism" (the following
account comes from Sloan 1985). The language poets were accused
of the former crime for their supposed denial of the self in the poem,
to which they opposed a conception of the socially constructed self
under heavy influence from the Frankfurt School and French poststructuralism. This attack raised issues surrounding the problem of
the postmodern aesthetic of the totally de-centred self, which was
seen by some as effectively denying the value of the individual and
collapsing universal value into particularity, a celebration of difference as such. On the other hand, language poets, in particular Ron
Silliman, accused the mainstream American poetry of being naive in
its assumption of self expression in language, which was advocated
for its humanism and championing of freewill and imagination. For
the language poets, the aesthetic of most mainstream contemporary
poetry in the United States, which assumed an inner voice, an iden-

tity unique and inseparable from all other entities, was also the aesthetic of conservative rhetoric, which has a narrow definition of what constitutes both a normal individual, and universal value.

The polemic over "crude personism" and "crude mechanism" thus went beyond the poetics and politics of language poetry to raise issues of more general concern amongst left-leaning intellectuals to the point where an opponent called Silliman the "Secretary-General of the Language Party".

In sum, language poetry was attacked on three grounds: its representation of self, its status as poetry, and its politics. It is important to note that language poetry itself encouraged those opposed to it to make connections between form and politics. There were two opposing views here: firstly a strictly autonomous view of poetry, and secondly a view of form and politics as connected but of language poetry as having the wrong form and politics. This argument can be understood partly as a struggle between different poets to assert their right to the legacy of 1960s activism. The argument partly grew out of what was seen as the attempt by some language poets to denigrate Robert Duncan's work. The use of the rhetoric of radical French poststructuralism allowed language poetry to effectively outflank any position less radical than its own and to accuse other writers of political and aesthetic complicity. Rather than losing its edge through a supposed "aestheticization of life", the neo-avant-garde language poets caused considerable upset through their challenge to the institutional autonomy of poetry, simply by increasing the level of rhetoric and the extremity of the solution on offer. As a result, the status of their poetry as art was for some time in question.

This record of reception, and the attitude towards the function and production of poetry amongst the language poets all are at least partly compatible with Bürger's description of the function, production and reception of the avant-garde. Moreover, the record of reception is a counterexample to Bürger's insistence that avant-garde acts are no longer possible and thus that the neo-avant-garde is "inauthentic".

It is a commonplace to observe that literary theory in the twentieth century emerged out of and with literary practice. In a recent review of a new history of the *TLS*, for example, James Wood uses a quotation from Wallace Stevens to refer to this phenomenon: "The absence of imagination has itself to be imagined" (2002: 12). As outlined above, Bürger's theory of the avant-garde recognizes both this relationship between theory and practice and the equally intimate relationship between modernism and the avant-garde in an intriguing way. For Bürger, the avant-garde revealed the institutional nature of art by both using and attacking the legacy of aestheticism and, having done so, ironically rendered avant-garde art impossible, because the new institutional criteria for art could encompass anything that radical artists might produce. Bürger's theory of the avant-garde thus contains an important insight into the relationship of the avant-garde to developments in both art history and art theory. Bürger linked the avant-garde to a specific moment in European art history, and particularly to the role of art as it was consciously defined by the Aesthetic movement.

As a result of the nature of this theoretical definition of the avant-garde, Bürger's theory is implicitly a theory of art, because it relies upon a view that definitions of art evolve historically and institutionally. This assumption seems to be based upon the observation that the predominant conceptions of art in twentieth-century have evolved with artistic practice. In pointing this out, the philosopher Noël Carroll calls the twentieth century, for the art theorist at least, "the age of the avant-garde". As Carroll sees it, in the twentieth century "the context that motivates theoretical activity in the branch of art theory concerned with the question 'What is Art?' is one in which change, transition, or revolution is a central problem" (2001: 84).

As Carroll freely acknowledges, his insight into the intimate relationship between definitions of art and avant-garde practice in the twentieth-century owes much to the work of Arthur Danto, whose view of modernism and the avant-garde was outlined above, although Carroll does not draw the same conclusions as Danto does from this insight. As I have pointed out, Danto's theory of the development of Western art in the twentieth century in turn bears some interesting similarities to and differences from Bürger's theory of the avant-garde. Danto argues that modern art has been a developmental process that "has attempted to use its own forms and strategies to disclose the essential nature of art". Bürger too seems to see the avant-garde as revealing the essential nature of art, which, as Bürger sees it, is essentially institutional. For Danto, "once an artist like Warhol has *shown* that artworks can be perceptually indiscernible from 'real things' and, therefore, can *look like anything*, there is nothing further that the artist qua artist can *show*." Thus "art history — as the developmental, progressive narrative of self-definition — ends" (Carroll 1999). Like Danto, Bürger focuses on the demonstration that art can be *anything*, though for him Duchamp's readymades are paradigmatic in this regard. He sees Duchamp and others as attacking aestheticism, in which art and life were seen as separate realms. By making this attack, according to Bürger, Duchamp revealed the institutional nature of art under aestheticism. But this shifted the conscious assumptions about what art was from aestheticism to institutional explanations. By attempting to destroy art, the avant-garde actually enlarged its realm and made art-watchers view it in a new, institutional way. Bürger sees the avant-garde as an attack on the institution of art that ends at the point at which the institutional definition is accepted. Danto, on the other hand, sees the same process as an attempt at self-definition. Whatever the aim, both agree that art reaches a point where intrinsic qualities are revealed as unnecessary for something being art. For Danto this point marks the end of art history, while for Bürger it marks the end of the avant-garde.

As Noël Carroll points out, definitions of art such as those suggested by both Bürger and Danto have been developed specifically to deal with the challenge of how to identify avant-garde art as art. Such definitions have been quite common in the twentieth century and tend to be either "institutional" or "historically reflexive" definitions of art, in the parlance of contemporary philosophy of art. In historically reflexive definitions, art is seen as having a historically changing definition whereby "something is an art work only in the event that it stands in the appropriate relationship to its artistic forebears" (Davies 2001: 173). Peter Bürger's theory is rather opaque but can be said to be a form of historically reflexive definition, in which he sees art as becoming "institutional" at a specific point. The main point, however, is that Bürger's theory of art *a priori* makes what he claims the avant-garde was trying to do incoherent. If art is merely art by virtue of its historical relationship to previous art, then to speak of an attempt to make art outside of this historical relationship makes little sense. To some extent it is possible to concede to this view, by claiming that avant-garde artists misunderstood the nature of art. It seems reasonable that the identifying of an artefact as art is, as Carroll argues, primarily governed by relationships of the historically reflexive variety. It is also reasonable to suppose that some avant-garde artists aimed to establish a clean break from such a narrative and to create artworks that performed the putatively original or basic functions of art. As part of this project, works that point out the importance of institution and narrative over function can be seen as playing an important role in undermining the credibility of art as understood in Western society, with the aim of re-establishing a functional form of art. But, if we are proceeding with a narrative understanding of art, then repudiation of existing art, is entirely compatible with being art, so that Bürger's understanding of art necessarily implies the impossibility of any work designed to repudiate art escaping the institution of art.

The problem with Bürger's definition may also lie in the way he appears to conflate competing ways of defining art, without adequately explaining how he intends these different definitions to be combined. As Davies has argued, contemporary definitions of art can broadly be divided into three types: functional, procedural, and the historically reflexive type that I have just discussed. On the one hand, functional definitions of art define art in terms of its point. Functional definitions define art in term of aesthetic goals or certain practically valuable skills in our everyday lives. This, I think, is what Bürger means by art when he writes of "aesthetic experience" (1984: 34). To be consistent such a definition of art will have to include a pleasing turn of phrase, a fascinating design, dressing up, and anything else in our everyday lives that is aimed at aesthetic experiences. But whereas it seems that art in this sense is very much a part of daily life, Bürger does not think it is, or if it is, it is only falsely sublimated. The reason that Bürger holds this opinion, I think, is because he conflates art in this functional sense with art defined procedurally.

Procedural definitions of art define art in terms of the way something is produced and presented. George Dickie has advanced perhaps the most comprehensive procedural definition of art (1972). Simply put, he thinks that art is best defined in terms of the institution of art; that art is art by virtue of it being placed in an appropriate place, say an art gallery, and of it being recognized as art by art critics. Bürger too broadly subscribes to this view, at least in the context of modern bourgeois Europe. But Bürger conflates the procedural definition of art, as the institution of art, with the functional definition of art, as "aesthetic experience". As a result, the avant-garde's aim does indeed appear paradoxical and thus impossible. But, as I have tried here briefly to point out, it is fallacious to move from the premise that art is institutionally defined to the conclusion that aesthetic experience is institutionally defined. The institution of art and objects that effect aesthetic experience may both be designated by the word "art", but these are two distinct uses of the word based on different definitions.

To conclude: Bürger's implied historically reflexive definition of art helps to explain the interaction between ideas about art and the direction of the development of art from aestheticism to the classical avant-garde. This insight in turn helps distinguish between some high modernist and avant-garde practices, while explaining that the latter aims not to destroy the former, but to mobilize for different ends. Bürger's theory up to this point is quite compatible with viewing a group such as the language poets as avant-garde, but he would object to this. The reason for his objection appears to be based on his view that there has been a complete acceptance of all new innovations as art, as a result of the "false sublimation" of art and life achieved partly thanks to the classical avant-garde, and that the neo-avant-garde is thus inauthentic. But, as I have argued, there are reasons for doubting his view at both empirical and analytical levels. At the empirical level, acceptance of new innovations is not complete, at least not in poetry. At the analytic level, Bürger justified seeing art as functionally restricted to a pleasure commodity because his theory ties the functions of art too closely to the procedural way in which art is defined at a given historical moment. Bürger sometimes seems to see the procedures, or social and historical context as determining the function of art absolutely, but the example of language poetry shows that this is not necessarily the case. If this is indeed not the case, then one is not obliged to accept Bürger's pessimistic view of the neo-avant-garde and of contemporary art in general.

BIBLIOGRAPHY

Allen, Donald M.
1960   *The New American Poetry: 1945–1960*, New York: Grove.

Bartlett, Lee
1986   "What Is 'Language Poetry'?" In *Critical Inquiry* 12, 741–752.

Bellos, David
2002   Abstract of "The Undermining of the Avant-Garde: Oulipo and the Future of Literary Movements". Conference on the Avant-Garde and Neo-Avant-Garde. Edinburgh University, March 2002. At: http://www.arts. ed.ac.uk/langgrad/rprojects/avantgarde/Edin%20abstract %2011.htm.

Bürger, Peter
1984   *Theory of the Avant-Garde*, Minneapolis: U of Minnesota Press.

1992   *The Decline of Modernism*, Pennsylvania: Pennsylvania State UP.

Carroll, Noël
1999   "Danto", 204, *Cambridge Dictionary of Philosophy*, 2nd edition, edited by Robert Audi, Cambridge: Cambridge UP.

2001   *Beyond Aesthetics: Philosophical Essays*, Cambridge: Cambridge UP.

Caws, Mary Ann
2001   *Manifesto: A Century of Isms*, Lincoln: U of Nebraska P.

Danto, Arthur
1997   *After the End of Art: Contemporary Art and the Pale of History*, Princeton: Princeton UP.

Davies, Stephen
2001   "Definitions of Art", 169–179, *Routledge Companion to Aesthetics*, edited by Berys Gaut and Dominic McIver Lopes, London: Routledge.

Dickie, George
1974   *Art and the Aesthetic: An Institutional Analysis*, Ithaca: Cornell UP.

Hejinian, Lyn
　1987 [1980]*My Life*, revised edition, LA: Sun and Moon.

Kivy, Peter
　1997　　　*Philosophies of Art: An Essay in Differences*, Cambridge: Cambridge UP.

Marwick, Arthur
　2002　　　*The Arts in the West since 1945*, Oxford: Oxford UP.

Maxwell, Glyn
　2002　　　"Make It Cohere: The Deep Confusion of the Avant-Garde". In *TLS* 5 Jul. 2002, 5–6.

Nicholls, Peter
　1991　　　"Spreading Difference: From Gertrude Stein to L=A=N=G=U=A=G=E Poetry", 116–127, *Contemporary Poetry Meets Modern Theory*, edited by Antony Easthope and John O. Thompson, London: Harvester Wheatsheaf.

Perelman, Bob
　1996　　　*The Marginalization of Poetry: Language Writing and Literary History*, Princeton: Princeton UP.

Perloff, Marjorie
　1970　　　*Rhyme and Meaning in the Poetry of Yeats*, The Hague: Mouton.

　1985　　　*The Dance of Intellect: Studies in the Poetry of the Pound Tradition*, Cambridge: Cambridge UP.

　2002　　　*21st-Century Modernism: The "New" Poetics*, Oxford: Blackwell.

Sheppard, Richard
　2000　　　*Modernism — Dada — Postmodernism*, Evanston: Northwestern UP.

Silliman, Ron
　1981　　　*Tjanting*, Berkeley: Figures.

Sloan, De Villo
　1985　　　"'Crude Mechanical Access' or 'Crude Personism': A Chronicle of One San Francisco Bay Area Poetry War". In *Sagetrieb* 4, 241–254.

Williams, Raymond
1989   *Politics of Modernism: Against the New Conformists*,
        edited by Tony Pinsky, London: Verso.

Wood, James
2002   "Phut-Phut". In *London Review of Books* 27 Jun. 2002,
        11–12.

IV.

BODY ARTS

From Futurism to Neo-Futurism: Continuities and New Departures in Twentieth-Century Avant-Garde Performance

GÜNTER BERGHAUS

Introduction

Looking back at the history of twentieth-century avant-garde performance, one notices periods of great artistic explosion, such as 1909–1928 and 1965–1985, interspersed with periods of creative lull. Received opinion has it that the last quarter of the twentieth century has been a period of stasis again. However, I do not share this view and regard the new developments in the electronic and digital media as having opened up novel and untried possibilities for performing artists. Although these new media were anticipated by concepts of virtuality in photography and cinema as far back as the nineteenth century, I would disagree with Richard Schechner's estimation that the new forms of electronic media are merely extensions and globalizations of visual and communication technologies that have already been in existence for the last fifty years (Harding 207).

Throughout history there has always been a lively exchange between art and science. Brunelleschi, da Vinci and Buontalenti — to mention just a few examples — were engineers who invented remarkable machines for military, civic and artistic purposes. The technologies of the industrial age gave birth to photography, the

panorama, cinema, radio and many other mechanical forms of reflecting the world. The futurists and constructivists made the
integration of art and science a fundamental principle of their aesthetics. But many of their Utopian concepts had to wait until the
invention of the computer before they could become reality. The
1960s saw the first artistic experiments with digital media (computer
graphics, computer dance, computer music, etc.), which soon
branched out into video performances and installations, virtual reality games, and so on.

For a while, critics categorized artistic developments in the
1970s and 80s under the rubric of "postmodernism". But as people's
living and work environments became more and more saturated with
electronic and digital technologies, and as the scope and scale of the
new media responding to this development increased, some cultural
historians suggested that the turn of the millennium may have served
as a threshold for a Second Modernity. Heinrich Klotz, for example,
promoted the idea that contrary to painting, sculpture and theatre,
which had only altered their shape and appearance by degrees,
media art was a fundamentally new phenomenon that ushered in a
new age of avant-garde experimentation. Although electronic media
in their commercial formats were rooted in traditional formulae of
fascination and visual appeal, their artistic branches proved to be a
minefield of genuine innovation. As any visitor to recent *Documen-
tas* or *Biennales*, not to mention the many specialized media art
festivals, will have noticed, the range of artistic experimentation has
considerably widened as a result of the digital revolution and has
finally overcome the long phase of postmodern stagnation. Rather
than recycling trends and fashions of the First Modernity, the avant-
garde at the fin-de-millennium moved into genuinely new terrain
that was "still modernity, although a modernity different from the
one at the beginning of the century" (Klotz 1996: 9).

I. The Role of Interactivity in Avant-Garde Performance

It was a fundamental concern of the historical avant-garde to explore
Kandinsky's idea of dismantling the mono-directional channel of
artistic communication and to turn the viewer / spectator into an active co-producer of the work of art. Futurism was the first avant-
garde movement to systematically explore this idea, both in the form

of theoretical reflections and practical experiments. In the area of the fine arts, painters and sculptors sought to "put the spectator into the centre of the picture" (Apollonio: 28) and to move away from static objects to "an emotive architectural environment which creates sensations and completely involves the observer" (Boccioni: 177). In theatre, they wanted to "eliminate the preconception of the footlights by throwing nets of sensation between stage and audience; the stage action will invade the orchestra seats, the audience" (Apollonio: 196). This aim was certainly achieved in the infamous *serate*, which provoked the spectators into lively and often violent reactions, allowing the performers, as in the Teatro Verdi in Florence (12 December 1913), to take a break on stage, smoke a cigarette and observe the main action unroll in the stalls (Berghaus: 122–8). A different type of interaction could be observed in the "Futurist Afternoons" (*pomeriggi futuristi*), where the acting took place in the midst of the audience and involved the spectators in a variety of participatory roles. The gallery spaces in which the performances took place knew no formal differentiation between stage and auditorium. The performances were therefore multifocal in orientation and employed the principle of simultaneity to merge the actions of both actors and spectators.

The reversal of the traditional stage-audience relationship pioneered by the futurists in 1910–1914 also became a key concern of the dadaists. In his *Zurich Chronicle* Tzara declared: "Our theatre will entrust the stage direction to the subtle invention of the explosive wind and the scenario to the audience" (564). A good demonstration of this principle was provided during a soirée at the Salle Gaveau in Paris (26 May 1920), where "the spectacle took place in the auditorium. We were gathered on the stage watching the audience let loose" (Tzara: 64). Hannah Höch recalls similar scenes in Berlin: "The audience and the actors on stage incited each other, and when the spectators began to join into the action or to vent their anger, the actors stood calmly at the proscenium arch and let the players in the hall run the show for a while" (204).

In the 1960s, interactivity was again a topical issue in the performing and visual arts. Members of the happening movement, theatre companies such as Living Theatre, Bread and Puppet Theatre, Chaikin's Open Theatre and Schechner's Performance Group, and special initiatives such as Billy Klüver's Experiments in Art and

Technology and Otto Piene's Center for Advanced Visual Studies, all sought to give the spectators an active agency and assign to them a variety of participatory roles. The first generation of artists who had a chance to experiment with the new electronic equipment coming onto the market felt an enormous excitement about its potential for building bridges between art and life in the information age: "The work of art is not to point to itself exclusively, it is to encourage the recipient to become active. This is the seed of dialogue that can be developed further, if the work of art becomes the interface of a dialogue of thoughts and perhaps also of common creation" (Lischka 1986: 17). Consequently, artists such as Peter Weibel, Roy Ascott, Jeffrey Shaw and Fred Forester, who had their roots in interactive forms of theatre, quickly realized the potential of the new media to "create a virtual space full of images, sounds, texts etc. which become (partly or fully) realized when a user is operating in and with the space" (Shaw 1989: 204).

Early interactive media art was rather basic in concept and execution and possessed only a limited range of operational possibilities. But as the technology became more complex, it enhanced the users' active and creative input. Simple stimulus-response mechanisms were replaced with more sophisticated hypermedia and VR interfaces, which made the work non-linear and open-ended, thus widening the range of interactions and creating scenarios of possibilities rather than finished products. In these creations, as in a theatrical performance, the performer vanishes once the task has been completed, and with him the work of art. But not all of these digital interactions become fully-fledged performances. Staged performances consist of presentations specially created for an audience (as in the theatre) and of demonstrations that other people can watch (as is often the case at media art festivals or in game arcades). If a media user "performs" a task for himself alone, he gives a concrete form to an otherwise virtual work of art. He therefore engages in a "performance", but one that knows only one actor and no audience. The artwork that requires such interactive input can be described as performative and has varying degrees of complexity and aesthetic quality. But as David Saltz rightly suggests, "we must stop considering computer interaction as a unified phenomenon and draw some distinctions between various kinds of interactive systems"(120).

When, in 1990, the Prix Ars Electronica introduced the new category of "interactive media art", Roy Ascott defined the medium thus:

> Interactive art presents a flow of data (images, text, sound) and an array of cybernetic, adaptive and, one might say, *intelligent* structures, environments and networks (as performances, events, personal encounters and private experiences) in such a way that the observer can affect the flow, alter the structure, interact with the environment or navigate the network, thus becoming directly involved in the acts of transformation and creation. (1991: 25)

Many of the works exhibited in Linz positioned the active user at their centre, and their artistic quality depended on the dramaturgy of interaction, the complexity of the participatory components, and the intellectual stimulation derived from the experience. As far as the content was concerned, the most convincing creations showed how these media alter the human experience of reality, how they influence our identity and psychology, and how they transform our relationships with our bodies and our environment. Moreover, the works not only reflected on these events but also allowed users to experience such changes and to develop a critical attitude towards them.

II. Primitivism and Technophilia in Twentieth-Century Performance Art

Much of twentieth-century avant-garde experimentation was characterized by various swings of the pendulum between the poles of technophilia and primitivism. No textbook on Modernism fails to mention how the great surge of expressionist art in the 1910s was followed by new objectivity and constructivist aesthetics in the 1920s. In the art and culture of the 1980s and 90s, the two trends seemed to coincide with, rather than follow, each other. On the one hand there were the neo-futurists, advocates of the electronic age, who saw in the new technologies a means of solving humanity's problems. They embraced the new developments with a Utopian optimism and propagated a euphoric scenario of increased communication by means of electronic mail, satellite telephone, the World Wide Web, etc. On the other hand, there were the neo-primitivists,

who deplored the influence of technology on our civilization and
professed a technophobic, pessimistic outlook on the twenty-first
century. They predicted a cultural Armaggedon, an erosion of humanistic values and traditions, and the demise of social institutions
and organic communities, all due to an increased isolation and alienation of the individual and a replacement of communal with
home-centred lifestyles. Their doomladen analysis of modern and
postmodern society favoured a rejection of the Moloch technology,
and in a distinctly neo-Luddite manner advocated a "politics of the
ejection seat" in order to prevent humanity's "march into Hades".

At a time when the individual was in danger of being disembodied, sucked into cyberspace or modified by the tools of
biotechnology, the rooting of the self in the physical body and an
organic community became a political as well as artistic issue. The
destabilizing effects of urbanization, mass consumerism and information overkill awakened a desire for re-establishing binding social
values and cultural continuities, a desire which often expressed itself
in a nostalgia for a pre-industrial past, the revival of earth-centred
pagan traditions, and the recycling of ancient goddess cults. A society characterized by an abundance and overproduction of goods,
images and works of culture encourages the rise of avant-garde
elites to reinstate the value of singular experiences and unrepeatable
acts of creativity. Vacuity of existence in a mundane world, crisis of
identity, and loss of spiritual certainties foster the search for com-
pensations in intensely personal and distinctly transcendental art
"events", which by definition are performative. Attempts at returning to a non-instrumentalized art by linking creative production to
personal, social and aesthetic concerns led the artists to a mythical
Ur-art, in which aesthetic and social processes were not yet separated from each other.

Technophiles were, of course, not unaware of the dangers and
negative aspects of modern electronic culture, but in their view this
was not to be seen as inherent faults of the media themselves but of
the way they were implemented, controlled and used. Mindful of the
Frankfurt School's critique of the "culture industry", they criticized
the frequently one-sided views of eschatological environmentalists,
who disregarded the dynamic diversity of modern capitalism and the
productive conflicts within postindustrial society. In their view, the
electronic market showed variety as well as uniformity. Besides the

multi-national monopolies, there was also a plethora of small companies which provided sophisticated services and products. And also the mass media offered not only soporific, escapist products but also reflected social realities and contributed positively to social change. Furthermore, the latest generation of interactive technologies opened up exactly those possibilities that Enzensberger had demanded from an emancipatory media practice.

Consequently, the technophiles attached great value to individual self-determination and independence in the flourishing, small-scale "electronic cottage industries" and trusted that isolation and alienation could be overcome through the construction of alternative social spheres, local support groups, civil rights movements, and so on. They believed that a positive valorisation of difference and a freedom of choice between multiple and situationally contingent identities would by necessity lead to the dismantling of hegemonic discourses of race, sex and class and thus to an obliteration of the universalizing social practices of dominant social groups. Reducing conformism and fostering a more pluralistic society, they argued, would shift difference from the margins to the centre of society, thereby creating a flourishing system of independent, market-oriented cultural sectors, which would allow for increased personal choice and greater democratic participation.

The two opposing tendencies sketched out above, as well as a wide spectrum of reconciliatory attitudes and startling hybrid positions, could also be found in the historical avant-garde. For this reason, I tend to avoid overly simplistic textbook histories that pitch futurism against surrealism, dada against constructivism, expressionism against new objectivity, high-abstraction against new realism, electronic media art against spiritualist Neo-Shamanism. The richness and diversity of the material in twentieth-century performance art defies any simple patterns of interpretation. From the futurists to the cybernauts there was a primitivist and even spiritual undercurrent in technophile thinking, and vice-versa: primitivists such as the expressionists availed themselves of the latest technologies, and much of their success depended on it. The same may be said of the Neo-Shamans who nowadays populate the internet, or of cybergurus such as Stelarc who also slip into the role of body artists. Although categories such as primitivism / technophilia, abstraction / construction, and body / media art offer some useful paradigms for analysis, they should not tempt us to overlook the considerable overlap that exists between them or underestimate their mutual dependency on one another.

In the following pages I shall use the example of the futurists and the neo-futurist artist Stelarc to demonstrate some of the complex interactions that exist between a primitivist art and a high-tech art, both of which focus on the body and its representation by performative means.

III. The Futurist Body on Stage

In the early years of the futurist movement, the plays written by its members looked no different from those to be found in the traditional repertoire. Similarly, the first dancer to join the group, Valentine de Saint-Point, made little attempt to develop a specifically futurist body language. The first futurist forays into the professional theatre were — and the futurists were among the first to realize this — imperfect demonstrations of their theory, as none of the performers were futurist actors equipped with an adequate training for the plays they were presenting. Soon, Marinetti and his colleagues began to realize that they would not be able to renew Italian theatre simply by writing new plays. What was required was an entirely new approach to the performative and scenic languages of the stage.

To overcome the handicaps of the professional theatre, the futurists took recourse to the popular stage. In 1913, Marinetti published his *Variety Theatre Manifesto*, which exalted action, instinct, intuition, and the use of *fisicofollia* (body madness) as the primary means of revolutionizing theatre. By choosing variety shows as a model for futurist theatre, Marinetti found an apt theatrical formula with which to fight the traditional dramatic forms in his country. No other form of theatre offered so much energy, dynamism, physicality and eroticism, and such an absence of seriousness, solemnity, or soberness. In variety shows, Marinetti experienced the effect of a presentation rather than representation. The actor operated with the overtly physical means of sound, movement, gesture and mime to create a desired effect. The viewer was taken in by the material aesthetics of the performance rather than by its signification. The collaboration with variety stars such as Petrolini revealed

ments of an aeroplane, impersonating the spirit of an airship fighting against the elements of the sky" (1931).

On other occasions she interpreted aeropoems by Marinetti, such as "Flight over Milan Cathedral", or aeropaintings by Prampolini, such as "Throwing the Propeller", "Ascending Speed", and "Simultaneity of Altitudes". Reviews of her performances indicate that her angular and concentrated movements employed every part of the body. She used a variegated rhythm of gestures and movement, producing an impulsive, energetic, jerky and uneven style and an impression of aggressive dynamism. But as Censi could not entirely forget her training at La Scala and still employed classical steps, jumps and turns, her dances do not fully qualify for being called futurist.

The closest approximation to the futurist body on stage was probably the dancer-robot, where the performer acted as a motor for a costume that had been designed and constructed with futurist principles in mind, or even a marionette, a sort of fully mechanized performer. But human beings had not yet undergone the "incalculable number of transformations" Marinetti had spoken of in *Man Extended and the Reign of the Machine* and had yet to discover "the laws of a true sensibility of machines" (1968: 256, 1972: 91). For this reason, what was described in the manifestos was rarely realized, and the futurist body on stage always remained more of an ideal than a reality. At least, this was so until the 1960s, when new electronic equipment and major advances in robotics indicated that a neo-futurist age was dawning.

IV. Stelarc's Reconstruction of the Human Body in a Digital Era

By the end of the twentieth century, some ten percent of the Western population was, technically speaking, cyborgs. They were kept alive by electronic pacemakers, made mobile by prosthetic limbs and synthetic joints, or interacted with the world by means of hearing aids, ophthalmic accessories, and artificial larynxes. The body, colonized by technology, had become a "post-human body". Evermore powerful human-machine interfaces, together with biotechnology and genetic engineering, gave rise to visions of conquering the physical and mental limitations of the human species by means of direct mind-machine connections (chip implants in the brain and neurological pathways connecting humans and computers). At the same time, these technical developments produced fears that the organic body would be reduced to mere "wet-ware" in a mind-machine symbiosis.

The dawn of a bio-cybernetic age not only introduced a wide range of new possibilities for humans to control virtual bodies and for new machines to regulate the human body; it also launched innovative developments in artistic media based on digital technology and prompted new departures in the performing arts. In past centuries, actors concerned themselves daily with the task of imagining themselves as a different person, and novelists conjured up travels to imagined lands. But in the age of "telepresence" in "artificial life-worlds", technological apparatuses and sophisticated software allow every person with access to Virtual Reality equipment to slip into the minds of other people, borrow their personality and act out alternative lives. Or vice versa: the human mind could become part of a feedback system controlled by exterior forces. The resulting schizoid condition — an ambiguous state of being two persons at once, of having more than one body, or of being an external part of a cybernetic system which can "steer" our body — has bewildering consequences for traditional concepts of personality and identity.

One of the first artists to explore in a practical way the consequences of a body being accessed and acted upon by cybernetic means and caught in a maelstrom of post-isms was Stelarc (artist name of Stelios Arcadiou, a Greek Cypriot who lived in Japan and Australia for most of his life). He trained as a sculptor in Melbourne and was principally interested in the body as an architectural structure, as an object in various magnetic, electrical and gravitational states, or as a container of rhythms and flows of energy. He began his career as a performer in 1968 with multimedia works and moved to "body events" in 1970 and to sensory deprivation events in 1972. In 1976–1988 he made a name for himself with 25 spectacular body suspensions of varying lengths and in a diverse range of locations. These "Events for Stretched Skin" usually involved inserting 18 hooks into his skin and then being hoisted into a horizontal position. He was very reticent about going public with these events and performed them only to small audiences, who watched him hanging suspended between trees, over the sea, in a Japanese Temple, or in an art gallery. He also performed the "Sun Dance", a trance technique practised for centuries by Native Americans, which had been reawakened by the Modern Primitives community in the USA. But Stelarc was adamant that he did not wish to play the role of a shaman. He regarded his hyper-engagement with the body as a response to the evaporation of material substance in minimalism and conceptual art and as a reaction to the decreasing role of physicality in an age of information overload (Stelarc 1978: 54). As a sculptor-turned-performer, Stelarc concerned himself with issues that are entirely pertinent to his profession: space, movement, weight. What makes it unusual is that his explorations of the inner space and the outer boundaries of the body, of the skin as membrane separating body from surrounding space, were conducted with the aim of re-designing the human body. This technological, genetic, and cybernetic project to liberate the body from its physical confinement pushed him increasingly into domains that no other artists had probed in such a systematic and dedicated manner.

Already in the 1970s, Stelarc introduced hi-tech components into some of his performances and gave lectures on artificial intelligence, robotics and prosthetics. His explorations of the limits of the body went hand in hand with experiments of how the physical capacities of the body could be extended. In the 1980s, he gradually shifted his focus from the suspension events to an examination of new relationships between technology and the body. His last suspensions included amplifications of body functions through ECG and EMG and activities carried out with the "Third Hand", a remote-control hoist to direct the ascent and descent of "The Body" (i.e. himself).

In a number of interviews, Stelarc suggested that it was time to escape the tyranny of biology and evolutionary development. Contrary to the critics of Western techno-civilization, who conjure up visions of humanity's descent into electronic incarceration (the postmodern equivalent of Dante's hell), Stelarc did not believe that the human race was enslaved by technology and advocated an even more technologically enhanced existence: "It is time to transcend human history, to attain planetary escape velocity, and to achieve post-human status" (Stelarc, Marsh 1987: 111). Copernicus shifted man from the centre of the universe to the fringe; since then, humans have travelled to extraterrestrial spaces, and new technologies now allow us to eclipse the carbon chemistry of our physical existence. Therefore it has become a realistic possibility to remodel our biological functioning and extend our operational sphere beyond our own planet.

In Stelarc's anthropology, the human species has evolved from the animal kingdom because bipedalism has given us the ability to handle tools. Our production of instruments and artefacts is intimately linked to our speciation and must be considered a defining criterion of humanity. If technology is the root of our existence, then humanity's future depends on its creative interaction with technology. Stelarc believes that the planet Earth cannot guarantee the survival of the species, and that we may well need to find habitats outside the terrestrial sphere. However, the scope of our five senses is currently too narrow for functioning effectively in macro and micro worlds. Our biological constitution is ill-equipped for the infosphere of cyberspace, and our body is not flexible and durable enough for extraterrestrial existence. Only successful body-machine symbiosis can release us from our biological and ecological containment. Therefore, moving into cosmic and cybernetic worlds will amalgamate the visceral and the mechanical, carbon chemistry and silicon-chip technology.

As an artist, Stelarc was particularly interested in the human-machine interface and the hybridization of the body with new technologies. His aim was to fuse man and machine, to make the machine a component of the body and the body a component of the machine: "Machines, bits of technology, will inhabit the internal tracts and soft tissues of the body, and the human body will become the landscape of machines" (Electronic Voodoo: 112). He calls the human being, when augmented, extended and enhanced by technology, a "bionaut". In his most radical visions he literally translates Deleuze's "body without organs" into a hollowed-out body, where biological functions are performed by computer software and technological life-support systems. His redesigned body will have enhanced connectivity and will link up with intelligent machines "as a kind of external nervous system that motivates and manipulates and modulates the body, both in its muscular motions and its acoustical and optical inputs" (Telematic Tremors: 197). Thus supplemented by computer-directed sensors directly implanted into the skin, the body will multiply its operational range.

Stelarc's ultimate aim is to "redesign the body to function in this intense information realm of faster and more precise machines" (Electronic Voodoo: 111). Once the neurological network that coordinates the various input nodes of our senses can be connected to the global telecommunication network, and once brain-chips make our thoughts compatible with computer memory, then a two-way communication system can be set up: humans entering electronic space, and the telematic world accessing, interfacing and uploading its terrestrial hosts. An operational system of spatially distributed but electronically interfaced bodies will be able to interact with remote agents. The Internet will not only be a means of transmitting information, but become an instrument of transduction, of affecting physical action between bodies. Electronic space will function as a realm of action rather than information, allowing intimacy without proximity and intercourse with both humans and machines. Once bionautics and cybernautics have completed our evolutionary development, "the body falls behind like a rocket stage as *Homo sapiens* accelerates into 'pan-planetary' posthuman evolution" (Dery: 159).

Stelarc demonstrated some of these ideas in a series of *Involuntary Body* performances, making use of a six-channel muscle stimulation system and a computer interface. The first version, called *Fractal Flesh*, was presented at Telepolis 1995, where audiences in the Pompidou Centre, the Helsinki Media Lab and the Doors of Perception Conference in Amsterdam were given remote access through the Internet to the main performance site in Luxembourg, where Stelarc's body could be "acted upon" via touch-screen interface. The feedback-loops allowed one side of Stelarc's body to be guided by the audience whilst the other was steered by himself, thus effecting a split physiology controlled by local and remote agencies. Stelarc could watch part of his body move without having to contract any muscle.

Stimbod (1995) was a related experiment that allowed audiences to direct Stelarc's body either by touching the muscles on the computer model or by pasting together a series of gesture icons. Video screens at different locations allowed the artist to see the face of the person who, through a six-channel muscle stimulation system, sent electric currents of 0–60 volts to the muscle sites (deltoids, biceps, flexors, thigh and calf muscles) to choreograph his movements. *Ping Body* (1996) was an Internet-actuated and uploaded performance, in which Stelarc's body was telematically scaled-up and stimulated by reverberating signals to over 30 global Internet domains. The pings[1] were mapped to his deltoid, biceps, flexors, hamstring and calf muscles and were used to determine his movements. Instead of having his body prompted by the internal nervous system or by people in other locations (as in *Stimbod*), it was the external ebb and flow of cyberactivity itself that choreographed and composed the performance. A more sophisticated version was *ParaSite* (1997), where a customized search engine was constructed to scan the World Wide Web to select and display images through a video headset. Computer analyses of the graphics (JPEG) files provided data that were mapped to the muscles, so that Stelarc effectively performed the images he was seeing without having control over the movements they were inducing in him. His body, optically stimulated and electrically activated, became a "parasite" sustained by an external nervous system operating in a global electronic space of information and images.

Movatar (2000) inversed the principle of a motion capture system, which allows a human body, furnished with electro-magnetic sensors on the limbs and head, to animate a computer-generated virtual body in cyberspace. Here, however, the virtual body, or avatar, could access a physical body and actuate its performance in the real world. The next stage, currently a work in progress, is an avatar imbued with an artificial intelligence who would not only be able to act but also to express emotions by appropriating the facial muscles of its physical body. As a VRML[2] entity it could be accessed and acted upon from anywhere; or, seen from the perspective of the Movatar, the virtual body could perform with several physical bodies in spatially separated locations. The result would be a global choreography conducted by an external intelligence, or a dance dialogue combining prompted actions from the avatar and personal responses by the host bodies. The performing body would also be, at the same time, a "performed" body.

With Stelarc's work of the 1990s, it appears that the avant-garde has gone full circle and returned at the end of the twentieth century to its futurist beginnings. His experiments, together with those of other media artists at the outset of the twenty-first century, point towards certain similarities between the cultures that emerged from the Industrial Revolution and develop out of the Information Revolution. They suggest that postmodernism was only an intermittent phase in the long trajectory from modernity to hyper-modernity and that the avant-garde may still have some lifeblood left. Stelarc, as a latter-day futurist, has committed himself to a modernist advancement of a techno-society. Like Marinetti, he became the prophet of a machine god and propagated a Utopian belief that technology will allow humans to transcend themselves and reach happiness in a radically transformed existence. Both content and style of his statements bear close resemblance to futurist manifestos and writings.

Stelarc's aesthetics of prosthetics, his redesign of the human body, and his practical experiments with mechanical extensions of the body and electronic link-ups to the nervous system originated in a futurist dream: "A synthesis of organic and synthetic to create a new hybrid human, one that can evolve with Larmarkian speed" (Paffrath, Stelarc: 52). Lamarck's theories of evolution, which suggested the mutation of species through the formation and modification of organs according to need, together with Alexis Carrel's revolutionary methods of transplanting organs, which won him the Nobel Prize in 1912, also convinced the Italian futurists "that the triumphant progress of science makes profound changes in humanity inevitable" (Apollonio: 24). The manifesto *Man Extended and the Reign of the Machine* (1967: 255–8, 1978: 90–3) suggested ways of remodelling the human mind and physique and of turning the New Humanity of the Machine Age into rulers over time and space. The futurists not only envisaged people as friends, masters and allies of the machine, but also dreamt of fusing the two in a symbiotic relationship. Humanizing the machine and mechanizing humans meant more than giving the machine an anthropomorphic character, or emphasizing the mechanical features of the human anatomy. It anticipated a new world, in which "everything has become mechanical, and life itself is like a whirlwind in a paroxysm of speed. Here, humans turn into machines and the machine tends to become human" (Alessio 1926).

From the many futurists who pursued this aim, Fedele Azari stands out as having the closest resemblance to Stelarc's fixation on an ultimate fusion of man and machine. Azari saw the human being as a "reasoning machine" (*macchina ragionante*) that could be perfected for survival in a world where the natural fauna, flora and habitats have been replaced by man-made forms that overcome "the imperfection, weakness and inconstancy of the organic world" (1992: 96). His concept of artificial life forms or his vision of a mechanized world peopled by robots equipped with computer brains and fed on artificial nutrition, could have inspired statements by Stelarc such as "Off the Earth, the body's complexity, softness and wetness would be difficult to sustain. The strategy should be to HOLLOW, HARDEN and DEHYDRATE the body to make it more durable and less vulnerable" (Involuntary, Alien and Automated). Such concepts also resemble Stelarc's ideas of an eviscerated body filled with medical software and a body covered in a synthetic epidermis that is able to turn light into nutrients and to absorb oxygen through its pores, thereby making lungs superfluous.

In presentational terms, the stage design of some of Stelarc's performances could come straight out of a futurist production in the 1920s or 30s. For example, Prampolini's designs for Marinetti's *Vulcani* showed the interior of a laboratory filled with test tubes and distilling bottles, and liquids bubbling colourfully in alembics and retorts (*Prampolini* 1992: 254). Idelson's designs for Vasari's *Angoscia delle macchine* combined semi-abstract constructions and irregularly shaped screens with realistic machine parts and selected props from factories and laboratories. The dominant colour was metallic-grey, but glowing reds represented the fusion of metals in the furnaces, colourful liquids indicated chemical substances, and sparkling light conjured the flow of electricity in the machines (Berghaus 1998: 505). These scenic ideas appear to have been resurrected in Stelarc's performances, some of which take place in the midst of sculptural installations of glass tubes crawling with plasma discharges or flashing and flickering in response to signals sent by his body. A cagelike structure, perched on the artist's shoulders, emits argon-laser pulses synchronized to the throb of his heartbeat. These beams, through eyeblinks, facial twitches, and head movements, scribble curlicues in the air. "Video shadows" — images captured by video cameras positioned above and around him and projected on large screens — are frozen, superimposed, or juxtaposed in split-screen configurations.

V. The Neo-Avant-Garde in the Age of a Second Modernity

As I have shown in the previous sections of this essay, some of the basic questions and fundamental concerns of the historical avant-garde are still topics of valid exploration under the changed conditions of the twenty-first century. Modernism, far from being a closed chapter, still continues to evolve an aesthetics based on assumptions of evolution, change and innovation — ideas that have dominated Western history since the Age of Enlightenment. To quote Heinrich Klotz again: "Modernism was not a style that comes and goes like fashion, but a concept which over a course of time finds multifarious realizations and explications" (1996: 10). Modernism revealed itself to have a broad potential for expressing the experience of Modernity in a variety of ways. At the end of the twentieth century it seized upon the opportunities afforded by the electronic and digital media to reflect upon altered modes of communication, their aesthetic and social implications, and upon people's radically changed practices of interacting with the world around them. In this respect, the Second Modernity bears close resemblance to its predecessor in the earlier part of the century. The only marked difference relates to its socio-political impulse: whereas the historical avant-garde promoted both an aesthetic and social Utopia and sought to overcome the dichotomy of art and life, artists of the Second Modernity are much more sceptical of the revolutionary potential of artistic discourses and have largely shed the "grand narratives" of former decades.

What concerns us here is whether any of the trends discussed above — those at the "cutting edge" of exploring the frontiers of a digitally based civilization and those which reinstate the aura of presence, individuality and performativity in art — are to be classified as "avant-garde". There is no doubt in my mind that the old concepts of the avant-garde have lost their relevance to twenty-first century artists. The speed of information exchange in a media-dominated society has shortened the shelf life of avant-garde schools and has produced an endless cycle of -isms, which by the end of the twentieth century had exhausted their *raison d'être*. When nothing new can be produced any longer, and the grand narratives of progress and development have been thoroughly deconstructed, there is nothing left to be "ahead of", and the pressure to produce something fundamentally different from preceding movements does not impose itself any longer on the new generation. Artists of the twenty-first century cannot make the same claims to originality or heterology as their colleagues did a hundred years ago. An avant-garde that has become absorbed into the fabric of bourgeois culture cannot be recuperated to fulfil its old functions.

Yet, writing off the history of twentieth-century avant-garde creativity as old hat would repeat a mistake that could be condoned in the case of starry-eyed futurists and constructivists, but not in the case of post-avant-gardists. The futurist battlecry "Let's Destroy the Academies"[3] has not brought down any such institutions; rather, it has led to the exhibition of works inspired by these sentiments in the very same temples of the arts. Hence, the new avant-garde (or post-avant-garde, or whatever it may be called) must be the result of a critique of the old avant-garde; but such a dialectic opposition also recoups substantive components of its predecessor and transforms them into a new gestalt. One does not have to be an advocate of a Hegelian concept of progress to acknowledge that present experiences do not cancel out previous developments but rather sublate them in a new synthesis. A productive relationship between old and new artistic practices would include the use of historical paradigms in order to comment on present conditions in the culture industry. It would, as Foster suggests, "*re*connect with a lost practice in order to *dis*connect from a present way of working felt to be outmoded, misguided, or otherwise oppressive" (3). Such strategies of historical appropriation do not equate to a recycling of the historical avant-garde (something for which Bürger censures the neo-avant-garde) but rather acknowledge the fact that there is no way out of the process of cultural confluence, and that two streams, which may have opposite origins, will in the end always flow into the same wide ocean.

Artists have begun to adopt attitudes towards the masters of the historical and postmodern avant-garde that are different from those the futurists or dadaists had taken *vis à vis* their predecessors. The avant-garde, or what remained of it in the late-twentieth century, was no longer characterized by an attitude of opposition. Rather, artists used the appellation "avant-garde" as a marketing device to promote their works; they applied for grants from the very same institutions that their predecessors had regarded as nests of incorrigible conservatism; they established their career on the strength of their avant-garde style of creativity. A large number of them became professors at art schools or universities and taught their strategies and methods of creation to the new generation. Similarly, art centres and festivals have sprouted everywhere in the world with the avowed aim of fostering avant-garde expression in the arts. The avant-garde, in short, has become an economic force, and one of the many hues in the wide palette of cultural manifestations.

From these facts one might conclude that a central objective of the avant-garde has actually been fulfilled: rather than having simply been absorbed by the mainstream, it has widened the spectrum of Western culture and has compelled the conservative majority to give recognition to innovative and untested forms of expression. Whereas a hundred years ago Europe boasted barely two handfuls of art theatres, nowadays every capital possesses dozens of them. There are probably more performers employed today in fringe theatres and experimental companies than in national, state and municipal theatres taken together, and a considerable portion of productions presented in these mainstream houses aims to be innovative rather than derivative.

These fundamental changes in the cultural landscape of most Western countries make an anachronism of the anarchical attacks on "the establishment" as promoted by the former avant-garde. This is not meant to justify blind acceptance of mainstream production methods, but rather to acknowledge that the stream has become very wide indeed and no longer consists solely of a commercialized culture industry. Does this intimate that there is no longer any need for an avant-garde? Some artists (and critics) would certainly agree; others, however, insist that as long as there are hegemonic elites and dominant ideologies, artists must continue to produce work that falls outside established structures and systems. The impulse not to be restricted by established canons and conventional discourses makes them venture into unexplored territory (although they may no longer be virgin soils, as they were in the nineteenth and twentieth centuries). This impulse propels them to work in those areas that are not occupied by the mainstream and have not been traversed by the historical avant-garde. What has changed, however, is the vision of

artists marching heroically under the banner of progress (exemplified by their ever more innovative techniques) into a brighter future,
and the belief that they can overthrow the status quo in artistic matters and achieve autonomy from the institution of art.

I would therefore disagree with Paul Mann's assessment:
"Without exception art that calls itself art, that is registered as art,
that circulates within art contexts can never again pose as anything
but systems-maintenance" (143). It does not seem to me that art has
reached a ground-zero point beyond which there is only no-art, or a
withdrawal from art. Poised between "daydreams of escape" and
"unprecedented silence" (Mann: 144), artists will escape discursive
suicide by exploring a third path. Dietrich Scheunemann, Hal Foster,
Peter Weigel, Heinrich Klotz and others have questioned the man-
tra-like proclamations of the death of the avant-garde and reopened
the chapter that Bürger so forcefully closed in 1974. Hal Foster, in
looking at developments post-1974, suggested that "the neo-avant-
garde has produced new aesthetic experiences, cognitive
connections, and political interventions, and these openings may
make up *another* criterion by which art can claim to be advanced
today" (14). Ben Highmore has taken on one of these criteria, which
Bürger thought he had dismissed once and for all: the sublation of
art into life. Drawing on Lefebvre's theory of modern everyday life,
he has shown that Bürger's "life" is not at all as homogenous and
monolithic as suggested. By restricting himself to a discussion of an
avant-garde economy within the institution of "art", Bürger failed to
recognize the potential of avant-garde intervention in the conflict
between the repressive and liberating aspects of everyday life. It is
common for individuals to be torn between the colonization of life
by capitalist forces and the tenacity of a festive, refreshing and in-
vigorating enjoyment of life. Similarly, artists develop a precarious
and ambiguous relationship with everyday life and find space for
creative operations in the interstices between alienation and jubila-
tion. Highmore concludes: "What Bürger misses, and what makes
his thesis less than adequate for an account of avant-gardism, is the
sense of ambivalence with which the avant-garde figured modern
everyday life" (2004: 249).

Scheunemann adds a further criticism and amplifies views promoted by the theorists of the ZKM in Karlsruhe. Whereas Bürger's
account ends with the neo-expressionists and neo-dadaists,

Scheunemann suggests a revised concept of the avant-garde based on the impact of technological innovations and the challenges of new media (cf. Scheunemann 2000). It is the avant-garde's mission to bridge the gap not only between art and life but also between art and technology. A history of the avant-garde focussed on the inter-action between art, literature, theatre and music on the one hand, and photography, cinema, telephone, television, video, computer on the other, will arrive at a periodization which is different from that of Bürger in 1974. This revised history will place centre-stage such techniques as montage and collage, which Bürger only discusses at arm's length, and will incorporate deconstructive methods, which Bürger does not mention at all.

What kind of artistic scenarios will eventually materialize from an enlightened modernity is impossible to predict. It may be a trans-formed avant-garde, or a practice to which the term avant-garde has lost all significance. It certainly will be the result of a critical exami-nation of the structural and discursive parameters of twentieth-century art production and reception, and not just a simple continuation of old trajectories.

Looking back at the twentieth century and looking ahead to the twenty-first, I'd suggest that an art which has, as yet, no prefix — and I prefer to avoid the term avant-garde here — will be both a cri-tique of the historical avant-garde and its safeguard, albeit under changed conditions. It will incorporate in a dialectic manner some substantive components of its predecessors and will merge them with forces that belong to the new age. Many of these, I have no doubt, will not stem from Western traditions, but will arise instead from developing countries. In a globalized world, new energies will emerge from those regions that currently play only a minor role in economic and artistic markets. The advances in the economic, social and political systems of such countries bear a structural resemblance to those previously observed in the West. Therefore, artists in these new centres will find opportunities to learn from the Western expe-rience and to avoid some of the worst mistakes made by their colleagues in the preceding century.

NOTES

[1] A 'ping' is a test signal used to assess the density of Internet activity by measuring the echo times of the signal on a scale from zero to 2000 milliseconds.

[2] Virtual Reality Modelling Language is a set of Internet protocols for converting virtual reality images into desktop 2D graphics.

[3] This was the title of a manifesto by Enrico Prampolini (*Bombardiamo le accademie*, 1913), in which he described his opposition to these strongholds of traditionalism, entrenched conservatism and enemies of true art.

BIBLIOGRAPHY

Mantura, Bruno, ed.
1989   *Aereo e pittura: Mostra dell'aria e della sua conquista.* Exhibition catalogue. Naples: Castel Sant'Elmo.

Alessio, Luigi
1926   *Aeroplani.* In: "Pagina d'arte futurista" of *La fiamma.* (Turin), no. 11, 4 April.

Apollonio, Umbro, ed.
1973   *Futurist Manifestos.* London: Thames and Hudson.

Ascott, Roy
1991   "The Art of Intelligent Systems". In: Hannes Leopoldseder (ed.), *Der Prix ars electronica: Internationales Kompendium der Computerkünste.* Linz: Veritas, 1991, 25–34.

Azari, Fedele
1992   "Per una società di protezione delle macchine". In: Lucia Collarile (ed.), *Fedele Azari: Vita simultanea futurista.* Exhibition catalogue. Trento: Museo aeronautico G. Caproni, 95–99.

Balla, Giacomo and Fortunato Depero
1958   "Ricostruzione futurista dell'universo". In: Maria Drudi Gambillo and Teresa Fiori (eds.), *Archivi del futurismo,* vol. 1, Rome: De Luca, 48–51.

Belloli, Carlo
1976 "Giannina Censi negli anni Trenta danzava la poesia futurista". In: *La Martinella di Milano*: *Rassegna di vita italiana*, vol. 30, no. 1–2, 3–18.

Berghaus, Günter
1990 "Danza futurista: Giannina Censi and the Futurist Thirties". In: *Dance Theatre Journal,* vol. 8, no. 1, 4–7, 34–37.

1993 "Dance and the Futurist Woman: The Work of Valentine de Saint-Point, 1875–1953." In: *Dance Research,* vol. 11, no. 2, 27–42.

1996 *Futurism and Politics: Between Anarchist Rebellion and Fascist Reaction, 1909–1944.* Oxford: Berghahn.

1998 *Italian Futurist Theatre.* Oxford: Clarendon Press.

Boccioni, Umberto
1973 "Futurist Painting and Sculpture (extracts) 1914". In: Apollonio, *Futurist Manifestos*, 172–181.

Corra, Bruno
1924 "L'affare della Baracca". In: *L'Impero*. 3 January 1924. Reprinted in: Francesco Bonanni, "Sul teatro di Bruno Corra". *Teatro contemporaneo*, vol. 3, no. 5, 189–200.

Crispolti, Enrico, and Rosella Siligato, eds.
1992 *Prampolini: Dal futurismo all' informale.* Exhibition catalogue. Rome: Palazzo delle Esposizioni.

Depero, Fortunato
1927 "Il complesso plastico motorumorista". In: *Depero Futurista.* Milan: Dinamo.

1969 "Appunti sul teatro". In: *Fortunato Depero: Opere 1911–1930.* Exhibition catalogue. Turin: Galleria d'Arte Martano, 58–61; translated in extracts in Michael Kirby, *Futurist Performance.* New York: Dutton, 207–210.

Dery, Mark
1996 *Escape Velocity: Cyberculture at the End of the Century.* London: Hodder and Stoughton.

Gori, Gino
1925 "La scenotecnica ne 'L'Angoscia delle Macchine'". In: *L'impero*, 3 April 1925.

Foster, Hal
1996   *The Return of the Real*. Cambridge, Mass.: MIT Press.

Harding, James, ed.
2000   *The Contours of the Theatrical Avant-garde: Perform-ance and Textuality,* Ann Arbor, Mi: University of Michigan Press.

Highmore, Ben
2000   "Avant-Gardism and the Dialects of Everyday Life". In: Dietrich Scheunemann (ed.), *European Avant-Garde: New Perspectives*. Amsterdam: Rodopi, 249–264.

Höch, Hannah
1989   "Erinnerungen an DADA: Ein Vortrag 1966". In: *Hannah Höch 1889–1978: Ihr Werk, Ihr Leben, Ihre Freunde*. Exhibition catalogue. Berlin: Berlinische Gallerie, 206–207.

Klotz, Heinrich
1994   *Kunst im 20 Jahrhundert: Moderne, Postmoderne, Zweite Moderne*. Munich: Beck.

1995   Lecture on "Medienkunst als Zweite Moderne". In: *Klotz, Eine neue Hochschule (für neue Künste)*. Stuttgart: Cantz, 43–57.

1996   *Die Zweite Moderne: Eine Diagnose der Kunst der Gegenwart*. Munich: Beck.

1997   *Contemporay Art*. Munich: Prestel.

Lischka, Gerhard Johann
1986   "Media Art". In: Gottfried Hattinger, Irene Judmayer, and Regina Patsch (eds.), *Ars Electronica: Festival für Kunst, Technologie Gesellschaft, Linz, 20. bis 27. Juni 1986*. Linz: Linzer Veranstaltungsgesellschaft, 16–17.

Mann, Paul
1991   *The Theory-Death of the Avant-Garde*. Bloomington, Ind: Indiana University Press

Marinetti, Filippo Tommaso
1968   "Lo splendore geometrico e meccanico e la sensibilità numerica". In: Luciano de Maria (ed.), *F. T. Marinetti: Teoria e invenzione futurista*. Milano: Mondadori, 84–92

1968   "L'uomo moltiplicato e il regno della macchina". In:
            Luciano de Maria (ed.), *F. T. Marinetti: Teoria e invenzi-*
            one futurista. Milano: Mondadori, 255–258.

1972   "Geometric and Mechanical Splendour and the Numeri-
            cal Sensibility". In: R. W. Flint (ed.), *F. T. Marinetti:*
            Selected Writings. London: Secker and Warburg, 97–103.

1972   "Multiplied Man and the Reign of the Machine". In: R.
            W. Flint (ed.), *F. T. Marinetti: Selected Writings.*
            London: Secker and Warburg, 90–93.

Paladini, Vinicio, and Ivo Pannaggi
1922   "Manifesto dell'arte meccanica futurista". In: *La nuova*
            Lacerba of 20 June 1922, reprinted in Anna Caterina
            Toni, *L'attività artistica di Ivo Pannaggi nel periodo gio-*
            vanile. 1921–1926. Pollenza: La Nuova Foglio, 1976,
            150.

Saltz, David
1997   "The Art of Interaction: Interactivity, Performativity, and
            Computers". *Journal of Aesthetics and Art Criticism,* vol.
            56, no. 2, 117–127.

Scheunemann, Dietrich
2000   "On Painting and Photography. Prolegomena to a New
            Theory of the Avant–Garde". In: Dietrich Scheunemann
            (ed.), *European Avant-Garde: New Perspectives.*
            Amsterdam: Rodopi, 15–48

Shaw, Jeffrey
1989   "Modalitäten einer interaktiven Kunstausübung".
            Kunstforum International, no. 103 (September – Octo-
            ber), 204–209.

Stelarc
1978   "Statement", dated 4 December 1977. *Flash Art,* no. 80–
            81 (February-April), 54.

1984   "Triggering an Evolutionary Dialectic". James D.
            Paffrath and Stelarc (eds.), *Obsolete Body / Suspensions /*
            Stelarc. Davis, Cal: JP Publications, 52.

1987   "Post-Evolutionary Desires: Attaining Planetary Escape
            Velocity". Unpublished paper, Yokohama, quoted in
            Anne Marsh, *Body and Self: Performance Art in*

Australia 1969–92. Melbourne: Oxford University Press Australia, 1993, 111.

1995 "Electronic Voodoo: Interview with Nicholas Zurbrugg". *21.C* (Melbourne), no. 2, 44–49.

1998 "Telematic Tremors, Telematic Pleasures: Stelarc's Internet Performances. Stelarc in Conversation with Nicholas Zurbrugg". Anna Novakov (ed.), *Carnal Pleasures: Desire, Public Space, and Contemporary Art.* San Francisco, Cal: Clamor Editions, 167–203.

n.d. "The Involuntary, the Alien & the Automated: Choreographing Bodies, Robots & Phantoms", published at http://www.stelarc.va.com.au

Tzara, Tristan
1975 "Chronique Zurichoise". In: *Œuvres complètes*, ed. by Henri Béhar, vol. 1, Paris: Flammarion, 561–568.

1975 "Le Surréalisme et l'après-guerre". In: *Œuvres complètes*, vol. 5, Paris: Flammarion, 59–108.

Vittori, Maria Vittoria
1990 Il clown futurista: Storie di circo, avanguardia e café-chantant. Rome: Bulzoni, 108–112.

Actor or Puppet: The Body in the Theatres of the Avant-Garde

OLGA TAXIDOU

In 1921 Oscar Schlemmer, the Bauhaus artist, wrote about the function of the human form in the theatre in an essay entitled "Man and Art Figure":

> The history of the theatre is the history of the transformation of the human form. It is the history of man as the actor of physical and spiritual events, ranging from naivete to reflection, from naturalness to artifice. (Schlemmer 1961: 17)

Indeed, writing in the 1920s Schlemmer is already referring to a well-established tradition of experimentation within the European theatres of the avant-garde. This project involves radically reconfiguring the art of acting. Is the human form the appropriate material for art, can it ever free itself from verisimilitude and psychological expressivism, can abstraction be ever fully rendered through the use of the human form? These and many more were some of the questions being tackled within a historical context that also saw the appearance of the figure of the director. The avant-garde helped to create, probably for the first time in history of the theatre, specific schools of acting, that almost always, however, were also creating the role of the director. One cannot really be read without the other. This debate about the best way to present the human form in the

theatre might be schematically drawn as the famous "man or marionette" debate.

And, of course, it is not a particularly modernist debate; it is at
least as old as Plato, and is often read as a reconfiguration of his attack on the theatre. The stage is held to create a double fantasy, a
world twice removed from the ideal by the operation of mimesis,
and the process of acting itself is seen as corrupting both the actor
and the audience (through empathy). Mimesis, particularly when it
involves enactment and the human body is seen as arousing the most
basic of human emotions, i.e. pity and fear. In turn this emphasis
that theatre places on enactment and physicality is viewed with suspicion, as it distracts from reason and philosophical thinking. In
other words the physicality of acting, its reliance on the human body
ushers in a type of "bad" philosophy: a philosophy that celebrates
emotion, physicality and in short elides the body-mind divide. Far
from expressing the pure reason of philosophy, mimesis as expressed through the agency of the human body relocates that
"reason" within the physical, the civic and the political, as theatre
also relies on an audience. Interestingly enough, the only type of
actors that Plato approved of were indeed puppets, the neurospasta,
which were probably used in the Eleusinian mysteries. Within modernism this debate acquires a new urgency as it is inflected by the
heated political discourses of the time, the discussions surrounding
the impact of technology and the desire to differentiate "performance" from the literary dimension of theatre. For the purposes of this
paper I would like to concentrate on two significant moments in this
debate about the representational efficacy of the human form: the
work of Edward Gordon Craig, probably the only instance of an
English theatre theorist of the avant-garde, and on the work of the
Russian/Soviet theatre visionary, Vsevolod Meyerhold.[1] The choice
might seem somewhat arbitrary, but I believe there are parallels in
these projects.

The work of Edward Gordon Craig occupies an ambivalent position within both British modernism and the European avant-garde.
The son of Helen Terry and the architect E.W. Godwin, Craig first
worked in the theatre as an actor with Henry Irving's company at the
Lyceum. By 1909, having directed several operas, he was ready to
abandon England and indeed one of its great theatrical families and
settle in Italy for the rest of his life,[2] turning himself into an exile

and consciously placing his work within the European avant-garde. He also distances himself from both the Victorian actor-manager tradition in the theatre and the modernist experiments in poetic drama conducted by Eliot, Yeats and later Auden and Isherwood.[3] Importantly he was not a playwright; he was more interested in creating a new language for the theatre than making plays. His work can be read alongside European figures like Reinhardt, Stanislavsky, Meyerhold and Artaud. Unlike any other theatrical project in the Anglophone world at the time, Craig's work embraced all the concerns of the theatrical avant-garde: exploring the relations of theatre, religion and politics; connecting with traditions of oral and popular performance and establishing relationships with the "theatres of the orient", as they were called at the time.

The Russian constructivists, and particularly Meyerhold, provide a fascinating parallel to Craigian experiment. Meyerhold's theoretical background was Russian formalism, which he combined with Marxism and Taylorism[4] to produce a highly original notion of theatre in general, and acting in particular, which designated both as forms of labour. This view might seem to be in conflict with Craig's concept of theatre as ritual and magic, a force that could transcend modernity (whereas Meyerhold celebrates it). However, Meyerhold was heavily influenced by Craig whose "First Monologue on the Art of the Theatre" had been pirated and published in Russia in 1906. Meyerhold wrote in 1909 that

> It is remarkable that in the very first year of this new century E.G. Craig flung a challenge to the naturalistic theatre. [...] This young Englishman is the first to set up the initial guideposts on the new road of the Theatre. (Senelick 1981: 114)

Craig was aware of Meyerhold's work but the two men did not meet until 1935, just before Meyerhold's disappearance and subsequent murder by the Stalinist regime. Both men were on a quest for "totality in the theatre", something that would recreate the "communal sacred". Meyerhold's utopian aspirations although embraced in the first years of the Soviet Revolution his affiliation with Trotsky made him undesirable to the Stalinist regime and he and his wife Zinaida Raikh were killed. Craig never suffered for his political affiliations although he did flirt with fascism (Taxidou 1998). The parallels drawn here between Meyerhold's romantic and utopian Marxism and Craig's albeit inarticulate fascism are in no way meant to be read as seeing these two projects as inextricably linked with ideas of totalization. Walter Benjamin's famous aestheticization thesis has been recently inverted and read critically (Benjamin 1973).[5] Instead of the aestheticization of politics leading to fascism, the politicization of aesthetics is viewed as flirting with fascism. In turn this inversion implies that formal experimentation, and the politicizing of form necessarily and inevitably lead to totalization. I in no way want to re-iterate the cold war notion — one that schematically equates Marxism with fascism — that the experiments of the avant-garde lead directly to the gulag, or the concentration camps. Instead, and in many ways continuing the legacy of the avant-garde itself the issue of autonomy or engagement is seen in the context of the ability or not of art to voice some form of critique.

The man or marionette debate is crucial in the above context as well (of politicizing form) as it is the version of the human form abstract or otherwise, that will render its representation humanist or not. From the turn of the century onwards there is a fascination with puppets as the alternative, in some cases, not only to acting, but as presenting the quintessential work of art. This is a legacy inherited not only from the aestheticist 1890s but also from such romanticist writers as Kleist, whose essay, "Über das Marionettentheater" (1810), saw its first English translation in Craig's journal *The Marionette* (1918). The importance of Kleist cannot be overestimated. The main question addressed is whether acting itself can be considered an art form. Craig writes in his equally famous essay "The Actor and the Über-marionette", which Kleist echoes even in its title, that:

> Acting is not an art. It is therefore incorrect to speak of the actor as an artist. For accident is an enemy of the artistic. Art is the exact antithesis of Pandimonium [sic], and Pandimonium is created by the tumbling together of many accidents; Art arrives only by design. Therefore in order to make any work of art it is clear we may work in those materials with which we can calculate. Man is not one of these materials. (*The Mask* 1908: 3)

And of course the puppet is. It can be molded, abstracted and schematized. As such, the response it will illicit from its audience will not necessarily be one of empathy and identification; it might be awe and wonder harping back to the puppets religious roots or it might be one of distance and estrangement. Both these responses of wonder (bringing back the naïve) and of distance, introducing the critical are what make the puppet an attractive model for acting. In Craig's case the actor would be substituted by the puppet. In the case of Meyerhold, the actor would copy the puppet. In both cases we witness an awe at the "cult of the puppet", which is specifically a concern about performance but also partakes in the general fascination of the time. The puppet comes to represent the emblem of an anti-humanist modernism that is concerned with abstraction and questions notions of agency and authorship in art. Oscar Wilde writes in his letters after a visit to the Petit Theatres des Marionettes run by Maurice Bouchor at the Galerie Vivienne in Paris:

> There are many advantages in puppets. They never argue. They have no crude views about art. They have no private lives. We are never bothered by accounts of their virtues, or bored by recitals of their vices; and when they are out of an engagement they never do good in public or save people from drowning; nor do they speak more than is set down for them. [...] They are admirably docile, and have no personalities at all. (Wilde 1962: 311)[6]

For both men, the idea of the puppet offered a way of resolving the particular difficulties that theatre sets in the way of the dramatist or director committed to the exploration and representation of abstract form. The physicality and "naturalness" of the human form make it resistant to abstraction and stylization. By contrast, the puppet allows the objective representation of abstract form on stage without tainting it with the subjectivity of psychological expressivism. For Meyerhold, supremely, the puppet provided a model for a mode of training. Mechanical, reproducible, functional, it could help transform the theatre from high art into a mode of production that resembled other forms of labour, ensuring, in Meyerhold's words, that "the work of the actor in an industrial society will be regarded as a means of production vital to the proper organization of the labour of every citizen of that society" (Braun 1969: 120).

The various traditions in puppetry, east and west, provided him with a basis from which to create his elaborate system of training, biomechanics. This was an attempt to mechanize the human form, to make it trainable, and hence turn it into an appropriate material for

Biomechanics in Action: Daesh Europa Production (1924)

constructivist form of theatre — one that, as in a constructivist painting, could deal with the materiality of people and things. At the same time, as the term suggests it was a homage to the popular, "organic" traditions of puppetry that Meyerhold was also heavily influenced by. The slightly uncritical adoration of technology implied by the use of mechanics is balanced against the return to the popular and carnivalesque traditions of puppetry, as the use of the prefix bio indicates.[7] Rather than ban the human form from the stage, Meyerhold sought to break it down, dissociate it from its conventional psychological and biological contexts, and turn it into raw material. This new kind of acting found its model, not its replacement, in the puppet. Meyerhold's experiments completed a full circle which, in the end, returned to the human form:

> The director came to his senses when he realized that there is a
> limit beyond which there is no alternative but to replace the pup-

pet with a man. But how could he part with the puppet, which had created a world of enchantment with its incomparable movements, its expressive gestures achieved by some magic known to it alone, its angularity which reaches the heights of true plasticity? (Braun 1969: 128)

The objective of a theatre pedagogy for Meyerhold was to re-produce in the human form the magic, the angularity and the plasticity of the puppet. He believed that "above all drama is the art of the actor". Craig on the other hand was more interested in con-solidating the role of the director. His views on acting are those of Plato: actors distort reality rather enhance or comment on it, and acting itself is a decadent and corrupting activity. As late as 1928, he prefaced an article entitled "Flesh, Blood and Marionettes" with a "Nineteenth Century Note" by Joseph Conrad:

> The actors appear to me like a lot of wrong-headed lunatics pre-tending to be sane. Their malice is stitched with threads. They are disguised and ugly. To look at them breeds in my melancholy soul thoughts of murder and suicide — such is my anger and my loathing of their transparent pretences. There is a taint of subtle corruption in their blank voices, in their blinking eyes, in their grimacing faces, in their light false passion, in the words that have been learned by heart. But I love a marionette-show. Mario-nettes are beautiful — especially those of the old kind with wires thick as my little finger, coming out of the top of the head. Their impassibility in love, in crime, in mirth, in sorrow — is heroic, superhuman, fascinating. Their rigid violence when they fall upon one another to embrace or to fight is simply a joy to behold. I never listen to the text mouthed somewhere out of sight by in-visible men who are here today and rotten tomorrow. I love the marionettes that are without life, and that come so near to being immortal! (*The Mask* 1928: 76)

While the futurist were writing and performing robot plays, Meyerhold experimenting with his biomechanics, and the Bauhaus mounting the Triadic Ballet, Craig turned his back on modernity and nostalgically revived a late-romantic vision of the function of the puppet. Kleist's essay of 1810, referred to earlier, was his main source of inspiration. Deploying, in the form of a polemic dialogue with a fictitious antagonist, an argument that Craig would later reiterate, Kleist had written that

> however clear his paradox might be he would never persuade me that there could be more grace in a mechanical doll than in the structure of the human body. He replied that a human being was simply incapable of rivaling the marionette in this respect. Only a God could ,measure himself against matter; and this was the point, he said, where both ends of the world's circle fit into each other. (Craig 1918)

The limitations of the human form are imposed by its materiality; the need then, is to de-materialise the body of the actor. For Kleist, this was the task of a God; for Craig, it was the work of the director.

Meyerhold, worlds away from both, rather than de-materialise the body of the actor, sought to re-materialise it with a theory of training that could be reproduced and developed. But for Craig, like Kleist, the marionette presented an ideal, which was not meant to be realised, let alone reproduced. Though he owned the best collection of puppets in Europe (Wyang, Bunraku, shadow puppets, Silcilian etc) and filled his journals with designs, reproductions and scholarly articles on puppets, he never tried to make the Ubermarionette that would displace the actor. Despite his theoretical preference for "men of the theatre" (as he called the new role of the director), and his radical influence on men such as Meyerhold, Craig never himself perceived the threads that connected his work to the larger context of European experiment; a tradition which would also have provided him with practical and theoretical solutions to some of the contradictions and dead-ends that his work led to.

Another source of inspiration in the attempts to puppetize the human form was the whole encounter with the "theatres of the orient". This east-west exchange has today to be reviewed within a theoretical context that takes on board notions of otherness and orientalism. In a familiar gesture that looks towards the east for inspiration when a European tradition is seen to be worn out and decadent, both Meyerhold and Craig saw in the theatres of China and Japan models of acting that would help them in their experiments.

I would like to investigate these encounters through the actual tours of two performers; one is Madame Sada Yakko from Japan and the other is Mei-Lan Fang from China.

> Madame Sada Yakko was the first lady to go upon the stage in Japan. The innovation was a pity. She then went to Europe to study the modern theatres there, and more especially the Opera House in Paris, intending to introduce such a theatre into Japan, [...] it is to be presumed with the idea of advancing the art of the Japanese theatre. There can be no hesitation in saying that she is doing both the country and its theatre a grievous wrong. Art can never find a new way of creating better than the primitive way which the nation learned as children from nature. (Craig 1910: 120)

Madame Sada Yakko was in fact not an actor but a geisha who was pretending to be an actor when her husband Kawakami realised how popular this was with "western" audiences. Sada Yakko was Europe's first encounter with Japanese acting in 1900, at the International Exposition in Paris. On her arrival in England she performed before Queen Victoria, and Ellen Terry was reported to have declared that the whole experience had been "a great lesson in dramatic art" (Pronko 1967: 120). Even Henry Irving, Craig's artistic godfather, was reported as saying, "I never had an idea of such acting" (Pronko 1967: 120).

The truth, of course, is that Sada Yakko had never performed in Japan. She only started acting with her husband Kawakami once they had left Japan. She had been trained as a geisha, which meant she had mastered traditional Japanese arts like dance and song. The company had initially left Japan in order to study western drama and acting techniques. There were only traces of Kabuki left. Instead they presented highly Romantic and slightly stylized melodramas. Yet she was hailed by the critics of the period as the Japanese Sarah Bernhardt. In a series of very interesting misunderstandings Madame Sada Yakko continued to tour the leading European capitals, presenting what was perceived as "oriental acting". Craig, of course, who thought that women acting was an act of blasphemy thought that she was going against her tradition. Ironically, she was, as she came from a theatrical tradition, of Noh and Kabuki, which had no female actors, but a complex and detailed legacy of female impersonators.

This brings us to the second orientalist encounter that of Mei Lan-Fang, who was also a famous female impersonator. Craig seems aware of Mei Lan-Fang even before he undertook his famous tour of the west. He writes in his journal, *The Mask*, in 1927:

> A writer living in Pekin reports to an American periodical that there is a remarkable Chinese actor called Mei Lan-Fang who performs, as did the Elizabethan, the principal female roles. He writes of this young actor that he deserves all his fame, and proceeds to tell us something (by now quite familiar to us); i.e. that the conventions of the Chinese Theatre are much like the Elizabethan — scenes, make-believe and all. (*The Mask* 1927: 73)

A few years later Mei Lan-Fang was invited to Moscow at one of the famous writers' conferences organized by Stalin, in many ways the start of the cold war. There he and his troupe performed for an audience of intellectuals and artists from all over the world. Those present were stunned. And amongst those present were Meyerhold, Brecht, Tretiakov and Eisenstein, all crucial in formulating theories of acting.

During this same visit (in 1935) Brecht, along with Meyerhold, Tretiakov, Eisenstein, and others, saw performances of the Chinese actor Mei Lan-Fang and his troupe. In his role (the woman warrior) Mei accomplished a sort of double alienation by impersonating a woman who impersonating a man. It may be that this performance, together with Tretiakov's interest in and experience of Chinese culture (as reflected in *Roar China!* and his 1930 novel *Den Shi-hua*), provided Brecht with certain ideas which bore fruit in The Good Person of Sezuan for which Brecht created a female-male central character.

Meyerhold was also taken by the performance of the Chinese actors, so much so that he dedicated to Mei his production, Griboedov's Woe to Wit, in which he incorporated "features from the theatrical folklore of the Chinese troupe". At a public discussion about the troupe's performance Meyerhold spoke on various aspects of Mei's art, in particular the use of gesture and rythmical movement (Eaton 1985: 22–3).

And so did Brecht in his important essay "The Alienation Effect in Chinese Acting" (Brecht 1964: 91–99). However, I think, that this whole encounter needs to be further scrutinized. Like Ito who inspired Yeats's Dance dramas, these performers were urged to stay "oriental", while in many cases they had gone to the west to study naturalist acting techniques. Mei Lan-Fang for instance was more interested in the naturalism of Stanislavsky than any of the experiments Meyerhold was undertaking at his studio. Indeed in China at the time the tradition of stylization that Mei Lan-Fang and his company utilized was considered old fashioned and dusty, in some cases even decadent; after all this was the eve of the Chinese revolution (another context within which this encounter needs to be read). Naturalism and psychological expressivism was the emblem of Modernity and not stylization and abstraction. Also this tradition in acting that inspired many avant-garde techniques in actor training was one where there were no female actors. It, was, however one where there was a detailed and long history of female impersonators. What intrigued Meyerhold and Brecht was primarily this aspect of their acting technique; the fact that through stylized gesture Mei Lan-Fang was able to create a female role. It is fascinating to note that Meyerhold's "dialectical actor", who can both be a role and comment on it, who impersonates rather than becomes the character might have a historical precedent in a tradition that has no female performers. Also Brecht's famous *Verfremdungseffekt* (which owes much to Meyerhold and the formalist notion of estrangement) finds inspiration in the same tradition. This is probably the most sustained and articulate anti-naturalist tradition we have in the twentieth century for actor training and it is one that in its conception might be implicated in ideas of orientalism, on the one hand, and might deploy a classic avant-garde gender blindness on the other.

The encounters with Mei Lan-Fang and Sada Yakko in many ways typify two classic problematic areas within the European theatrical projects of the avant-garde; an uncritical orientalism and an unwillingness to engage with issues relating to gender and representation. All this talk about bodies or puppets treats the body as a, more or less, empty space; a blank canvas for the actor and / or director to work with. And this neutral body, usually mechanized, was also usually based on the male body. In turn this has created a legacy of actor training that, in many respects continues and duplicates the same problems. Although the relationship between gender and representation in performance has been more recently addressed in feminist and queer performance, in many cases this has involved radically re-writing the Brechtian/Meyerholdian model while also paying homage to it (Tony Kushner or Heiner Müller are characteristic examples of this trend).

The man or marionette debate has generated a body of work that in crucial is rethinking the role of the human body in theatrical representation. From the Romanticism of Kleist to the utopian Marxism of Meyerhold it has also created a legacy for training actors; one that we still inhabit today. It is, however, a tradition that we need to revisit critically. It has created some of the most exciting and radical performances in the early twentieth century and provides examples and techniques that are constantly renewed today, for instance in the whole issue of multicultural or intercultural performance. If we believe we are continuing the debates about form and content; about the politicization of form; about the relationships between politics and aesthetics that were initiated in the fervor of the avant-garde, then we need to be both critical and appreciative of this legacy.

Heiner Müller, who continues Brecht's legacy, said that in order to be faithful to Brecht we need to betray him (Müller 1990: 124–33). I would suggest the same attitude of critical faithfulness and skeptical betrayal towards the renditions of the human body and the theories of acting they embody in theaters of the historical avant-garde.

NOTES

[1] Vsevolod Meyerhold (1974–1940) was one of the visionary theatre makers of the Russian/Soviet avant-garde. He trained with Eisenstein and started his career with the naturalist director Stanislavsky. In 1921, he set up his own studio, the Moscow State Higher Theatre Workshop, where he sought to create a revolutionary theatre incorporating the latest technological developments. In 1937 he was criticized by *Pravda*, and a year later the Meyerhold Theatre was closed down. In 1939 he and his wife were arrested and later murdered. For many years information about his life and work was suppressed. Now there is a Meyerhold Museum in Moscow.

[2] Before leaving for Germany and later Italy he had directed operas and masques: *Dido and Aeneas* (1900); *The Mask of Love* (1901); *Acis and*

Galatea (1902); Laurence Housman's nativity play *Bethlehem* (1902), and Ibsen's *The Vikings* (1903).

[3] There is a considerable body of work in Anglophone modernism which can be termed as "poetic drama". See David Edward Jones, ed. *The Plays of T.S. Eliot*, (London: Routledge and Kegan Paul, 1960). On Yeats see Richard Cave, ed., *Selected Plays by W.B.Yeats*, (London: Penguin, 1997); for the influence of Noh on Yeats see Richard Taylor, *The Drama of W.B.Yeats. Irish Myth and Japanese Noh,* (New Haven and London: Yale University Press, 1976).For Auden and Isherwood see Edward Mendelson, ed., *Plays and Other Dramatic Writings by W.H. Auden and Christopher Isherwood,* (London: Faber and Faber, 1989).

[4] Meyerhold's view of technology was similar to that of Walter Benjamin. It is read as almost inherently critical and emancipatory. There is in his work a fascination with Taylorism, which ironically gave rise to the "assembly line" in the USA. See Frederick Winslow Taylor (1856–1915), *The Principles of Scientific Management*, (New York and London: Harper and Brothers, c1911).

[5] For a critical account see Boris Groys, *The Total Art of Stalinism: avant-garde, aesthetic dictatorship and beyond,* (Princeton: Princeton University Press, 1992). For a response see Lutz Koepnick, *Walter Benjamin and the Aesthetics of Power*, (Lincoln and London: University of Nebraska Press, 1999).

[6] A letter to the editor of *The Daily Telegraph,* 19 February, 1892. In the same letter Wilde writes, "I saw lately, in Paris, a performance by certain puppets of Shakespear's *Tempest*. […] Miranda was the image of Miranda, because an artist had so fashioned her; and Ariel was true Ariel, because so had she been made. Their gestures were quite sufficient, and the words that seemed to come from their lips were spoken by poets who had beautiful voices. It was a delightful performance, and I remember it still with delight, though Miranda took no notice of the flowers I sent her after the curtain fell."

[7] Meyerhold was greatly influenced by popular traditions in puppetry and acting as diverse as the *commedia dell'arte* and the circus. The impact of these can bee seen in productions like *The Puppet Show* (1906–7), *Columbine's Scarf* (1910), *Mystery-Bouffe* (1918, 1921), and many others.

BIBILIOGRAPHY

Benjamin, Walter
    1973   "The Work of Art in the Age of Mechanical Reproduction", trans. Harry Zohn. In: *Illuminations*. London: Fontana Press, 219 – 253.

Brecht, Bertolt
    1964   *Brecht on Theatre*, trans and ed John Willett. London: Methuen.

Craig, Edward Gordon, ed
    1908–1929 *The Mask* 1–15. Florence.

    1918   *The Marionette*. Florence.

Eaton, Katherine Bliss
    1985   *The Theatre of Meyerhold and Brecht*. Westport, Conn.: Greenwood Press.

Kleist, Heinrich von
    1982   "Über das Marionettentheater". In: Kleist, *Sämtliche Werke*. Munich: Winkler, 945–951.

Meyerhold, Vsevolod
    1969   *Meyerhold on Theatre*, ed Edward Braun, London: Methuen.

Müller, Heiner
    1990   *Germania*, trans. Bernard and Caroline Schutze. New York: Semiotext(e), 124–133.

Pronko, L.C.
    1967   *Theatre East and West*. Berkeley: University of California Press.

Schlemmer, Oscar
    1967   "Man and Art Figure". In: Walter Gropius, ed., *The Theatre of the Bauhaus*, trans Arthur S. Wesinger. Middletown, Conn.: Weslyan University Press, 17–48.

Senelick, Lawrence
    1981   "Moscow and Monodrama". In: *Theatre Research International 6*.

Taxidou, Olga
    1998   *The Mask: A Periodical Performance by Edward Gordon Craig*. Amsterdam: Harwood Academic Publishers.

Wilde, Oscar
    1962   *The Letters of Oscar Wilde*, ed Rupert Hart-Davies. London: Rupert Hart-Davies.

Fragmentation of the Body in Spanish Surrealism

UTA FELTEN

A man is being harassed by a crawling hand in his apartment. Several attempts to rid himself of it fail. The man tries to throw the hand out of the window, but shortly after is shocked when he sees it crawling out of his shirt. Infuriated, he reaches for a dagger, intending to nail the body part to the table. He pierces his own hand:

> Loco de rabia, coge con decisión el organo mutilado y lo sujeta furiosamente con su mano izquierda mientras empuña una daga con la derecha. Se dirige a la mesa y coloca la mano muerta sobre ella. Los dos manos izquierdas, la viva y la muerta. El espectador desconoce cúal de las dos manos es la muerta. [...] Primer plano de las dos manos izquierdas. El puñal atraviesa una de ellas. Alarido de dolor. Una de las manos ha quedado clavada contra la mesa por la daga. La otra comienza a deslizarse. El hombre ha atravesado su propia mano. (Buñuel 1982: 209)

Dream fantasies of dismembered and pierced bodies, such as those seen in Buñuel's shock montage *Alucinaciones en torno a una mano muerta*, are omnipresent in surrealistic texts, pictures and films by García Lorca, Salvador Dalí and Luis Buñuel. The famous first sequence of a cut-up eye and the sequence of a cut-off hand in Buñuel's and Dalí's renowned filmic co-production *Un chien andalou* are among the best known presentations of disintegrated body parts in Spanish surrealism.

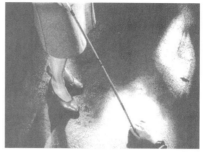

Stills from *Un Chien Andalou*, dir. Luis Buñuel (1928)

Buñuel's less known *Obra literaria*, e.g. his anthology of poetry *Un perro andaluz*, also offers a wide variety of examples of the surrealists' delight in dismemberment, analogous to experience in dreams. In Buñuel's *poeme en prose Palacio de hielo*, a lady who is polishing her fingernails tears out the narrator's — Luis Buñuel's — eyes and throws them into the street:

> La ventana se abre y aparece una dama que se da polisoir en las uñas. Cuando las considera suficientemente afiladas me saca los ojos y los arroja en la calle. Quedan mis órbitas solas sin mirada, sin deseos, sin mar, sin polluelos, sin nada; Una enfermera viene a sentarse a mi lado en la mesa de café. Despliega un periódico de 1856 y lee con voz emocionada: „Cuando los soldados de Napoleón entraron en Zaragoza en la VIL ZARAGOZA; no encontraron más que viento por las desiertas calles. Solo en un charco croaban los ojos de Luis Buñuel. Los soldados de Napoleón los remataron a bayonetazos. (Buñuel 1982: 141)

That García Lorca's surrealistic text production — his theater play *El Publico*, his movie script *Viaje a la luna* and his experimental prose texts *Degollación de los innnocentes*, *Degollación del Bautista*, *Nadadora sumergida* and *Santa Lucía y San Lazaro* — can be situated in the domineering surrealistic dismemberment discourse of Buñuel and Dalí is barely mentioned in Lorca research.

However, rather than present a motif history of the dismembered body in surrealism, I intend to explore the surrealistic representations of the body not as subjective and isolated products but as manifestations of literary imagination, as a dialogical examination of the literary and pictorial tradition. The frequent images of a disintegrated body in Lorca's text stand amidst a wide array of links to the pictorial and literary tradition of pre-modernity, whose pleasure in fragmentation Lorca actualizes. Besides Hieronymus Bosch's *The Temptation of Saint Anthony* and the famous representation of martyrs by Sebastián de Llanos y Valdés, *Cabeza cortada de Santa Catalina* (Severed Head of Saint Catherine), and by Fransisco de Zurbarán in *Santa Águeda* and *Santa Lucía*, Quevedo's *Sueño del juicio final* (Dream of the Final Judgement) belongs to the essential reference points of the surrealistic aesthetic of dismemberment.

Sebastián de Llanos y Valdes, *Severed Head of Saint Catherine*
(c. 1670)

In these body images, which were seized by the Tridentine Council, the surrealists rediscover their inherent ambiguity and interpret it as an anticipation of an aesthetic of the grotesque multiplication of meaning. In this paper, I will address questions of reception, actualization and transformation of pre-modern body dismemberment myths in the surrealistic dream aesthetic of Luis Buñuel and Federico García Lorca. The concept of intermediality, which is here understood in line with Volker Roloff's definition as a "mixture of various discourses and media charged with tension" (Roloff 1994: 4), offers a suitable premise for answering these questions. Using the example of García Lorca's text production I will show how intermediality functions as an actualization of pre-modern body images of disintegration when freed from psychoanalytic and ideological meanings.

Francisco de Zurbarán, *Saint Agatha* (1630-33)

The pleasure in representing dismembered bodies and in the cheerful representation of cruelty manifests itself above all in Lorca's prose texts *Nadadora sumergida, Suicidio en Alejandria, Santa Lucia y San Lazaro, Degollacion del Bautista*, in the film script *Viaje a la luna* and in his theater play *El Publico*. In the prose dream text *Nadadora sumergida*, a surrealistic newspaper report, the narrator tells of the monstrous find of a corpse on the beach. It is the corpse of a countess, whose neck was pierced with an absinth fork by a "strange murderer":

A la mañana siguiente fue encontrada en la playa la condesa de X
con un tenedor de ajenjo clavado en la nuca. Su muerte debió de
ser instantánea. En la arena se encontró un papelito manchado de
sangre que decía. „Puesto que no te puedes convertir en paloma,
bien muerta estás". Los policías suben y bajan las dunas
montados en bicicleta. Se asegura que la bella condesa X era muy
aficionada a la natación, y que esta ha sido la causa de su muerte.
De todas maneras podemos afirmar que se ignora el nombre de su
maravilloso asesino. (García Lorca 1986 : 160)[1]

Suicidio en Alejandria, a cinematographic poem, begins with a
decapitation scene, in which the placement of a cut off head on an
office desk is depicted:

Cuando pusieron la cabeza cortada sobre la mesa se rompieron
todos los cristales de la ciudad. (García Lorca 1986: 156)

The narrative *Santa Lucia y San Lazaro*, the only instance of a
marked, explicit intermediality, attempts the visual staging of a
martyr painting by Zurbarán, which shows Saint Lucy carrying her
gouged eyes on a tray:

Santa Lucía fue una hermosa doncella de Siracusa. La pintan con
dos magníficos ojos de buey en una bandeja. Sufrió martirio bajo
el cónsul Pacasiano, que tenía los bigotes de plata y aullaba como
un mastín. [...] Los ojos de la Santa miraban en la bandeja con el
dolor frío del animal a quien acaban de darle la puntilla. [...] Ojos
de Santa Lucía [...] Merecedores de la bandeja que les da realidad
y levantados, como los pechos de Venus [...]. (García Lorcas
1986: 144–146)

In *Degollacion del Bautista* the separation of a head from the
torso is enacted:

Bajo un cielo de plantas de pie. La degollación fue horripilante.
Pero maravillosamente desarrollada. El cuchillo era prodigioso.
Al fin y al cabo, la carne es siempre panza de rana. Hay que ir
contra la carne. Hay que levantar fábricas de cuchillos. Para que
el horror mueva su bosque intravenoso. El especialista de la
degollación es enemigo de las esmeraldas. Siempre te lo había
dicho, hijo mío. No conoce el chicle, pero conoce el cuello
tiernísimo de la perdiz viva. El Bautista estaba de rodillas. El
degollador era una hombre minúsculo. Pero el cuchillo era un

cuchillo. Un cuchillo chispeante, un cuchillo de chispas con los dientes apretados. (García Lorca 1986: 153–154)

In the sado-masochistic plays *Figura de Cascabeles* and *Figura de Pámpanos*, both of which are presented as homoerotic interpretations of Amor in *Cuadro segundo* of *El Publico*, Figura de Pampanos orders her lover to take an axe and cut off her legs: "FIGURA DE PÁMPANOS. Toma una hacha y cortame las piernas" (García Lorca 1988: 132–139).

Figura de Pampanos' dismemberment fantasies culminate in the final scene of the second act, where the character suggests decapitating herself in order to offer her own head as an object of pleasure to the emperor: "FIGURA DE PÁMPANOS. [...] Si me besas yo abriré mi boca para clavarme después tu espada en el cuello. [...] Y deja mi cabeza de amor en la ruina" (García Lorca, 1988, 132–139). In Lorca's film script *Viaje a la luna* sequences of screaming, gaping mouths, phalli, vomiting bodies, eyes, legs, feet, hand and heads are interlocked with one another:

> 3: Pies grandes corren rápidamente [...] 4: Cabeza asustada que mira fijamente un punto [...] 5: [...] un sexo de mujer con movimiento de arriba abajo [...] 9: Dos piernas corren con gran rapidez. 10: Las piernas se disuelven sobre un grupo de manos que tiemblan. [...] 14: Al final un gran plano de un ojo [...] 19: [...] una cabeza que vomita y abre y cierra los ojos [...] 32: [...] aparece una cabeza enorme dibujada de mujer que vomita. (Lorca 1980)

Lorca's taboo-breaking pleasure in the fragmentation of the body becomes particularly apparent in the picture sequences of strangled fish, bird, and toad heads, which are intertwined with images of vomiting women, screaming mouths and phalli:

> 27: [...] Un pez vivo sostenido en la mano de una persona, en gran plano, que lo aprieta hasta que muere [...] 44: aparece una cabeza de un pájaro en gran plano a la cual se estruja hasta que muere frente al objetivo [...] y aparece en la pantalla una luna [...] que se disuelve sobre un sexo y el sexo en la boca que grita. 51: Una cabeza mira estúpidamente. [...] Y se disuelve en una rana. El hombre de las venas estruja la rana con los dedos [...]. 54: Una cabeza que vomita. (Lorca 1980).

The picture sequences of disembodied legs, hand, eyes, phalli, strangled fish and toad heads in Lorca's script *Viaje a la luna* recall Hieronymus Bosch's *The Temptation of Saint Anthony* and realize in a certain way the "system of asceticism developed there, desire structured through prohibition" (Gendolla 1994: 139). In Bosch's painting this desire finds expression in the fantasies of the animals and demon bodies dismembering and devouring one another that inhabit the imagination of the hermit and are his own fantasies of asceticism.

Hieronymos Bosch, *The Temptation of Saint Anthony* (c. 1500)

Also obvious in Lorca's script are the implicit intermedial references to Buñuel's literary and cinematic productions, which portray visions of desire and the carnivalesque pleasure of breaking taboos. One need only think of the widely quoted sequences of the cut-off hand, the cut-up eye or the decaying donkey corpse, initiators of pleasure, fear, laughter and shock in *Chien andalou*. In the complementary pairs of pleasure and fear and taboo and taboo-breaking, Peter Gendolla recognizes the primary picture-producing principles, the *generateurs* of a desire determined through prohibition, which Buñuel's *Chien andalou* attempts to clothe in rhythmical pictures:

> So gibt es im Chien andalou unentwegt plötzliche Übergänge von neutralen zu tabuisierten Bildern, anstößig vor allem aufgrund der Verknüpfung, die das neutrale Bild denunziert, eine verbotene Beziehung, heimliche Komplizenschaft aufdeckt. Der Schnitt oder die Überblendung gibt einen Zusammenhang frei, der verdrängt und mit Angst aufgeladen war. Eben diese Angst bildet die den Film beherrschende Emotion, unauflösbar verbunden mit der Lust. Die Angst ist nur die unters Verbot geratene Lust, genau diese Überlagerung gibt der Film fürs Auge frei. [...] Tabu und Tabuübertretung werden vom Film rhythmisiert. (Gendolla 1994: 138)

Pleasure and fear, asceticism and ecstasy, taboo and the breaking of taboos, and laughter and shock are the primary *generateurs* that define production of pictures in Lorca's filmscript *Viaje a la luna* and at the same time instruct the reader, or the imaginary spectator, how to view and understand such images. The surrealists have fun playing conscious, ironic games with the taboo desires of the spectator and with his or her possible expectations, obsessions, and fantasies. This desire determined through a ban, already realized in Bosch's *Temptation of Saint Anthony*, manifests itself in Lorca's œuvre by means of a Lacanian structure of desire. In *La signification du phallus,* Lacan elaborates on the process of desire in which the subject elevates the Other, thus making him the phallic signifier and acknowledging his desire:

> Que le phallus soit un signifiant, impose que se soit à la place de l'autre que le sujet y ait accès. Mais ce signifiant n'y etant que voilé et comme raison du désir de l'Autre, c'est ce désir de l'Autre que est imposé au sujet de reconnaitre, c'est à dire l'Autre en tant qu'est lui même sujet divisé de la Spaltung signifiante. (Lacan 1971 : 112)

The basic structure of Lacanism as it manifests itself in *Viaje a la luna* can be described as follows: An imaginary hermit — I understand the hermit as an inner authority that controls the mental production of pictures — fills various objects, heads, mouths, phalli, strangled fish heads with his desire. Once filled with desire, the pictures themselves turn into phallic signifiers. Yet, because of the phallic over-determination of the sequences of the pictures, the film script becomes impervious to a serious lacanian interpretation which rejoices in pathologizing and constructs a pathological individual behind the pictures of fragmented and dismembered bodies. As he explains in his most famous essay *Le stade du miroir*, Lacan views dream fantasies of dismembered or pierced bodies as regressions to a time prior to the mirror stage, as "symptomes de schize ou de spasme, de l'hystérie," as symptoms of a sick, aggressive, hysterical individual:

> Ce corps morcelé [...] se montre régulièrement dans les rêves, quand la motion touche à un certain niveau la désintégration agressive de l'individu. Il apparait alors sous la forme de membres disjoints [...] cette forme se [...] manifeste dans les symptomes de schize ou de spasme, de l'hystérie. (Lacan 1966 : 97)

The surrealists counter Lacan's pathologizing of the dream of dismembered bodies with a carnivalesque pleasure in the dismemberment of the body into its desirable composites. The fragmented body is aestheticized and liberated from principles that only pathologize and rationalize it. The surrealistic pictures of corporal fragmentation are ambiguous and cannot be pinned down to a single signifier of psychoanalytic provenance. In their ambiguity they incarnate the obsessive aspect of asceticism and of a desire that is determined by prohibition. The heterogeneous picture sequences of fragmented bodies in *Viaje a la luna* re-actualize the carnivalesque chaos of body parts searching and misplacing each other, enacted in Quevedo's *Sueño del juicio final*. As Bernhard Teuber shows in his study on the carnivalesque tradition in Quevedo's œuvre (Teuber 1989), one encounters a high number of pictures of dismembered bodies in *Sueño del juicio final*. From a hill, the dreamer of *Sueño del juicio final* watches the resurrection of the dead, in which bones rise from the grave and begin searching for their various body parts. The dreamer, however, is not interested in the assembly of the body parts into a perfect whole guided by the Divine Providence but rather in laughing at the sight of the chaos in which bones search for matching bones, often mistaking one for the other:

Al punto comenzó a moverse toda la tierra y dar licencia a los
huesos, que andaban ya unos en busca de otros. [...] Después noté
de la manera que algunas ánimas venían con asco y otras con
miedo huían de sus antiguos cuerpos. A cual faltaba un brazo, a
cual un ojo y dióme risa ver la diversidad de figuras, y admiróme
la providencia de Dios en que, estando barajados unos con otros,
nadie por yerro de cuenta se ponía las piernas ni los miembros de
los vecinos. (Quevedo 1991: 93–95)

Even though the dreamer is not very interested in the recombi-
nation of the body parts into a perfect whole by Divine Providence,
it does in fact take place, effectively resolving Christian theology. In
Lorca's *Viaje a la luna*, on the other hand, the ideologically Christian component is entirely absent; the assembly controlled by God
of the disintegrated body into a perfect whole no longer takes place.
The Divine Providence that can re-integrate the body is absent. Instead, a monstrous, deformed, disintegrated body is created.

NOTES

[1] Cf. in this context also Uwe Scheele, who compares selected sequences
from *Un chien andalou* and *La voie lactee* with Valdes Leal's *Fin de la
gloria del Mundo*. Scheele states that Buñuel's surrealistic transposition of
motifs from Sebastián de Llanos y Valdés' pre-modern paintings freed
themselves of Christian dogmas, which had been forced on baroque art by
the counter reformation, and achieved "instantaneous, uncontrollable
expression" in Buñuel's movies. (Scheele 1994: 155)

BIBLIOGRAPHY

Buñuel, Luis
    1982   "Alucinaciones en torno a una mano muerta". In: *Obra
                literaria*. Introducción y notas de Agustín Sánchez Vidal.
                Zaragoza : Edición de Heraldo de Aragón, 209–211.

García Lorca, Federico
    1986   *Obras completas* III. Notas de Arturo del Hoyo. Madrid:
                Aguílar.

    1988   *El Público*. Edición de María Clementa Millán. Madrid:
                Cátedra.

    1980   *Viaje a la luna*. Loubressac: Braad Editions.

Gendolla, Peter
    1994   "Begegnungen im Traum. Buñuels Transformation der Versuchungsgeschichte in den Film". In: Volker Roloff/Ursula Link Heer (ed.), *Luis Buñuel: Film — Literatur — Intermedialität*. Darmstadt: Wissenschaftliche Buchgesellschaft, 137–145.

Lacan, Jacques
    1966   *Écrits I*. Paris : Éditions du Seuil.

    1971   *Écrits II*. Paris: Éditions du Seuil.

Quevedo, Francisco de
    1991   *Los Sueños*, Madrid: Cátedra.

Scheele, Uwe
    1994   "'El Obispo podrido'. Buñuels Schock-Ästhetik zwischen Hyperrealismus und innerer Bildwelt". In: Volker Roloff/Ursula Link-Heer (ed.), *Luis Buñuel: Film — Literatur — Intermedialität*. Darmstadt: Wissenschaftliche Buchgesellschaft, 145–159.

Teuber, Bernhard
    1989   Sprache — Körper — Traum. Zur karnevalesken Tradition in der romanischen Literatur aus früher Neuzeit. Tübingen: Niemeyer.

V.

THE VANGUARD IN CINEMA AND ARCHITECTURE

The Surface of Illusion: Avant-Garde Apperception and Antecedence in Structural/Materialist Film

DAVID MACRAE

Cinematic illusion and celluloid surface, although physically bonded, seem to require perceptual detachment to attain conventional apprehension. Cinematic illusion, or representation, is perceived as the delivery of coherent and specific instances of captured visualisation. The celluloid surface, the mediating material, exists in a hidden sanctum of perceptual denial which lurks beneath an inelegant veil of coldly technical extraction where the constituents of image are dissected into chemical configuration. This chemical configuration cannot, it may seem, be directly represented, but rather exists as the dutiful vehicle of redirected presentations. The objects of cinematic illusion are actuated by the perceptual processes of representation, yet such a representational status seems perpetually denied to the opaque concreteness of the celluloid surface. The dynamic illusions of cinematic representation are frequently ascribed as perceptually transparent procedures which intuitively revitalise technically recorded visual data into an ongoing stream of responsive sensation, whereas the mechanical apparatus of the base medium is somehow devoid of prominent sensory significance and thus, by necessity, rendered perceptually non-existent. Apparently then, film's illusory visual content flourishes upon the implicit invisibility of its supporting mechanical structures.

In the early 1970s, the critic P Adams Sitney first applied the term 'structural film' as a definition of experimental forms which privilege the importance of film structure over content. The film-works made by Andy Warhol in the early 1960s, which emphasised the extremities of filmic duration, were a precursor of the North American structural films of Michael Snow, Hollis Frampton, and George Landow. Their work was structural in the sense that it concentrated upon the moulding of film form itself — light, process and temporality. In this way, conventional symbolic narrativisation was transcended by formal self-reflexivity. In Europe, structural film tendencies were developed to particularly profound and intensive levels. Here the focus of concern was directed toward the foregrounding of film's pure physicality of corporeal presence — its status as malleable, exposed material. The illusory imagery of filmic representation was obscured by the factural characteristics and factual textures of the celluloid surface. Such experimentation was theorised and specifically defined as 'structural/materialist film' by Peter Gidal, whose own works, along with those of Malcolm Le Grice, Kurt Kren, Peter Kubelka and William Raban, are most prominently associated with the form. Indeed, the numerous intriguing films made in this vein of progressive scrutiny, seem to reach straight into the historical origins of film innovation, experimentation, and avant-garde material manipulation.

Thus, it is possible to reveal a direct legacy of conceptual relationship running form the early European avant-garde film-works of Hans Richter, Fernand Léger, Man Ray, and Marcel Duchamp, to the structural/materialist films made in the 1960s and 1970s. The avant-gardist impulse which connects these areas may be located to the axiomatic function of apperception: the self-evident, media-specific awareness and recognition of the processes of perceiving. The term 'apperception', of course, may also be used in the sense of fundamental knowledge acquisition in which new concepts are contextualised and contrasted with existing elements of prior knowledge. This concept of contextualisation can additionally be related to the historicising notions which Peter Bürger has attempted to apply to the historical avant-garde and its relationship to what he terms the neo-avant-garde. For Bürger, the historical avant-garde is a phenomenon statically rooted to a temporal location, and the so-called neo-avant-garde is dismissed as merely a form of "consumption fad"

(Bürger, 1984:63) — a muted mimic of earlier lofty aspirations which serves only to consolidate the perceived limitations of aesthetic revolution and institutional abolition. By exploring examples of the origins of structural/materialist film, it may be possible to elucidate the nature of a range of significant relational factors deriving directly from the early film-works of the historical avant-garde. In this way, a vital artery of developmental avant-gardist innovation may be exposed to new attention and Bürger's characterisation of avant-garde/neo-avant-garde historicisation may be challenged and critically reassessed.

There are a variety of valuable reasons to scrutinise and interrogate the validity of the sweeping term 'avant-garde film'. Indeed, the very use of the term itself often results in little more than obfuscatory reductionism. Historicisation of the avant-garde film tendency has frequently assumed the existence of a perpetual process of irresistible developmental innovation. Yet even elements of the so-called avant-garde film phenomenon rely heavily on the reciprocal impacts and influences of historical retrospection and reflection, rather than an unbridled trajectory of dazzling visionary revelation. Stephen Heath has stated that

> the practice of 'structural/materialist film' is defined in the *presentation* of a film's process, 'the presentation of the material construction of film;' process, construction are displayed reflexively, not displaced uniformly into the pattern of a narrative, bound up for the stable subject-centred image. Important to presentation of process is an attention to temporality (time is 'film's primary dimension'), duration (how long something lasts). It is usual in this connection to begin by adducing the exposition of the possible one-to-one relationship between shooting time and reading time, equivalence between the duration of the event recorded and the duration of the film representation of that event. [...] Durational equivalence, however, is itself a turning back in cinema's history (accepting for a moment the idea of a progressive development), right back to the practice of the films screened by Lumière in the Grand Café. (Heath, 1978, reprinted in O'Pray, 1996:171-2)

Heath's suggestion of the historicising implications of durational equivalence between originary event and representationally reconfigured form, draws into question the apparent disparity between surface and illusion, between the presented film-time and the recollected real-time. This comparison between these frequently discordant temporal frameworks serves as a valuable complementary template for the broader analysis of cinematic evolution — both within specific screen texts and across the wider expanses of film history. Indeed, these questions of durational equivalence and ambivalence, accentuate the requirement for a more thorough-going examination of the nature of the film material with the filmic subject.

The experimental film-maker, in historical terms, has often been perceived as the mediator between the apparently polarised extremities of authenticity and artifice, document and deconstruction. Thus, the experimental film-making tendency may be seen to emphasise the reification of transient optical sensations. The experimental film has often been characterised as the attempt to draw forth central elements, or key components, of an array of visual experiences in order to generate a newly solidified confrontational awareness of the constructed act of witnessing visuality itself in operation. In this confrontational, and revealing, act of witnessing visuality, there is the assumption of an implicit separation between an objectively tangible reality and a subjectively experiential imagining. The filmic object itself, in this regard, exists as a descriptive entity exposing its own presence in a particular place and time, yet is simultaneously relocated within the purely filmic dimension of the screen-fixed medium. Experimental film, thus, has historically been recognised as the location of perceptual procedures in fusion with mechanical reproduction enunciated through the media-specific language of the camera. The intuitive artistry of the experimental film-maker, therefore has become characterised as that which is quintessentially influenced and modulated by the ever-present tension between record and reconfiguration; fragmentary facets of visual sensation become thrust into the foregrounded factuality of the material status of filmic apprehension. Peter Gidal states that

> the concept of materialism cannot be covered by the concept and concrete reality of physicality. The attempt here is by fits and starts to elucidate a materialist process. The questions pertaining to representation–systems and codes has to do with the *physical* reproduction and transformation of *forms*, a reproduction, at

some level, of the profilmic, that which the camera is aimed at —
a transformation *to* the filmic, the filmic event, so to speak. This
transformation has to do with codes of cinematic usage which for
the most part are not yet clearly delineated in the case of experimental film. For example, there is no questioning that the
dissolution of imagery through extremes of darkness and light
also (and equally) has to do with the flattening of the screen-sur-
face, bringing that screen-surface-ness into play against the
(however momentarily) held depth-illusions, i.e. representation of
the real world via cinematic photochemical means. It is thus un-
questionable that a certain usage of grain and contrast can
produce itself *vis-à-vis*, and through, the *image*. The duration of
that "image", and that image's transformation, always preceded
by other mages, always effecting other images, and their meanings and uses, is inseparable from the material-physical support.
(Gidal, 1989: 15-16)

This acquaintance, though, or conventionalisation of the supporting
status of the filmic material, has become something of a staid
mechanism for the exposing capacities of cinematic experimentation. Indeed, it has perhaps developed into a static formula for the
ability of screen abstraction to become, itself, a representation of the
optical reality of the medium. This apparent reductionism brings the
evolutionary nature of the avant-garde film form into question and,
thereby, calls forth the necessity of the influential genealogy of film
experimentation as a vital factor in the understanding of a creative
"vanguard" of film innovation. The inseparability of the image from
its material and media-specific, support may be seen as part of a
broader impulse within cinematic experimentation, forming a series
of presentative typologies whose layers have become increasingly
impacted and congested. These generalised typologies have succes-
sively impinged upon the originary status of the exposing medium,
so that factors of duration and reflexivity gradually come to refer to
their own historiographic location in a manner similar to the representative status of illusory cinematic presentation: their innovation is
enveloped within generic recognition. The requirement therefore
emerges to scrutinise questions of relativity, both within the evolution of experimental film history, and the parallel implicit relativity
of image and medium.

Gidal suggests that "the importance of the history of each viewing is inseparable from the subject/viewer's own history but not somehow determined by it. This gives the material of film power through which the cinematic event persists" (Gidal, 1989:11). Malcolm Le Grice has written of the seminal influence of Fernand Léger's 1924 film, *Ballet Mécanique*:

> Possibly as a by-product of the rhythmic editing of sequences, Léger, also for the first time in a film, introduces lengths of film with no image — strips of black film — as elements of the rhythmic and optical interchange and thereby also prefigures a concern with abstract cinema, which later almost takes on the proportions of a 'genre', the flicker effect. There are two other firsts which can probably be claimed for Ballet Mécanique, and which have an important place later. One of those is almost an aside within the film and may have been the result of an accident, though some of the implications may well have appealed to Léger when he saw the result. In one sequence a mirrored glass ball is swung backwards and forwards […] as the ball swings, the camera and its operator are mirrored in its surface, creating the first direct reference to the machinery of cinema as part of the content of film. This is a notion which Vertov developed more consistently later, and which anticipates some of the most recent formal notions occupying contemporary film-makers.
>
> The other 'first' is the multiple repetition of a sequence, again prefiguring what is now almost a 'genre' — exploration of the 'loop'. The sequence is of a woman, with a bag on her back, climbing a set of steps, filmed from above. Certainly, the repetition in this sequence is prophetic, for example, of Warhol's multiple repeat paintings. (Le Grice, 1977, reprinted in 2001:43)

These elements of flicker-effect, material self-reflexivity, and multiple repetition, represent the inception of an array of core practices distinctive to experimental film phenomena. Certainly, their seminal influence is crucial and eminently salient. Yet beyond the level of their creative resonance through the century, there emerges the notion of technical procedures in film "experimentation" which in themselves are efforts to regenerate a specific conception of generalised tendencies of cinematic subversion, whose own devices are themselves predelineated and thus circuitously self-referential. The flicker-effect, reflexivity of mechanical exposure, and repetition are all devices which draw attention to the specific nature and capacities of the material medium of film. As such, these devices become part of an established grammar through which a recognition of the broad concept of film as material is grounded.

Fernand Léger, *Le Ballet Mécanique* (1924)

However, although these elements may be recognised as part of a creative genealogy which might, by definition, deny the vitality of innovation necessarily specific to avant-gardism, the elements themselves operate in both individual and collective manners which extend beyond mere historical continuity. Filmic reflexivity is more than a perceptual effect, which problematises the simplicity of illusory transparency. It simultaneously bonds the understanding of an

The tension which emerges here, between durationality and spatiality, crucially engages the perceptional process itself in terms of the temporal requirements of viewer attention for optical signification of the viewed image. Indeed, in the work of Warhol, durationality seems to amplify the innate sensory data of the viewed material. From this phenomenon emerges an apparent ambiguity between intellectual discernment of the optical data and the related role of duration in the operation of that discernment. Indeed, the implications of these factors are particularly significant in the apperceptive nature of experimental film, even in its broad historical sense. Similar to the latent nature of thought patterns themselves, formal structures of filmic spatio-temporality emerge most profoundly at the purest, most elemental, level. Where time passes at an apparently unmodulated pace, and spatial forms are contained within that circumscribed sphere of time, the central essence of film as an abstracted expanse of direct experience prominently emerges. This contrasts significantly with a cinematic lineage of conventionalised codes involving phrasing and intonations of formally coherent temporal transitivity — of time as a convention of film grammar. The Warholian filmic "stare", then, may be interpreted further as a perceptual surface of awareness. It presents an experience of time within time, bonded by the filmic surfaces of enveloping imagery which exist in a directly indexical relationship to optical immediacy. This indexicality places the optical dimension in an intensive proximity to the containing parameters of open time. In this way, the films present an experience of that which is known as well as that which is seen. The knowledge of the facts of temporal duration fuse with the facts of the optical imprint of the objective environment. The film-work loses its status as fabricated exposition, and becomes organic observation. The film experience which Warhol initiates is one which draws heavily on awareness of space and time as an immediate conceptual experience, rather than a series of recollections or expectations about a plasticised re-rendering of passing facets of space and time, which are detached and mutually excluded within their collective media. Warhol achieves a distinctive cinematicity which negates the status of film merely as memory, and revitalises it in the form of the confrontational unravelling of direct knowledge, perpetually relentless awareness.

Configured as an aspect of memory, or chemically captured recollection, film exists as a further detached layer of opacity, a mesh
through which direct perception is further obfuscated or distanced.
The film strip, as pure material, blurs as well as contains the objects
of its mechanised scrutiny. This language of recollection, as it may
be perceived, settles into the soft dusty dimensions of the archive, of
the secondary strata of a bygone impression of time's ephemeral
passage. Warhol's approach to film is less as memory than temporal
immediacy and inevitability. His film-works are propelled by the
profound pictoriality of time's presence, rather than the recollected
reflection of its evasive distance. Thus, works such as *Sleep* (1963),
Eat (1963), *Empire* (1964), and *Beauty #2* (1965), present Warhol's
attitude to film as a rendering of visible elements dependent upon
the temporality of direct perception, rather than the fragmentary facets of indirect recollection or presupposition. This durational
'materiality' of Warhol's early films generates the central area of
influence upon subsequent experimental film-making which emphasise notions of cinematic substance; the substantive experience of
the facts of film as physical material and psychological activity. In
Material, Materiality, Materialism (1978), Malcolm Le Grice wrote
about the contrasting, and related, levels of these substantive filmic
components:

> In its simplest sense, the question of materiality is seen in rela-
> tionship to the: *physical substances* of the film medium, the film
> strip itself as material and object. Work in this area drawing and
> paying attention to the physical base (acetate), emulsion surface,
> sprockets, joins etc, easily shades over into an awareness of: *me-
> chanical and physico-chemical processes*. In this case attention is
> drawn to the photochemical response and its chemical develop-
> ment, the transfer of image through printing, the transformation
> of image through these processes and the mechanical systems of
> film transport in camera, printer, or projector.
>   The earliest example of this awareness is to be found in Man
> Ray's *Retour à la Raison* (1922) through his incorporation into
> film of the direct photography 'Rayogram' technique, by laying
> small objects like dust, nails, pins and springs directly onto the
> film before exposure without the use of a camera. Distancing the
> representational image in this way draws attention to film sub-
> stance and process as an element of content. (Le Grice, 1978,
> reprinted in 2001: 165)

What is particularly intriguing about Le Grice's treatment of the vital importance of Man Ray's seminal materialist influence through the 'Rayogram', is the implication that this apparently indexical practice of image capturing has a distancing effect upon representation. This engages as important concept regarding the possibility of cinematic materialism depending upon image generation directly from originary visual objects, yet crucially also involving a perceptually complex trajectory through mental imagery, through purely cerebral conception of pre-existing imagery. In this regard, Man Ray's 'rayogrammed' imagery initiates a detailed process of perceptual assimilation of the originary optical data, which simultaneously engages conceptualisation of form, structure, scale, dynamics, and velocity, all of which interact with the immediate recognition of the data at the solely visual filmic level. The sustained impact of these materialist issues, stemming directly from Man Ray's original innovation, may be largely due to the fact that whilst cinematic perception is frequently understood as a passively receptive process of absorption, potently radical evasions of that conception emerge from the realisation that filmic imagery can be further directed by the pervasive elements of multiple transcendent perceptual procedures including conceptualisation, reconfiguration, recollection and anticipation. All of these elements gain their incisiveness from the direct perceptual exposure of the physical substance of the medium. Le Grice continues:

> Another relatively simply definable area of attention to filmic materiality is: *optic functioning* [...] Duchamp's *Anémic Cinéma* (1926) is the initial historical point of reference [...] This area of exploration which shifts the question of materiality from the film–material to the material functioning of the viewer, in a primitive sense, is made possible by the location of film's frame/projection rate at the threshold of optical discrimination. (Le Grice, 2001: 166)

This threshold of optical discrimination is the territory wherein cinematic experience may oscillate between symbolic recollection and indexical cognition. The status of film as a material modulator of memory, as a surface of visual resonance, intertwines explicitly with the status of film as a transparent illusion of self-contained meaning and visual sustenance, significance stemming solely from presentation. The emergence of materialist film simultaneously signals an experimental process of reconsidering film as the site of the physical manipulation of the previously elusive ethereality of memory. Indeed, film as 'memory' becomes reconstructed as the formalisation of modes of optical recollection. Along with the apparent surface simplicity of exposing the medium itself, or fusing the sustaining surface with the supporting content, so the symmetries and conditioning patterns of the passage of time through image are rediscovered within the veiled vehicle of screen-based communication.

The indexical status of May Ray's rayogramming technique, however, is complicated by the nuances of their simultaneity of memory and materiality — the objects within the rayogram are simultaneously present and distant, both index and symbol. Indeed, this curious nuance is extended in the experiments of materialist film-works into the 1970s. In materialist film, attention tends to fixate upon the surface of the medium, but the objective status of the film-strip reacts to the objects captured upon this surface. Objective status, then, becomes a site of competing dominance, a perpetually tensioned exchange between surface and object, significance and subject. Therefore, materialist film may be understood as a process by which objects of attention are stripped of their originary objective status to become granular vestiges of a fading memory, a bygone engagement with an enveloping medium. Furthermore, the medium itself, the film-strip, attains the status of object. It is an object whose foregrounded position confronts the viewer not as transparent illusion, nor as ethereal recollection, but directly tangible visibility — itself objectified. This nuance, or ambiguity, points to the pictoriality of memory as well as to the objectivity of illusion. Here materialist film begins to expose issues of considerably greater magnitude than the straightforward aesthetic recognition of the supporting modulations of the medium. Observational directness, or cinematic clarity, become subsumed by the burgeoning gravity of film material which in itself is part of a wider dimension of exchanges between subject and object, between surface and illusion. If the cinematic experience crucially deploys processes of awareness and suspensions of disbelief, then so too does the film strip depend upon forms of containment for the validity of its expressive content. Whilst the materiality, and material recognition, of the filmic medium is an empowerment of the terms of representation, it is additionally a submission to its limiting capacities. Thus, materialist film's expansive perceptual project concurrently embraces the stasis of objects captured within the fixative gaze of the lens, and releases the medium itself into the dimensions of its own objectivity — another object amongst many. Materialist film collides with the fluidity of temporality in a manner similar to the collision of objects with the surface of Man Ray's 'Rayogrammed' film strip. The materialist conception of film is an optical enunciation of the physicality of perception.

This colliding optico-temporality finds particular relevance in the work of Kurt Kren. *Trees in Autumn* (1960) is a film which demonstrates Kren's ability to build an awareness of the materiality of time within the context of cinematic constraint and propulsion. Peter Gidal describes the film thus:

> *Trees in Autumn* is a series of shots, each shot a density of trees and branches, the rhythm of montage combined with the rhythm of movement or stillness within each shot dominating any inferences (narrative or otherwise) from the represented space. This is also because the speed of shot following shot at half-second bursts flattens out the represented spaces seen. The relations of this film are shot-to-shot, rather than any internal editing complexities. A shot becomes a piece of time. (Gidal, 1989: 6)

Kren's style of temporal materiality utilises the tension between stasis and motion, inverse fixity of the gaze and mobility of subject, in such a way that the bond of image and duration deviates from conventions of cinematic time-space progression. Thus, as Gidal suggests, the individual shot itself exists as a time fragment. Yet, crucially, it is a fragment whose *location in* filmic space is more perceptually prominent than its *progression through* that space.

The conventional modes of temporal advancement traditionally propelled by optical succession, are replaced not by repetition but by revision. The camera-eye engages and re-engages originary optical data in a manner which denies succession of temporal focus, and lends primacy to a revising tendency which accentuates the stifling dependency of filmic time upon visual evolution. An added nuance of this phenomenon emerges from the acknowledgement that a structural wholism of the shot as time elaborates the entwinement of film material and perceptual motion. It becomes a dynamic friction of surface symbol and sensory response. Gidal points out the relation between Kren's *Trees in Autumn* and Malcolm Le Grice's 1967 film entitled *Yes No Maybe Not*. Indeed, Le Grice himself has described *Trees in Autumn* as the first film he regards as generally of structuralist significance. In Le Grice's own work, the materialist

Kurt Kren, *Trees in the Autumn* (1960)

impulse surges toward a heightened discourse of the dimensional status of time within the destabilisation of pictorial conventions. *Yes No Maybe Not* is apparently a work of crafted superimposition, yet it is the disposition of the film's layering devices which generate a transcendent space for the scrutiny of durational transformations. Peter Gidal describes the film as comprising two basic sequences, which are:

an image of water splashing against a wall or barrier, and a long
shot of Battersea power station, with its huge smoke stacks,
smoke rising out of them. [...] The film starts with a negative image of water superimposed upon the image positive. [...] The
space between two equal opposite images that are several frames
out of synch makes for the effect of bas-relief; also, the separation of two images, one negative, one positive, makes for a line-
determined space of grey that varies in shape and tone according
to the change of synchronisation. The interplay of *same* images
creates a dialectic, which becomes more complex via the viewer.
(Gidal, 1989: 124)

The channelled complexity of this dialectic crucially actuates
through the viewer's engagement with the spatial circuits which the
film pervades. The superimposition initiates the dispositioned spatial
depth arising through alternate channels of temporal velocity. Here a
direct bond of time and space depends upon surface perception and
separation. Intriguingly, this process seems to engage the eye with
greater immediacy than the emerging detail of the depicted representational imagery. Thus, a form of perceptual transfer occurs from
the specificity of content to the conceptual spatiality of form, and it
is in this regard that materialist film may rightly be historically located at the crux of purely percept-based screen responsiveness. The
inception of materialist film, drawing as it does on apperceptive antecedents in the cinematic avant-garde, signals a critical shift in the
conceptual criteria of screen dimensionality and time-based media.
It additionally expands upon the core qualities of optical perception
by distillating the documents of vision into an intellectualised scope
of object and subject, recognition and reconfiguration, medium and
modulation. Of course, materialist film proliferated into the 1970s
and developed its own internal discourses and intertextualities, its
own creative influences. Yet the apparent requirement for a historiographic chronology of structural/materialist film, now seems to be
outweighed by the need to acknowledge its central location in the
apperceptive status of avant-garde visual phenomena of the twentieth century. It is the legacy of conceptual thinking which remains
the most potent genealogy feeding into, and flowing out from, the
evolution of experimental film-making.

BIBLIOGRAPHY

Bürger, Peter
  1984   *Theory of the Avant-Garde.* Minneapolis: University of
            Minnesota Press.

Curtis, David
  1971   *Experimental Cinema: A Fifty Year Evolution.* London:
            Studio Vista.

Danino, Nina and Maziére, Michael, eds.
  2003   *The Undercut Reader: Critical Writings on Artists' Film
            and Video.* London: Wallflower Press.

Foster, Hal
  1996   *The Return of the Real.* Massachusetts: MIT Press.

Gidal, Peter
  1989   *Materialist Film.* London: Routledge.

Le Grice, Malcolm
  2001   *Experimental Cinema in the Digital Age.* London: British
            Film Institute.

MacDonald, Scott
  1993   *Avant-Garde Film: Motion Studies.* Cambridge:
            Cambridge University Press.

O'Pray, Michael, ed.
  1996   *The British Avant-Garde Film, 1926 to 1995.* Luton:
            University of Luton Press.

Rees, A.L.
  1999   *A History of Experimental Film and Video.* London:
            British Film Institute.

Sitney, P. Adams
  1979   *Visionary Film: The American Avant-Garde, 1943 –
            1978.* Second Edition. New York: Oxford University
            Press.

Tyler, Parker
  1995   *Underground Film: A Critical History.* New York: Da
            Capo Press.

Wollen, Peter
  1982   *Readings and Writings: Semiotic Counter-Strategies.*
            London: Verso.

WHAT AVANT-GARDE?

GÉRARD LEBLANC

May 1968 marks in France, more still than in any other European country, a return to politicisation within the polemic of the artistic avant-garde, and more particularly the cinematographic avant-garde. This polemic came about in the aftermath of the social movement which had given rise to the development of so-called "militant" films, devoid of any avant-gardist characteristics. This situation was radically opposed to that of the Soviet Union during the 1920s. There was no revolutionary political party, nor indeed one that claimed to be, in power. Quite to the contrary, the bourgeoisie, greatly aided by the French communist party and the General Confederation for Labour, had resumed its domination after the great fright which led it to consider military action. The revolution appeared both immediate and inaccessible. The numerous organisations — Marxist-Leninist, Maoist, Trotskyite — who claimed to lead it, were only mildly developed and merely exerted a derisory influence upon the social movement. Within this context, revolutionary filmmakers, notwithstanding the fact that they were few, were never tempted to place themselves under the banner of a non-existent revolutionary party, despite various self-proclamations, like it happened in the Soviet Union with Dziga Vertov for instance.

Hence the novelty and paradoxical character of the situation. In 1970s France, two avant-garde cinema groups — the Dziga Vertov group and the Cinéthique group — acted out, without claiming it to be so, the political role generally held by political organisations. These groups, not able to establish working relations or collaborations with these organisations, turned inwardly in order to attempt "to make politically political films". It is not to say that these groups lived in theoretical autarky: they were strongly influenced by Althusserian Marxism (mainly on the issue of the ideological apparatus of the State), by Lenin's analysis of the transformation of capitalism into imperialism, and by the philosophical writings of Mao Tse Tung — in particular *Of Contradiction*. They complained that these references, both theoretical and practical, were not really taken into consideration by the political organisations with which they were in discussion. This placed them in a position of political solitude, but it was far from isolationist. Despite the very limited means of production at their disposal — all their films were shot in 16mm on exceedingly low budgets — the two groups succeeded in producing films and their distribution gave rise to numerous debates.

Insofar as avant-garde cinema around that time failed to meet up with a political avant-garde, that in fact did not exist, it then strove to constitute itself as an aesthetic and political avant-garde. The political orientations and directives no longer emanated from an external organisation or party, they were the result of setting up cinema within the contradictions of 1970s society. Such attempts cannot be discredited by the cutting accusation of "formalism", as it had been the case against Dziga Vertov. Those that formulate such accusations are immediately confronted with their own political ineffectiveness. For the first time in history, and without the support of any sort of political authority, filmmakers interacted with their avant-garde political orientations and their cinematographic practice indissociably. The result was an original questioning of the place cinema held in society and on the way it acted upon its revolutionary transformation.

The initial dominant theme of the triangle relationship, filmmaker-film-spectator, was work. The work asked of the spectator harked back to the work of the filmmaker and that of the film. The filmic body had to bear the trace of the technical, as well as the artistic work — a work borne out of the determined conditions of production of the filmic body. The film had to break away from its status as consumable, as merchandise, and as cultural merchandise intended for a cultivated audience. We tended to demand that a film set forth everything about itself. Film was envisaged as a work process that met up with spectators-cum-individuals engaged in other work processes. The entertainment function ascribed to cinema overshadowed the work of the film and the filmmaker can only thwart this by developing film's potential as critical operator of representation.

The paradox lies in that this concept of work was applied to films that were for the most part freed of the constraints of industry, where the notion of play held an important part. It was precisely about consolidating the playing potential of cinema in order to reconcile the unity between work and play in all aspects of life. It was about freeing work from constraints that were similar to a sacrificial ritual, constraints which were particularly noticeable at the level of production. Conceived in this way, film, as work process, itself became the condition of a non-alienated aesthetic pleasure.

If only these work relations were not governed by business relations. The so-called "technical" division of work was contested from within the film production team (the filmmaker acting as "manager of meaning" in opposition to the technicians who follow orders and directives without voicing their opinion), but also from within the "team" formed by the filmmaker and the spectator: the filmmaker no longer directing the spectator as an actor, but placing him on the same level as himself. The journal Cinéthique advocated that cinema should no longer conceal the production work, root of an increase in value. It is to this condition that cinema could meet other forms of work exploitation that occurred in capitalist society.

The never-accomplished project for elaborating a theory of value for cinema, on the basis of the Marxist theory of increase in value, did not comprise only of purely analogical and mechanistic aspects. Its primary quality was to redeem usage value from practical exchange value. The usage value of films should no longer be governed by an "escapist" practical exchange value. Cinema should no longer allow imaginary escapism from the real conditions of existence, on the contrary, it should confront them with a view to transform them.

Before directing their own films, the Cinéthique group distributed a number of them — interacting with very different groups of spectators, both socially and culturally — and this allowed Cinéthique to establish its own polemic. At the forefront of these films there

was *Méditerranée*, directed by Jean-Daniel Pollet in 1963, a genuine
fake avant-garde film which was rejected by the audience of the
avant-garde film festival of Knokke-le-Zoute, in Belgium, the year
of its release. The work presented by the film to the spectator consists of attaining the viewpoint that no image could ever be constituted as a representation bearing preconstrued meanings and
generating interpretations based on the recognition of the already
known. Strictly speaking, the spectator no longer identifies with the
images presented for his recognition. He no longer identifies with
these images although they are perfectly identifiable: a pyramid, a
Greek temple, a bull-fighting ring, a tangerine, the smile of a young
woman, and other, apparently banal, visual motifs. The spectator no
longer controls what is being showed to him, just as much as the
filmmaker feels dispossessed by what he is filming. In a constantly
renewed whirlwind, the film alternates between the known and the
unknown and, in order to be understood, demands of the spectator to
explore alterity within him. The most decisive effect produced by
Méditerranée is that it allows the spectator to discover himself differently than he is, and this, through the constant return to his self.

Ten years later, Jean-Daniel Pollet directs *L'Ordre*, a film that
pushes to the extreme the questioning of the spectator. The film tells
the story of lepers in Greece, first recluse on an island off Crete, the
island of Spinalonga, then treated in a hospital that, de facto, they
could not leave in order to return to a world that does not want them.
Although they are all cured, they continue to frighten those that we
dare not call their fellow men, because of the traces of bodily decomposition present on their faces. The film asks: "Do you think
death is contagious?"

L'Ordre could have played the card of compassion, dealt a thousand times in other films. Pollet forbids himself to do this — aided
by Raimondakis, a leper who, for many long years, has developed a
raw thought process: the exclusion of his group by the "healthy people". Raimondakis refuses to become an object of spectacle and
starts off by questioning the filmmaker. Will he — like so many
others who have come to the island throughout the years — get picturesque images in a rush and accompany them by a personal
commentary, a thousand miles removed from the preoccupations of
the lepers? Or, on the contrary, will he listen to their discourse and

make a film that corresponds to this very same discourse? As long as the film remains unfinished, doubt will linger.

Through his questioning, Raimondakis will place the filmmaker and the spectator on an equal footing. This is also the approach of the filmmaker. Of course we watch the face of leprosy that presents itself before our eyes, we are at the cinema, but it is the leper that guides the gaze we cast on him. It is a fantastic inversion: the film watches us as we watch it, moreover, it questions the nature of our gaze. In the end, it is the political self of the spectator that is questioned. Raimondakis launches at us: "Soon you will become detersive and live in filth", he follows with the command: "Stop, while there is still time, stop".

Other cinematographic approaches aim at rendering the position of the spectator unbearable. The most radical and the most systematic one is certainly that of Jean-Pierre Lajournade, who directed *Cinéma, cinéma* in 1969, *Le Joueur de quilles* in 1968, and *La Fin des Pyrénées* in 1971. We are no longer dealing with the diversion of the spectacle as advocated by the situationists, for whom everything has become spectacle; but to divert the spectator from the spectacle. The spectator is not longer invited to partake in the work of the film; instead he has to refute it, including the work that would involve him in a fiction of revolt — like in *La Fin des Pyrénées*. The only way to rebel is to live out one's revolt in reality.

La Fin des Pyrénées is a refractory film, not because it expresses revolt but because it formulates, through a representation of revolt that society can accept and integrate as representation, the actual organisation of the envisaged society in its essential structure. *La Fin des Pyrénées* fights off the illusion of a possible emancipation of society through the imaginary. Any fiction harks back to the organisation of society, and any revolt experienced by proxy, through characters, only reinforces the idea of a society whose imaginary is increasingly dominated by advertisement. The film does not tell the tale of a failed revolution, it tells the tale of the failure of fiction, the failure of the world of surrogate satisfactions.

We are not dealing here with a dissolution of art into an aesthetised everyday life. Rather it is a matter of turning the cinema into an impossibility in order to attain the realisation of the impossible in everyday life. It is this utopia that Jean-Pierre Lajournade's cinema prompts us towards. This type of utopian dimension is a major constituent of the avant-garde cinema that developed at this time. The revolutionary transformation of cinema is immediately linked to the revolutionary transformation of society or to that of the spectator-cum-individual within society. Any form of separation between art and life is violently refuted, as was done by previous avant-garde movements, but this time such a refusal encompasses all the aspects of life and integrates its political and ideological dimensions. Art itself is no longer separate from politics and ideology. The work of the film precisely consists of allowing for the interaction of these different dimensions, having for only goal actual reality.

Cinema thus becomes the locus of reflection and transformation of all social practices. Cinema works on states of life which are questioned in their relation to ideology, politics and economics. It also becomes an operator for the analysis of contradictions that are visible only in their effects. Such is the orientation which prevails in the films of the Dziga Vertov and Cinéthique groups. In *Vent d'Est* (1969), the critique of representation is thought out in terms of class system and the spectator must first of all situate himself in relation to the theoretical and practical stakes which makes up every individual, questioned as subject, in an imaginary relation with his real conditions of existence (*Luttes en Italie*, 1970). Intimately linked to the Athusserian analysis of the ideological apparatus of the State, this approach leaves pending the question of the desire of individuals — or at least a great number of them — wanting to live within this imaginary relation. In any case, this is one of the most justified hypotheses that could be put forward in order to explain the failure of the revolutionary movement at that time.

"When you love life, you go to the cinema" (Cinéthique group 1975). This statement engages in a systematic dismantling of dominant representations, against the background of a critical analysis of the social function of cinema. If the huge majority of films offer representations true to the renewal of an existing chaos, the first of these representations remains foreign to this. It deals with the social programming of the desire for cinema. What can one expect, or hope for, in moments of cinema that life spares us? We buy tickets for a journey organised by specialists of the imaginary, whether this journey allows us to cross landscapes or faces, the journey is segmented into codified relations through slow-maturing genres where the spectator has become unaccustomed to fictional leeway, where the smallest discrepancy becomes an aggression, as if the lights were switched back on during the projection.

QUAND ON AIME LA VIE ON VA AU CINEMA

Mainstream cinema has constructed a spectator who corresponds to its choice in films. It would never have succeeded had it not highlighted the existence of a rooted need, both social and physiological. The success of entertainment cinema rests on the need for escapism felt by the public, to whom life has not brought the satisfactions hoped for. Entertainment cinema provides surrogate satisfactions. Its mission consists of making life more bearable than it is. The imaginary is just as subservient, as the relation to the real is disguised.

Any internal critical discourse of cinema, and even a discourse which aims to analyse its mechanism, is incapable to fight off, because of its conceptual strength, mechanisms of projection and identification that numerous authors have investigated under different lights. Spectators who are more or less clearly conscious of their existence nonetheless fall for this trap. Action must be taken on the reality of this need sustaining these mechanisms, so that a significant transformation can be operated on spectatorial behaviour. This presupposes action external to the film. This presupposes that cinema be lived and thought of as a locus for the transformation of society.

It is a historical tradition to mark the simultaneity of historical disturbance with artistic disturbance. Cinema would change either in response to social changes or in order to announce them. The interaction between art and politics within 1970s cinematographic avant-garde particularly highlights distortions and discrepancies. A film that calls into question "cinema as leisure", opposes itself to immediate political efficiency. And still, there is no revolutionary political practice possible without this calling into question.

Unless it is reduced to a shadow of these possibilities, cinema is a tool that tolerates little manipulation when the aim is directly political. A film is not politically productive, in the sense that it is not a political practice and cannot substitute itself for itself. The political space of film is composed of the relations of confirmation, or of opposition, that it maintains with world conceptions that are formed in contemporaneous cinema: not only in the relations established with the cinema as an outing and as a spectacle; but also in the spectatorial behaviour induced by the functioning of films; as well as in forms of montage. Film's relation to politics is mediated by philosophy. And if the same world conception lays the foundation for both a political line and the making of a film, its function is not to resolve the same problems in one situation as it will the other. In the first case, it is about translating an analysis of society into orientations, directives and slogans. In the second, it is about transforming according to a given political orientation, the system of representations, both internal and external, that links the cinema to its spectator. If only this political orientation did not attempt to represent itself in a form that remained external to it, if only it became that form, and it reproduced it.

Film finds its political efficiency in the movement of transition from a world conception to a cinema practice that is likely to suit it, even if this efficiency is limited by the historical situation in which the film is produced and distributed. The avant-gardist experimentation of the 1970s nonetheless taught us that no revolution can ever take place if it does not affect the whole of the social practices of the individuals that find themselves involved in it.

Translated by Jennifer Valcke

BIBLIOGRAPHY

Cinéthique
1969-85   37 issues published between January 1969 and October 1985. Read in particular issues 17-18, 19-20 and 23-24 about the film *Quand on aime la vie on va au cinéma*.

Comolli, Jean-Louis, Gérard Leblanc and Jean Narboni
2001   *Les Années Pop, Cinéma et Politique 1956-1970.* Centre Pompidou: Paris.

Faroult, David and Gérard Leblanc
1998   *Mai 68 ou le cinéma en suspens.* In: *Syllepses*, Paris.

Leblanc, Gérard
1972   *Sur trois films du groupe Dziga Vertov.* In: *VH* 101, number 6, Paris.

1972   Lutte idéologique et "Luttes en Italie". In: VH 101, no. 9, Paris.

The Limits of "Non-Plan": Architecture and the Avant-Garde

RICHARD WILLIAMS

Peter Bürger's *Theory of the Avant-Garde* has been thoroughly interrogated here and in the previous volume. Its stated desire to reconnect art and life is, as has been argued, too narrow, too reductive, too bound up with the desire for political action rather than formal innovation in the arts. Its prescriptiveness has little to say about the 1960s neo-avant-garde other than to dismiss it as inauthentic. In place of Bürger's theory, Dietrich Scheunemann has proposed that the avant-garde is conceived in terms of changing "modes of perception" which involve "communication and interaction between the world of arts and other life spheres" (2000: 43). In this scheme, the realm social by no means disappears, but its relationship with avant-garde art is redefined. It could be said that art is no longer — as it is in Bürger — to be regarded as an instrument of social change, but as both a manifestation of the social world and a representation of it. This would concur with existing attempts to explain avant-garde art, by for example, Fred Orton and Griselda Pollock. For them the avant-garde is a social phenomenon, a product of the self-consciousness of an intellectual group, but also:

> a range of social postures and strategies for artists by which they could differentiate themselves from current social and cultural structures whilst also intervening in them. To be of the avant-garde was to participate in complex and contradictory tactics of

involvement with, and evasion of, immediate forms of metro-
politan social and economic life. (Orton and Pollock 1996: 142)

Thus the avant-garde does not have the objective of bridging the
perceived gap between art and life (and in so doing achieving a
healing closure in our fragmented world) but, rather, an open-ended
critical engagement with the culture which produces it. This is
Clement Greenberg's position in the classic 1939 essay "Avant-
Garde and Kitsch" (Greenberg 1939). It is also, to give one much
later example, Thomas Crow's position on the essay "Modernism
and Mass Culture in the Visual Arts," in which he imagines art and
life in a dialectical relationship (Crow 1996: 3–37). Like Greenberg
he sees the dialectic in terms of mutual antagonism or even hostility,
but the avant-garde by definition exists in this condition. The surrounding culture may actually need the avant-garde, for it can act, as
he put it in an unforgettable phrase, as the "research and development arm of the culture industry" (Crow 1996: 35). The relationship
is therefore complex and contradictory, but necessary for the existence of both parties. As Ben Highmore pointed out in the last
collection of essays to emerge from these conferences: "within the
various avant-gardist formations, everyday life registered a contradiction: it was something to be decried and denounced, yet it was
also the possibility of salvation" (Scheunemann 2000: 249).

In this essay, I focus on architecture, an arena in which the complex relationship between the avant-garde and everyday life is most
publicly played out. Specifically I want to look at one particularly
inflammatory and controversial essay published in Britain in 1969,
"Non-Plan: an Experiment in Freedom". Not only does this essay
have much of the character of an avant-garde manifesto (its demands are superficially futurist in their intensity), but it makes
everyday life central to its argument, indeed, spectacular. Yet its
relationship with any existing concept of the avant-garde is prob-
lematical. It is this difficulty, I argue, that makes it a useful thing to
think with, helping us define what we mean by avant-garde. I have
two broad questions here, first being simply: is "Non-Plan" avant-
garde? Second, can there be an avant-garde in such a public and
comprised art as architecture?

"Non-Plan: An Experiment in Freedom" was published in the 20
March 1969 issue of *New Society*, a bi-weekly political journal sym-

pathetic to the libertarian left, although resolutely non-partisan according to its editor (Hughes and Sadler 2000: 2). Its authors, Reyner Banham, Peter Hall, Cedric Price and Paul Barker had already had some success in baiting the English architectural establishment. Banham, possibly the only Courtauld-trained art historian also to have been an aerospace engineer was a regular contributor to the journal on such diverse topics as the bolo tie, aeroplane design, and the quality of motorway food. His acclaimed book *Theory and Design in the First Machine Age* had rewritten modern architecture from the point of view of building services rather than art history (Banham 1960). The planner Peter Hall was the author of the widely-read futorology *London 2000* which advocated remaking London as a vast motorised region rather than a city of monuments (Hall 1969). The architect Price had proposed, without building very much, a modular university on wheels for the English midlands (Potteries Thinkbelt, 1964), and an inflatable replacement for the Houses of Parliament (1965). Barker, the journal's editor, kept the others under control.

Exasperation with English planning law was the essay's pretext. A booklet, Banham et al wrote, had just been published by the Dorset County Council on the appropriate forms of building in rural areas. It illustrated a set of place-specific designs for houses in that part of the world, but paradoxically these designs closely resembled the houses found in any speculative builder's suburban estate. The local area society of architects has complained and asked for the booklet to be withdrawn. "This illustrates," they continued, "the kind of tangle we have got ourselves into. Somehow, everything must be watched. Nothing must be allowed simply to happen. No house can be allowed to be commonplace in the way that things just *are* commonplace." (Banham et al 1969: 435)

Their solution was simple: abolish planning, starting with a set of three large-scale experiments limited in time and place in which the normal restrictions are removed. At the end of the experiment, assess the result, and continue or not as appropriate. The relative civility of this proposal — there are chronological and geographical limits — was aggressively undermined by the ironic character of the three areas selected for the experiment. The first, "Constable Country", was Banham's proposal, an area surrounding what is now Stansted airport. "Lawrence Country", chosen by Peter Hall was a large chunk of the east Midlands, just south of the Peak District. "Montagu Country", Price's choice, was the Solent between Southampton and Portsmouth, and perhaps the most urbanised of the three zones. Constable, Lawrence, Montagu, three names which in different ways represent a peculiarly English and quasi-aristocratic attachment to the land: Constable, the painter responsible for *The Haywain*, that most sacred image of English rural life; Lawrence, a singularly anti-urban modern novelist; Montagu, a hereditary peer with a well-known country estate. Each name identifies Englishness with the rural scene rather than the city. To choose these names, and to add the label "country" in each case, to represent zones which will become intensively urban is a calculated provocation, the sacred attachment to the countryside being perhaps England's greatest taboo.

Within each of these zones, anything would be possible, not just new building, but previously unimaginable pleasures. Price's "Montagu Country" is especially striking in this regard. He foresees a society of motorised nomads, liberated from work and sexual repression, drifting from one attraction to another with no preconceived plan. He imagined "tree-top rides through the (New) Forest", "*son et lumiére*" on Fawley oil refinery (then the largest in Europe), "retractable marinas with sail-in movies and row-in bars", "convoys of computer-programmed holiday houseboats", "Britain's first giant dome on the Isle of Wight" containing the first all public nudist scene in the country — thermostatically-controlled and ten bob a head", "pot shops instead of all those declining tobacconists" (Banham et al 1969: 441). The liberation from repression, through regression to a quasi-infantile state, is elaborated in the essay's conclusion. "We seem so afraid of freedom," they write, but

> Britain shouldn't be a Peter Pan Edwardian nursery. Let it at least move into the play school era: why should only the under sevens be allowed their bright materials, their gay constructions, their wind-up Daleks. In that world Marx is better-known as a maker of plastic battery powered dump trucks. Let's become that sort of Marxist. (Banham et al 1969: 443)

"Non-Plan's" title alone seems to make it a good candidate for avant-garde status. Its primary purpose seems to be to antagonise the architectural establishment, attacking the most deeply held views.

The prospect of building on large sections of the countryside is a calculated affront to two centuries of ingrained culture. Its solutions are futurist in their boldness. The activity they imagine will take place in the non-planned zones, especially that in Montagu country, involves a Marcusian release of the libido, which is then directed at activities — nude bathing, smoking cannabis, aimless wandering — likely to be regarded with suspicion by right-thinking people. Likewise the call to regress psychologically to infancy is a familiar avant-garde tactic. Dada, surrealism and later neo-avant-garde artistic tendencies made such regression a specific part of their programmes, refusing the conventions of adult bourgeois society at the most profound level by, for example, representing the excremental or scatological. This reading of "Non-Plan" is supported by the book on it which appeared in 2000 edited by Jonathan Hughes and Simon Sadler. Here in many contributions it is clearly a cultural avant-garde, an English flowering of the same kind that produced the Situationist International and the events of May 1968 (Hughes and Sadler 2000: 156–65).

As an avant-garde manifesto, however, it has limits. While stylistically it resembles one, its position vis-à-vis the surrounding culture is more affirmation than critique. In retrospect, Paul Barker recognised its ambiguity. Its "rampant neophilia" was radical, he wrote, but its argument that planners should give in to popular taste without imposing their own judgements could be regarded as "rampant conservatism" (Hughes and Sadler 2000: 2). I want to explore these limits further as they help describe some larger problems to do with architecture and the idea of the avant-garde. The limits of non-plan fall into two general areas — its unwitting re-enforcement of existing aesthetic values and its failure to produce a new mode of perception.

Let me take the first point first. "Non-Plan" was an attack on the architectural establishment, but it also reinforced some long-established architectural values. Take, for example, the opening passage which expresses frustration with Dorset County Council and their document on permissible styles of building. Their frustration is clear enough, and their solution extreme ("abolish planning"). But at the heart of their complaint lies an assumption of a natural state of affairs which will simply reassert itself if planners leave the built environment alone. "Nothing must be allowed simply to happen," they wrote, "No house can be allowed to be commonplace in the way that things just *are* commonplace" (Banham et al 1969: 435). Large parts of London, they continue, simply are commonplace in this way, unplanned but regarded with approval by planners.

The instinct to leave things be is generally conservative, as Barker suggests. The idea of naturalness presupposes the futility of change, or the possibility of human action. There is understood to be a natural order to things which cannot be overturned. The English aesthetic position that this relates to is the picturesque, most associated with two eighteenth century English philosophers Richard Payne Knight and Uvedale Price. Principally a set of formal values for viewing landscapes, it emphasised intricacy, formal variety, roughness, variation of texture, variation of light and shade, and irregularity (Price 1794–8). These were developed through the close observation of the existing scene. What Alexander Pope termed the *genius loci*, or genius of the place was an essential element that differentiated from other aesthetic modes (Pevsner 1964:181). It was essentially a visual aesthetic, whose values could not be transposed to any other sense, and it was facilitated by special equipment, especially the Claude Glass, a darkened mirror which the picturesque tourist could use to make a picture (by simple reflection) out of a view.

It was enormously influential and popular, becoming in one account "the universal mode of vision for the educated classes". (Watkin 1982: vii) However, it was, and is an exclusionary mode of perception that puts the viewer in a position of power. It provides, for example, a means of neutralising social of political conflict by aestheticising it. This is seen a particularly clearly in the way eighteenth and nineteenth century landscape painters represented the urban poor (for this argument developed in detail, see John Barrell's *The Dark Side of the Landscape*, 1982). Poverty could be made to seem a source of aesthetic pleasure for the privileged viewer, rather than a social or moral problem in need of a practical solution.

In the twentieth century the mode was revived in specifically architectural terms by the British journal the *Architectural Review*, in the polemical articles by its editor Hubert de Cronin Hastings, illustrated with appropriate drawings first by Gordon Cullen and then by Kenneth Browne. The urban picturesque favoured by the *Review* was called "townscape" and like the eighteenth century theory on which it was explicitly modelled, it was exclusively visual, and favoured formal irregularity. A certain amount of decay and disorder was to be encouraged, as was the sight of traditional forms of labour when it helped make a picturesque scene (Cullen 1961: 112–4). In the hands of the *Review* it provided a way of looking at existing urban landscapes, and these acted as models for future practice. The theory was outlined first in a de Cronin Hastings' editorial in 1949 (written under his usual pseudonym Ivor de Wolfe) and then Gordon Cullen's influential and popular book *Townscape* (de Wolfe 1949, Cullen 1961). The Festival of Britain (1951) staged on London's South Bank, which presented a picturesque version of the Modern Movement to the world, was the ideology of "townscape" realised on a grand scale.

Banham, who joined the permanent staff of the *Review* in 1952, regarded "townscape" as a failure of nerve that would lead to a "collapse in creative energy". A compromised Modernism, it had, he thought, little future (see Whiteley 2002: 11). But having said that, there are contradictions in his position which surface in "Non-Plan" as a residual sense of the picturesque. "Non-Plan" may superficially appear radical, but its assumption of a natural order in a site is practically the same as the picturesque *genius loci*, in both cases there being a deep aversion to idealism. Further, the elevation of popular taste parallels the interest in the vernacular characteristic of both the eighteenth century theorists of the picturesque and modern advocates of "townscape" (Banham, in fact was deeply concerned with the vernacular too. It just happened to be the American, rather than English, variety). Finally there are the illustrations, a mixture of specially taken photographs of neon signs at night by Christopher Riley, and a cartoon-like perspective view of a "non-plan" roadside scene in "Constable Country". These both belong in the tradition of "townscape". Cullen had been long interested in the visual potential of public advertising which he regarded, as in Piccadilly Circus or Time Square, as a free spectacle to be enjoyed by the sophisticated viewer, who, needless to say, had the education to remain unaffected by the commercial messages. The perspective drawing by Graham Percy is crudely done, but in its compositional and formal values (surprise, irregularity, and liveliness) belongs in the same tradition.

The picturesque is a mode of perception, and in the form of townscape it may even be a new mode of perception. De Cronin

Graham Percy: *Constable Country* (1969)

Hastings at the *Review* thought it was, and made great, if spurious, claims for its "radical" nature (de Wolfe 1949: 358). But it cannot, in my view, be avant-garde because it affirms the existing social order, and the avant-garde, however it is defined, must stand in some kind of critical relationship to its cultural context. "Non-Plan" offers a different way of looking at the world, but the difference is of viewpoint within an accepted frame — the frame itself remains the same.

Let me be more precise about this: what "Non-Plan" does is sub-stitute a post-war English working class perception of the world for the usual middle class professional one. That mode of perception already existed, as evidenced in the growing working class con-sumption of material goods, especially the developing taste for spectacular items like cars and suburban houses. Similarly, the activities Cedric Price imagined in his "Montagu Country" were principally the consumption of goods, services and leisure. The scale of this consumption, and the extremes of bad taste that it would, no doubt, involve were new, but none of this imagined anything but an extrapolation of existing consumer trends. It posed no threat to the deep order of things. "Non-Plan" proposes some new emphases, but leaves the terms of perception fundamentally unchanged. Planning, paradoxically, remains a matter of taste, that of one class' over another's.

"Non-Plan" is undoubtedly radical, but it is the radicalism of capital that it celebrates. Just as Marx marvelled at capital's ability to strip authority away from every social institution, so the authors of "Non-Plan" were awe-struck by its effect, if unfettered, on the built environment (Marx and Engels 1985: 82). All had been profoundly affected by the experience of Los Angeles. Banham had already written about it for the *Listener*, and was in the middle of writing a book which would appear in 1971 as *Los Angeles: the Architecture of Four Ecologies*. Banham's writings on the city are remarkable — he is the first European critic to take its architecture seriously — but his residual instinct for the picturesque leads him to judge it as a series of visual incidents. There is a bit of downtown here, an observation about freeway driving there, or elsewhere a discussion of the eccentricities of "dingbat" architecture and the Watts Towers. The city may appear formless on the surface, but has the requisite variety, roughness and irregularity to keep the picturesque tourist happy, of which Banham is one. On this latter-day Grand Tour everything and everyone is available for aesthetic consumption.

It is all good aesthetic fun and in this respect it closely resembles Robert Venturi and Denise Scott-Brown's book *Learning from Las Vegas* (Venturi and Scott-Brown 1972). The authors, at that stage teaching architecture at Yale took a group of students to Las Vegas in 1968 to investigate the actual nature of the city's built environment, rather than prescribe what it ought to look like from a conventional modernist position. Their premise, and their gaze upon the subject was picturesque — they remained essentially distanced from the city, which remains a kind of exotic specimen, a source of pictorial imagery for their own architecture. That they will return at the end of the book to Yale is never seriously in question: they are tourists after all. As in Banham's view of the city, the viewpoint is different from the norm, radically so, but the perceptual frame stays unchanged. Their picturesque mode means they affirm rather than critique the established order of things.

But can there be an avant-garde perception of the city? Can there be a mode of viewing that resists the picturesque, that provides a different perceptual frame? From within architecture it is unlikely that such a mode could develop given the compromised nature of that profession, the need to seek and maintain clients, to work within a body of legal restrictions, and to acknowledge, in the most material way, the surrounding culture. Given such restrictions as these, could "Non-Plan" have more closely approached the condition of the avant-garde?

In retrospect, one way that it might have done so would have been to engage more closely with the idea of formlessness, something which it at first seems to promise. Contemporary with "Non-Plan" there developed in the United States a rich body of ideas about the dissolution of form in sculpture. It arose in response to the changing condition of urban life, and which was explicitly anti-picturesque. The key figures are New York-based sculptors Robert Morris and Robert Smithson (both of whom wrote extensively) and critics sympathetic to their work. Their sculpture of the later 1960s involved large arrays of heterogeneous matter, arranged informally on the floor, which specifically lacked a single point of focus. There were superficial similarities to Jackson Pollock's later drip paintings, but these works could not be possessed in the same way, and they came with more theoretical baggage. For Morris, the works were explicitly about changing modes of perception. The new mode, with its large scale, and its resistance to traditional forms of composition, would envelop the viewer in a situation in which it was not clear where the work's limits lay. In the somewhat bleak essay that theorised this work, "Notes on Sculpture Part 4: Beyond Objects", Morris wrote of the need to make work that resisted commodification as image or object — by making a seemingly formless environment, an artist would maintain a critical relationship with the surrounding culture. To make an art of "chunks, particles, and slime" (Morris 1969: 54) was also a realistic means of representing a culture, which at that moment seemed to be falling apart (for a more detailed account see Williams 2000: 59–80). For Morris' friend, Robert Smithson, entropy was the key term — looking at the seemingly endless sprawl on the fringes of New York, he wondered in a series of witty, eclectic essays if there was any point in building anything of fixity when the city's natural condition was entropy. It was the artist's job to explore the entropic city, rather than attempt to resist it with monuments that Smithson saw as heroic but futile (Smithson 1966).

This sculptural engagement with formlessness was avant-garde in that it aimed at new modes of perception, rather than different viewpoints within an existing mode. It also clearly stood in critical relation to the culture that produced them. Transpose these ideas to the level of the city and it could bring about a radically different kind of urban pathology. Horizontal extension and temporariness might be advanced as the natural conditions of the city, rather than its unfortunate consequences.

But "Non-Plan" falls short of advocating the entropic city. In fact it imagines the urban less in terms of entropy than containment, its authors being at pains to show that it is an experiment, limited in space and time, and that even within the experimental zones, development can be controlled. The results of "Non-Plan" will not, its authors admit, look very different from the present environment. Peter Hall wrote of "Lawrence Country" that it would be "probably a pattern which intensified the present one, but without the planning rigmarole" (Banham et al 1969: 438). And Banham's contemporaneous project on Los Angeles shows deep resistance to entropy from the beginning, asserting that Los Angeles has a "comprehensible, even consistent quality to its built form" (Banham 1971: 21). Why this backing away, this retrenchment? Despite "Non-Plan's" title, and the superficial drama of its demands, its aims were actually local and modest. The pretext was a specifically English one, the failure of the local planning system to be anything other than restrictive, a response to what Barker concludes is "the English vice of bossiness" (Hughes and Sadler: 7). It has the look of an architectural avant-garde, but in fact is a form of radical pragmatism. The liberatory promise of "Non-Plan" must be realised elsewhere.

BIBLIOGRAPHY

Banham, Reyner

    1960   *Theory and Design in the First Machine Age*. New York: Praeger.

    1971   *Los Angeles: The Architecture of Four Ecologies*. London: Penguin.

1996   *A Critic Writes: Essays by Reyner Banham selected by Mary Banham, Paul Barker, Sutherland Lyall and Cedric Price.* Berkeley and Los Angeles: University of California Press.

Banham, Reyner and P. Barker, P. Hall, C. Price
1969   "Non-Plan: An Experiment in Freedom". In: *New Society*, 20 March, 435–43.

Bürger, Peter
1984   *Theory of the Avant-Garde.* Minneapolis: University of Minnesota Press.

Cullen, G.
1961   *Townscape.* London: Architectural Press.

Crow, T.
1996   *Modern Art in the Common Culture.* New Haven and London: Yale University Press.

Greenberg, C.
1939   "Avant-Garde and Kitsch". In: *Partisan Review*, VI, 6, Fall, 34–49.

Hall, P.
1996   *Cities of Tomorrow.* Oxford: Blackwell.

Hughes, Jonathan and Simon Sadler
2000   *Non-Plan: Essays on Freedom, Participation and Change in Modern Architecture and Urbanism.* London, Architectural Press.

Lynch, Kevin
1960   *The Image of the City.* Cambridge (Mass.) and London, MIT Press.

Marcuse, Herbert
1956   *Eros and Civilization: a Philosophical Inquiry into Freud.* London: Routledge.

Marx, Karl and Friedrich Engels
1985   *The Communist Manifesto with an introduction by A. J. P. Taylor.* London: Penguin.

Morris, R.
1969   "Notes on Sculpture Part 4: Beyond Objects". In: *Artforum* 7, 8 (April), 50–4.

Orton, F. and G. Pollock
    1996   *Avant-Gardes and Partisans Reviewed.* Manchester: Manchester University Press.

Pevsner, N.
    1964   *The Englishness of English Art : an Expanded and Annotated Version of the Reith Lectures Broadcast in October and November 1955.* London: Penguin.

Price, U.
    1794–8   *An Essay on the Picturesque as Compared with the Sublime and the Beautiful.* London.

Smithson, R.
    1966   "Entropy and the New Monuments". In: *Artforum*, 5, 10 (June), 26–31.

Tafuri, M.
    1976   *Architecture and Utopia: Design and Capitalist Development.* Cambridge (Mass.) and London: MIT Press.

Venturi, Robert and Denise Scott-Brown
    1972   *Learning from Las Vegas (revised).* Cambridge (Mass.) and London: MIT Press.

Watkin, David
    1982   *The English Vision : the Picturesque in Architecture, Landscape and Garden Design.* London: Murray.

Whiteley, N.
    2002   *Reyner Banham: Historian of the Immediate Future.* Cambridge (Mass.) and London: MIT Press.

De Wolfe, I.
    1949   "Townscape". In: *Architectural Review*, CVI, 636, December, 363–74.

Williams, Richard
    2000   *After Modern Sculpture: Art in the United Sates and Europe 1965–70.* Manchester: Manchester University Press.

VI.

CROSSING THE GENRES

Montage in the Arts: A Reassessment

JENNIFER VALCKE

The term "montage" has been used to refer to the formal principle at work in many of the most distinctive cultural products of the early twentieth century. These include the dada images of George Grosz, John Heartfield, Hannah Höch and Raoul Hausmann; the fragmented literary narratives of Dos Passos's *Manhattan Transfer* and Döblin's *Berlin Alexanderplatz*; the cinematic editing techniques of Dziga Vertov, Sergei Eisenstein and Walter Ruttmann; the episodic theatrical structure of Ernst Toller's *Trotz Alledem*; the multi-layered exhibition spaces conceived by El Lissitsky and Herbert Bayer; and the multiple exposure photographs of Edward Steichen, to name just a few. The technique of montage is an aesthetic practice of painting, literature, photography and film that suggests a new way of seeing and perceiving the world. Through images that at times integrate text, often conjure unreal space, and always include a degree of narrative breakdown, the technique of montage invokes the discontinuous and the ruptured as symbols of our century. At the same time montage is seen as the epitome of avant-garde art. Jochen Schulte-Sasse therefore states in his introduction to Peter Bürger's *Theory of the Avant-Garde* that "the success of any theory of the avant-garde can be measured on how convincingly it can anchor the avant-garde formal principle of the collage and montage" (Bürger

1984: xxxix). Montage has become a symptomatic and formal structural precept of artistic development since the end of the undisputed supremacy of Renaissance perspective. While highlighting images with radical distortions of scale, it is argued that montage practice seeks not merely to represent the real, but also to extend the idea of fragmentation to the real. Montage offers a kaleidoscopic expanded vision which, by collapsing many views into one, suggests an experience of unfolding time. In effect, montage replaces the image of a continuous life glimpsed through a window frame — the heritage of the fine arts since the Renaissance — with an image or set of re-assembled images that reflect a fast-paced, multi-faceted reality. Klaus Honnef, in his essay *Symbolic Form as a Vivid Cognitive Principle: An Essay on Montage*, states: "This new space is a mixture of geometry and symbolic representation, where technological knowledge is the tool of individual and collective beliefs" (Pachnicke and Honnef 1992: 53). Montage thus serves as a sign of an old world shattered and a new world in construction, of the fragmentation of the once-reigning unities of life and an everyday reality that has suddenly burst the frame of experience.

Bürger, whose *Theory of the Avant-Garde* has moulded our perception of the historical avant-garde for the past two decades, recognises the significance of theorising montage as a formal precept because "without the avant-gardist notion of montage numerous realms of contemporary aesthetic experience would be inaccessible" (1981: 22). Surprisingly, however, this is where Bürger's theoretical framework fails most spectacularly. Although his *Theory of the Avant-Garde* establishes an integrating framework and a valuable set of categories for many avant-garde art practices, his assessment of montage clearly calls for a re-evaluation of the technique. Bürger's conception of montage suffers from three major problems: firstly, it confuses the technique of montage with that of collage; secondly, the discussion of photomontage revolves around John Heartfield's political works of the 1930s, works no longer concerned with the avant-gardist conception of art; and thirdly, Bürger does not take into account the importance technological innovations had in the elaboration of a new concept of artistic production, thus disavowing the crucial importance of photomontage and film montage.

It should be emphasised at the outset that the visual devices employed in montage in the early decades of the twentieth century represented no absolute novelty; in many cases they predate the appearance of photography itself. As early as 1840, for example, British caricaturists employed the mismatching of heads and bodies for comic effect. By the 1850s and 60s, there appears in the well-known work of such professional artist-photographers as H.P. Robinson and O.G. Rejlander the practice of combination printing — the making of a single photographic print from a number of different negatives. These were all fairly limited and specialised practices, however. As these precedents suggest, the later disputes among figures like George Grosz, John Heartfield, Raoul Hausmann and Hannah Höch about who "invented" photomontage should be understood as having mainly to do with the introduction of a specifically avant-gardist visual idiom into montage. In this regard, the wide artistic interest awakened by the cubist collage techniques pioneered by Picasso and Braque since 1912, as well as the influential adaptations of collage by the Italian futurists and the early Russian avant-gardists, should also be seen as crucial sources for the subsequent development of photomontage. One result of this mixed ancestry of photomontage has been a lasting confusion of terminology that attempts to make general formal distinctions between *papier collé*, *Klebebild*, *Fotoklebebild*, *Wirklichkeitsausschnitt*, photocollage and photomontage, all of which yields little in the way of helpful clarification.

Bürger also seems to suffer from the same confusion when he states that "montage first emerges in connection with cubism" (1984: 73). This misconception is most likely due to the fact that collage and montage — as well as filmic montage — share the common technique of cutting and gluing as the main artistic procedure in structuring the work of art. While emphasising the common construction principle of several of the new avant-garde art forms, Dietrich Scheunemann, in his essay on *Montage in Theatre and Film*, also points to the differences between them, the different materials and media being used:

> Eisenstein was not the first to [...] practice such an alternative mode of assembling a work of art out of various independent elements [montage]. One can find correspondences in the technique of "collage" which the cubist painters developed by inserting a piece of oil-cloth, a strip of wall-paper or coloured

papers into their pictures. The Dadaists [...] composed their pictures with the help of, or completely out of, photo-bits [...] Kurt Schwitters preferred to call his collections of old buttons and tram-tickets, wheels and wooden strips, wires and strings "assemblage". Collage, montage, assemblage are just three ways of referring to the same constructive principle of artistic production which emerged in various art forms of the avant-garde since 1912. (1991: 114)

The constructive principle of which Scheunemann speaks is that of fragmentation and multi-perspectival space. Yet, Bürger exemplifies his theory of montage in terms of "art and life", using Picasso's *Still Life with Chair Caning* (1912) as the prime example of the technique: "The selection of a piece of woven basket that Picasso glues on a canvas may very well serve some compositional intent. But as a piece of woven basket, it remains a reality fragment that is inserted into the painting tel quel, without substantive modification" (1984: 77–78). Bürger confuses the piece of oilcloth, whose design shows a photographic imitation of chair caning, for a genuine piece of "woven basket". This has dramatic consequences in relation to Bürger's understanding of Picasso's intent, and has painful ramifications when considering the *materiality* of art production. Indeed, instead of inserting a piece of "reality" into his composition, Picasso's interest focused on the interplay between photographic imitation and a multi-faceted notation of objects. Around the piece of oilcloth imitating chair caning, Picasso painted wooden strips to enhance the illusion of a piece of furniture. These *trompe-l'oeil* effects strive to depict different views simultaneously, resulting in compositions of a many-sided, unreal pictorial space; not, as Bürger puts it, to insert "reality fragments into the work of art" (1984: 78).

For the purpose of this paper, a more useful starting point is that provided by the German art historian Franz Roh in 1925. Roh described montage as a precarious synthesis of the two most important tendencies in modern visual culture: those of extreme fantasy and extreme sobriety, or put another way, the pictorial combination of avant-gardist abstraction and the realism of photographic fragments (1925: 45–6). Equally helpful is Sergei Tretiakov's definition of photomontage, which he advanced in the 1930s. Writing about John Heartfield, Tretiakov proposed that photomontage begins whenever there is a conscious alteration of the obvious first sense of a photograph — by combining two or more images, by joining drawing and graphic shapes to the photograph, by adding a significant spot of colour, or by adding a written text (Tretyakov 1936, in Siepmann 1977: 178). Photomontage thus seems to be a practice that includes photography as one of the materials of a composite image, complemented by planes, lines, cut-outs, and *objets trouvés*, and incorporating the printing of two superimposed negatives. The photomontage can then be photographed and printed, thus producing a flat surface that eliminates the unevenness of the cut-out of collage. Instead of defining montage with the help of cubist collage it thus seems more appropriate to differentiate both in terms of the materials that they use and the effects that they achieve. For Dawn Ades it is even clear that the dadaist photomontage was invented in opposition to collage: "The name [photomontage] was chosen," she writes, "to distance the two activities, and Dada recognized a very different potential in the new technique" (1976: 15). One of the most important potentials was to divert the photograph from what it naturally seems to say, and to underscore the need for the viewer's active reading of the image.

When dealing with photomontage, Bürger analyses two of John Heartfield's photomontages: *Adolf — the Superman — Who Swallows Gold and Spouts Junk* (1932) and *Germany is Still Not Lost!* (1932). Both of these works were produced in the 1930s, when Heartfield's work was no longer concerned with avant-garde art, when indeed dada was well and truly over. Heartfield was now producing political art, and as Raoul Hausmann points out in his essay *Peinture nouvelle et photomontage*:

> The technique of photomontage markedly simplified itself according to its field of implementation. Above all its area of implementation is political propaganda and commercial advertisement. The clarity called for by political or commercial slogans will increasingly influence its capacity to counterbalance the most startling contrasts, and depart from the whims of early times. (1958: 48–49, trans J.V.)

Indeed, when Heartfield's photomontages became politicised, form became subservient to content. The clear conveyance of the political message became all-important, and experimentation with form, the

essential characteristic of avant-garde photomontage, was abandoned.

Bürger's analysis of photomontage focuses exclusively on
Heartfield's political work in the 1930s. It shows no interest in the
genuine dadaist photomontage of the years 1920 to 1924. The work
of Raoul Hausmann, Hannah Höch, George Grosz, Heartfield's earlier work, the photomontages of Man Ray and Max Ernst and of the
Russians Alexander Rodchenko and El Lissitsky are simply over-
looked. One of the earliest examples of the dadaist photomontage is
Hausmann's *Dada-Cino* (1920), which was exhibited at the First
International Dada Fair in 1920. It is a montage of cut-out photographs, newspaper bits, advertisements and typography with a
number of themes and allusions that recur throughout Hausmann's
subsequent work: the birth of dada (Hausmann insists on the mechanical functions of the body: gestation, birth, brains), fashion and
elegance (shoes, suits), the New World and war. In *Dada-Cino* and
Syntetisches Cino der Malerei (1918), one can notice Hausmann's
quest for synthetic film: although the photomontage is static, the
unique circular construction provides an impression of movement.
This explains why Hausmann described photomontage as "a motionless moving picture" (Richter 1965: 118), and why he
retrospectively called photomontage "static film" in an article published in the journal *A bis Z* of May 1931. Other photomontages
illustrate the intrinsic link between photomontage and film, such as
Paul Citroen's 1923 *Metropolis* series or George Grosz's and John
Heartfield's *Leben und Treiben in Universal-City um 12Uhr 5 mit-
tags* (1919). The latter is a montage composed of photographic
fragments: icons of technology and industry feature among direct
references to Hollywood and cinema. Under this light, photomontage can be understood as an anticipation of effects that the cinema
was about to develop. In the early phases of its development, photomontage strenuously worked towards effects that later were
attained by film. Walter Benjamin supports this point by stating that
"Dadaism attempted to create by pictorial — and literary — means
the effect which the public seeks in film" (1973: 230).

Although Bürger recognises montage as an artistic principle in
painting, he describes montage in film as a "basic technical procedure. It is not a specifically artistic technique, but one that lies in the
medium" (1984: 73). The distinction between montage in painting

and montage in film reveals itself to be misguided in categorical terms, but also if one takes into account that by the 1920s cinema had become a powerfully influential art. Its reverberations were felt in theatre, in literature, in art, in photography, as observed by Hans Richter: "Roads lead from painting to film and from film back to art, from abstract art, cubism, dadaism, surrealism [...]. Film was not only a region for a painter's experiments, but a part of modern art, the expression of a new total experience" (1965: 38). Film was suddenly thrust forward as the example to be followed by other media: "Even before montage techniques were fully unfolded as the film's aesthetic device, the traditional art forms of literature and theatre adopted [cinema] and anticipated its most favourable effects" (Scheunemann 1991: 116). Bürger's argument appears particularly short-sighted in the light of the practice and theories of avant-garde cinema from the works of Walter Ruttmann and Man Ray to the works of Sergei Eisenstein and Dziga Vertov, in which montage became the dominant technique of composition, or in Eisenstein's words "the axiom", of the culture of cinema. When Bürger notes that "within the frame of a theory of the avant-garde, the use to which film puts the concept [of montage] cannot become relevant because it is part and parcel of the medium", he fails to recognise that cinematic montage is not merely a technical operation inherent to filmmaking but also a creative principle, a way of thinking, a way of *conceiving* films by associating images. This fragmentary dimension of film aesthetics is a feature that it shares with other contemporary art forms.

Bürger shrinks from an investigation of photomontage and film because of their intrinsic link with photography. He insists on separating the realm of technology from that of art, and refuses to acknowledge the importance the advent of photography and technological reproduction played in the development of the new concept of art production. The mutual penetration of art and technology is precisely one of the most important revolutionary functions of photomontage and film; nothing indicates more strikingly that art has left the realm of *beautiful semblance,* previously assumed to be the only sphere in which it could thrive. At the very moment when technology, in the guise of photography, challenged the limits of art, the mimetic function of art was abandoned. André Breton wrote: "The invention of photography has dealt a mortal blow to the old modes of expression" (Scharf 1968: 253). Because they are permeable, art's boundaries are open to influence from other forms and are in a state of constant change. Hannah Höch explains that the main aim of photomontage was to "integrate objects from the world of machines and industry in the world of art" (Scharf 1968: 281). Her claim is supported by Walter Benjamin, who wrote in his essay *The Work of Art in the Age of Technological reproduction* that the invention of technological reproduction caused "the most profound change in the impact [of works of art] upon the public" by devaluing traditional categories of art — while at the same time establishing "a place of its own among the artistic processes" (1973: 213–214).

It becomes evident that Bürger, in his dismissal of photomontage and film because of their intrinsic link with photography, fell prone to the dispute opposing photography as art. Instead of realising that photography marked a new beginning that rendered obsolete categories of art and aesthetics, Bürger attacks photomontage and film on the terrain of art. This strategy radically avoids the basic question raised by Benjamin of "whether the invention of photography had not transformed the very nature of art" (1973: 220). Indeed, the introduction of photography as discourse fragment into an artistic form does not strip it of all meaning; on the contrary, it invests it with new signification: it has become available for an infinity of messages, just like a letter is available to form, in association with other letters, an infinity of words. Benjamin Buchloh adds: "The procedure of montage is one in which all allegorical principles are executed: appropriation and depletion of meaning, fragmentation and dialectical juxtaposition of fragments, and separation of signifier and signified" (1982: 44). An analogous phenomenon can be observed in film montage, which is, without a doubt, at the origin of the rapid expansion of photomontage and the new form it takes in the 1920s. It was the Russian filmmaker Lev Kuleshov who through his famous experiment showed that the effect obtained through the montage of two shots is not reducible to the apparent content of these shots.

In France, the term *montage* entered filmic vocabulary as early as the 1910s, defined as the simple end-to-end joining of disparate elements or as a sequence of tableaux. It was only at the end of this decade that the meaning of the word expanded in conjunction with the evolution of cinematic practices. From then on, *montage* dealt with the last stage of the elaboration of a film, the stage at which the shot elements are synthesised into a whole. This synthesis consists of three different operations: *cutting*, the material operation of cutting and pasting; *editing*, the organisation of visual and sound elements which gives the film its true face; and *montage*, the relation between sequences from an essentially aesthetic and semiological perspective. Dziga Vertov's *Man With a Movie Camera* (1929) epitomises this technique. Anyone who has seen the film will remember a number of episodes attesting to shifts in street traffic with all sorts of objects shifting in various directions of movement, and where the structure of movement goes not only further toward the horizon but also develops vertically. Vertov magnificently understood the idea or the task of the new montage. The film de-objectifies the city centre. Everything results from shifts, everything comes unexpectedly. Vertov does not attempt to analyse or justify the machine; rather he shows motion itself, dynamism itself. This is quite different from the city symphony by Walter Ruttmann. Ruttmann's *Berlin: Symphony of a Great City* (1927) essentially shows the development of the dynamic from a "symphonic" perspective: an initial moment of static rest builds to a high point of tension. As Vsevolod Pudovkin describes:

> The film seems to begin with interesting landscape pictures seen from the window of a train; but they yield to the rhythmic and hypnotic turning of the wheels, and certain barely visible optical images light up on screen. Before the viewers know it, they have arrived in Berlin. The virtual starting point is a tunnel in the morning, but this gives way to masses of people hurrying to work. Their movement is continual and is set once again to a special rhythm… [Ruttmann's] purpose is not to present Berlin but the *life* in Berlin. Even short, isolated shots which could arouse the suspicion of mere presentation turns out to be of strict rhythmical design. (Schobert 1989: 86)

Today montage is unanimously considered not only an essential element of cinematic language but also its most specific element. Montage is also a creative process, a way of thinking, a way of conceiving art through an association of images. According to Rosalind Krauss, montage revealed itself to be *the* "structuring principle of spacing" (Buchloh 1982: 56). Without an extended scope of analysis, the full importance of montage to avant-garde art will not be understood.

BIBLIOGRAPHY

Ades, Dawn
    1976   *Photomontage*. London: Thames and Hudson.

Benjamin, Walter
    1973b   "The Work of Art in the Age of Mechanical Reproduction". In: Benjamin, *Illuminations*. London: Fontana, 219-253.

Buchloh, Benjamin
    1982   "Allegorical Procedures: Appropriation and Montage in Contemporary Art". In: *Artforum*, September 1982.

Bürger, Peter
    1981   "The Significance of the Avant-Garde for Contemporary Aesthetics: A Reply to Jürgen Habermas". In: *New German Critique*, number 22, Winter 1981.

    1984   *Theory of the Avant-Garde*. Minneapolis: University of Minnesota Press.

Hausmann, Raoul
    1958   "Peinture nouvelle et photomontage". In : *Dada*. Paris: Editions le Terrain Vague.

Honnef, Klaus
    1992   "Symbolic Form as a Vivid Cognitive Principle: An Essay on Montage". In: Peter Pachnicke and Klaus Honnef (eds.), *John Heartfield*. New York: Harry N Abrams, 49-64.

Richter, Hans
    1965   *Dada Art and Anti-Art*. London : Thames and Hudson.

    1965   *Hans Richter*. Neuchatel: Editions du Griffon.

Roh, Franz
    1925   *Nachexpressionismus*. Leipzig: Klinckhardt   und Biermann.

Scharf, Aaron
    1968   *Art and Photography*. London: Penguin Books.

Scheunemann, Dietrich

1991   Montage in Theatre and Film: Observations on Eisenstein and Brecht. In: *Avant Garde*, vol. 5/6, 109–135.

Schobert, Walter

1989   *Der deutsche Avant-Garde Film der 20er Jahre*. Munich: Goethe-Institut.

Tretiakov, Sergei

1977   "John Heartfield montiert". In: Eckard Siepmann, *Montage: John Heartfield*. Berlin: Elefanten Press Galerie, 168-175.

Means and Metaphors of Change: Technology and the Danish Avant-Garde of the 1960s

TANIA ØRUM

This paper addresses the question of the relation between the avant garde and the technological development in the post-war period. It focuses on the Experimental School of Art, which is the central group of avant-garde artists in Denmark in the 1960s, and discusses the relative importance of technological change and aesthetic ideas.

I

The Experimental School of Art, often referred to simply as the Ex School, was founded in 1961 as an independent art school, unconnected to the official education at the Royal Academy of Fine Arts in Copenhagen. Organised teaching was, however, soon abandoned as the Ex-School turned into a collective work place. Quite a lot of young artists passed through the Experimental School in the early days, but the nucleus was a group of 6–8 painters and sculptors plus an art historian, Troels Andersen, who was the first Western historian permitted to study the Russian avant-garde in the Soviet Union and thus transmitted an important piece of avant-garde history to the Danish post-war avant-garde (Andersen 1963,1967). The Russian background pops up as a constant frame of reference in the early writings of the Ex-School group and in fact proved crucial for their specific outlook and optics: They perceived for instance the strong impulses from American minimalism, pop art and happening through the filter of Russian avant-garde concepts.

This small group of self-educated visual artists turned into an avant-garde movement (in Bürger's sense) as they were joined in the early sixties by writers, composers, an architect, and in the late sixties by filmmakers and political activists — and so became a cross-aesthetic experimental group working across genres, styles and art forms as well as across the boundaries dividing art and life, aesthetic and political action. The Ex-School circle was characterised by great stylistic and individual heterogeneity, but held together by dynamic (often quite harsh and heated) discussions, collaborative efforts and collective experiments. Through these discussions and collaborations a common aesthetic outlook or programme was generated, which was also a view of life or a code of ethics. And this aesthetic programme had its own logic, leading the Ex-School group on from the formal and material experiments of the early sixties to the artistic-political actions of the late sixties and early seventies. As the art critic Thomas Crow has rightly observed in *The Rise of the Sixties*, in the context of the 1960s

> every decision that an artist might make was henceforth open to question on principles that might as readily be ethical, political, or bearing on fundamental questions of honesty and falsehood in representation; every serious artistic initiative became a charged proposition about the nature and limits of art itself. (Crow 1996: 11)

Having worked their way through the experiments of the 20th century, historically as well as personally, as part of the Ex-School's self-organised education programme, these artist found themselves in a zero situation where every kind of gesture, material and technique had lost its grounding in a metaphysical or historical value system. The artist was thus free to use any kind of material and move into any sphere of life, as long as it was an open-ended process.

One of the participants, the writer Erik Thygesen, once remarked that the entire development of the Ex-School from the early sixties into the seventies (i.e. the avant-garde period) could be seen as a response to contemporary technological developments. I think this is largely true, and I shall try to develop this relation between avant-garde and technology in the following.

In keeping with the general outlook just briefly sketched, the avant-garde of the sixties tended to take a positive view of modernity and new technologies. There was, indeed, a certain fascination with new technological developments and theories — ranging from the expanding mass media as heralded by Marshall McLuhan to cybernetics, information theory and thermodynamics — a fascination which was part of the whole cultural context in this period. In the 1960s there was a definite sense of living in an era of irreversible change, an at times ecstatic or almost apocalyptic sense of rupture or even revolution, which the avant-garde came to share with other youth groups of the sixties, whether they were involved in the new youth culture, the many groupings of the new left or the student revolt. And this sense of change, which in the sixties could still be measured against a memory of greater stability and against the opposition of a conservative cultural establishment, was undoubtedly related to the technological development.

The first issue of the journal *ta'* (take), which launched the larger cross-aesthetic group in 1967, characteristically carried an editorial announcing a broadening of cultural perspectives (to include several arts and intermedia experiments as well as "low" cultural phenomena such as pop music, pulp literature, television and the mass media) and a programmatic article heralding new concepts of a mobile subject in a changing world. The feeling that stable traditional hierarchies of knowledge, art, subjectivity and society were rapidly being replaced by more flexible and temporary constructions is almost invariably related to the appearance of new media and technologies in the writings of the avant-garde of the 1960s. The changes brought about by the technological, social, economic and educational restructuring of the post-war period, which have often been discussed under the heading of "post-modernity", started making themselves felt in the 1960s. They were registered by the avant-garde not only as changes requiring new artistic strategies, but as fundamental shifts in concepts of identity, human relations and modes of perception.

II.

The relation between avant-garde and technology and the implications of the technological fascination felt by many avant-gardists in the sixties may be seen for instance in a review of the first volume of concrete poetry by Hans-Jørgen Nielsen (*at det at*, 1965) written by the Swedish avant-garde novelist and critic Torsten Ekbom under the heading "New media — new poetry". According to Ekbom, concrete poetry should be viewed in the context that "we live in a transitional age between a mechanical and an electronic civilisation". We are, so he argues with reference to Marshall McLuhan's influential book *Understanding Media*, "moving towards a visual-auditive civilisation, characterised by instant communication and direct visual-auditive contact with people and societies all over the globe." This globalisation implies, as Ekbom points out, a complex reorientation process:

> we had to get used to events on the other side of the globe being of immediate relevance for us (the Vietnam debate is inconceivable without electronic mass communication). The artists, too, have to adjust to this development. (Ekbom 1966)

As McLuhan notes, there is, however, little awareness of the radical psychological, social and political changes which take place in society when new media are introduced. McLuhan suggests that artists are the first people to react to the changes, but Ekbom modifies this by arguing that

> it would be more correct to say a few avant-gardists. If the notion of avant-gardism is still relevant, it would be in this context. It is the artists who will have to teach us how the media function, either by using the old media in a new way, by creating hybrid forms between different media or by working directly with the new media. (Ekbom 1966)

Ekbom finds this kind of artistic sensitivity in "the concrete poetry appearing exactly as the electronic media are pushing the written page towards the periphery" — just as abstract painting emerged at the moment when photography appeared. He points to Hans-Jørgen Nielsen's concrete poetry as "an advanced example of how poetry that has abandoned the Gutenberg tradition may look. Traditional aesthetic standards have no relevance to this poetry. But it may be grasped from the perspective of Marshall McLuhan." Ekbom is referring here to McLuhan's famous dictum "The medium is the message", i.e. the medium is not just a neutral transmission channel through which the contents of the message is conveyed, on the contrary the medium imposes new conditions which largely determine the kind of message sent.

A poet who insists that "language is the message" thus need not be an aestheticising "purist" who turns his back on society and politics, Ekbom goes on to argue. Such criticism levelled at concrete poetry confirms the general unawareness of the effects of new media pointed out by McLuhan. In popular aesthetic discussions, Ekbom says, content is always the main thing, while formal experiments are seen as more or less irrelevant.

> But it is the formal experiments which challenge the conventions of the medium and thus break with customary ways of thinking and habitual psychological patterns. So to challenge language is to challenge a social convention and all the value judgements inherent in this convention […] The expression (the content, the message) thus inheres in language, in the play with linguistic conventions. To break up the syntax for instance equals breaking with the rationalism and the rigid conception of time and space which according to McLuhan go with the printing principles of Gutenberg. To *describe* this new world picture is only a half measure, since through the medium you inevitably conserve the concept of reality you raise doubt about. (Ekbom 1966)

Poems like "efter før efter" (after before after)

```
efter   før   efter
efter         efter   efter
efter   før                   før
        før   efter
        før                   før
```

therefore demonstrate in Ekbom's view "not feelings or moods but the mechanisms of the medium", in this instance, as he says,

> by making syntax represent the spatial relations which are simultaneously described. The texts are quite de-individualised,

> like a programming code for a computer. Nielsen deliberately abstains from all personal expression. [...] After the romantic individualism of the Gutenberg epoch follows fragmented, machine-made information. (Ekbom 1966)

Torsten Ekbom's review is a fairly characteristic example of a widespread feeling in the mid-sixties of standing on the threshhold of a new era, marked by technological innovation and change. From this perspective the formal experiments of the avant-garde of the 1960s represent a much larger cultural and historical shift. Looking back to-day, it is indeed obvious that much of what goes on in the avant-garde of the 1960s anticipates broader lines of development in the modern world — if not exactly in the way envisioned then.

From this example I would like to return to the artistic development linking the Ex-School more specifically to contemporary technology. My scope here permits me only a brief outline.

III.

The Experimental School of Art started out in 1961 and 1962 with experiments in etching. Some of the more radical experiments were carried out by Paul Gernes, who made a series of etchings produced by applying 100 hammer strokes to each graphic sheet, and another series for which the sheets were left in the street for cars to drive over and leave their tyre marks on. The rather beautiful etchings consist of the accidental patterns resulting from these procedures. When off-set printing became available in the second half of the sixties, Ex-School members turned from etchings to producing posters, handbills, newsletters, journals and books and increasingly used photography. The use of these media was often an integral part of the collaboration between members of the avant-garde (especially the sculptor and performance artist Bjørn Nørgaard) and the various youth movements involved in critical and subversive activities and attempts to form alternative communities in the years 1967–1972. These printing techniques also signal the move from the garage and gallery exhibitions of the art world (however limited, unrecognised or shabby) to demonstrations, art and art-political actions, alternative life styles and political organisations in a larger social arena.

The journals are an important forum for cross-aesthetic collaboration, discussion and experiments. They should be considered principal avant-garde works of the Ex-School group, comparable to the
manifestos of the historical avant-gardes. Besides, they are among
the more durable works. Many other individual and collective avant-
garde works from the sixties were thrown out or otherwise de-
stroyed, many of them even without previous photographic documentation since the experimental process was considered more important than the product. But most of the journals still exist to-day.
Leafing though these publications in chronological order, one may
see how forms of expression change as the off-set printing process
offers technical possibilities of writing and drawing across the
printed texts and pictures, cutting out and pasting in pictures and
other collage elements etc. — techniques which were new and exciting then, but are nowadays available to anyone as ready-made
software programmes. The respectable printed matter (such as the
journal *ta'*) meant to launch the group in the cultural arena in the
mid-sixties and published by regular publishing houses, although
open to playful experiments unsual in publishing to-day — was replaced in the late sixties by self-made publications (such as the al-
most-daily newsletter *Hætsjj,* 1968–70) or plastic bags (the art journal *Ta'box,* 1969–70) filled with contributions from the Ex-School
circle, ranging from texts and pictures to cakes, fir cones and as-
sorted small objects.

  The cheap printing techniques aroused considerable enthusiasm
and encouraged the production of several artist's books, issued in a
few copies by the artist himself and sometimes reprinted by publishing houses in experimental editions. The easily accessible off-set
printing process was seen as facilitating democratic access to publishing, so for the 200 years' anniversary of the exhibition building
Charlottenborg in the summer of 1968, a small printing press was
established as part of the exhibition (along with Paul Gernes' public
showers and photo lab where everyone was invited to sit down and
have their behinds photographed). This printing press issued daily
bulletins, posters and statements by the artists involved, but was also
open to anyone in the public who wanted to print or distribute messages or pictures, thus demonstrating the ideal possibilites of
interactive communication made possible by new technology and
envisioned as part of a new society. In fact, one of the smaller

groups branching off from the Ex-School circle in the beginning of
the 1970s in order to do more political and collective work ended up
establishing themselves as a printing firm, Eksskolens Trykkeri,
which still exists to-day as an ordinary co-operative business, but
was meant originally to serve as a utopian model for new ways of
organising work, leisure and communal living.

When cheap tape recorders became available, members of the
Ex-School group moved into sound experiments. The group published a series of tapes in 1969 containing a mixture of sound recordings from performances (for instance by Beuys and Herman de
Vries), talks on various subjects, a so-called "novel in time" (by Erik
Thygesen), and several compositions by Henning Christiansen,
sometimes played on self-made instruments, toy instruments or
kitchen utensils, or conceptual compositions like for instance "I am
no. 1, I am no. 2...", created for one of the early happening sessions
in 1965, which keeps counting for two days. Really advanced text-
and-sound-experiments, however, still required expensive technical
facilities available only with professional assistance from Radio
Denmark in order to produce interesting results. In the advanced
sound studios, however, avant-garde experimentation is often difficult, the machinery is too expensive to play with, and technical specialists take over, giving machinery priority over experiment. These
days sampling is simple and electronic recordings can easily be
made at home with available standard technology. But in the 1960s
concrete music, sound poetry or collage pieces produced outside the
electronic studios often had to be performed manually or with the
help of simple tape-recorded sequences to be switched off and on
during the performance.

Some members of the Ex-School, Erik Thygesen for instance,
move on from formal sound experiments to media experiments involving interactive, democratic access to national radio and the
establishment of local or alternative radio stations.

With the introduction of small, cheap super 8 cameras which
were easy to operate, the group around the Ex-School and the journal *ta'* joined with actors, photographers and film directors to form
the film association ABCinema in 1968. Now people from all the
arts began making, showing and distributing films. The small port-
able cameras meant that filmmakers could move around more freely,
and the highly specialised and hierarchical organisation in the film

industry, which made traditional film so expensive and inaccessible, could be dispensed with. The technical development thus made it possible to use the camera much more directly, "like a pen", so the slogan went — without going though the process of first producing a script, then shooting the film and finally editing.

The result was film exploring the possibilities of the medium and very often abandoning what was seen as the overly "literary" reliance on a previous script. Many sculptors and painters agreed with Per Kirkeby's dictum that "film is pictures" and treated film as a primarily visual medium, as painting in motion, or a chance to carry out experiments of "seeing differently" by testing the technical possibilities of the camera. Poets like Jørgen Leth and others made films trying out varying combinations of picture, sound and text. While people from the film and music world explored the effects of coordinating several cameras to form a "film band", making use of parallel or contrasting images like musical instruments or trying to create a continuous view of 360 degrees. Many members of AB-Cinema took their cameras with them everywhere, documenting hitherto unfilmed activities of everyday life or art blending into political actions.

Many of these films were produced under primitive circumstances: The standard 8 mm films of 3 minutes' duration were "cut" in the camera, sent out to be developed and then glued together to form a longer sequence. And experiments also went on as films were shown several at a time, accompanied by music and very often in rooms outside the cinema, thus permitting what was seen as more democratic ways of viewing, or turning the films into parts of an environment through which the audience was free to move. The best of these films, for instance those by the poet and filmmaker Jørgen Leth, still look surprisingly fresh and experimental compared to most recent films.

To-day's state support system for films in Denmark and the open workshops intended to provide public access to filmmaking date back to principles introduced by ABCinema. And the present wave of successful Danish so-called "dogma films" (i.e. simple, cheap films) by Lars von Trier and others, although much more conventional, owe much to these experimental films of the late sixties. But the ideas of democratic access to filmmaking promoted by the avant-garde filmmakers of the 1960s were not technically realised until the much later introduction of the modern video cameras, computer editing and dvd techniques which enable everyone to make their own movies. And the attempts by the avant-garde of the 1960s to make interactive use of communication channels as diverse as film, radio and television, art exhibitions and concerts or to include people in the planning and construction of their own houses, playgrounds, institutions and cities have had to wait until recent years before being picked up by new generations of artists or by the mass media. Radio and television these days is full of (often heavily edited and manipulated) "interactive" programmes urging the public to participate by phoning in, sending e-mails, entering competitions or participating in various kinds of "reality" shows. This is hardly the democratic access to the media dreamed of by the avant-garde. Modern architects, decorators and constructors come closer to implementing the ideals of the sixties in their use of modern visual technologies to help people imagine their future homes before they are built or re-decorated.

These examples illustrate the ambiguous way in which avant-garde movements are assimilated historically and culturally. The ambiguity of this reception leads to equally ambiguous assessments of the impact and importance of the post-war avant-gardes, ranging from dismissive views — like Peter Bürger's claim that the post-war avant-garde is merely repeating the original gestures of earlier avant-gardes (Bürger 1974: 71), or Lev Manovich's statement that the historical avant-gardes have turned into the software of to-day's computer industry and media technology (Manovich 2000) — to more appreciative evaluations like Hal Foster's claim that the ideas of the pre-war avantgardes are fulfilled only by the avant-garde of the 1960s (Foster 1996: 30).

IV.

As I have indicated, it can indeed be argued that technology plays a significant role in determining the development of the post-war avant-garde in Denmark — directly, by providing new technological means of expression, new communication channels and new material, and indirectly, by providing new models of thinking, seeing and imagining the world, metaphors for change.

But this is only half the story, I would suggest. Obviously the relation between technology and avant-garde is not simple. The technological changes during the second half of the 20th century have elicited varying responses from the arts in different periods. It is hardly possible to draw a single development line through this period based on avant-gardist responses to technological innovation. Indeed, a plurality of co-existing tendencies has been characteristic of the arts in the last decades of the 20th century, some re-appropriating historical styles, genres and gestures, others trying to continue and renew the experiments of the avant-gardes, which have now themselves become a historical tradition, whether they belong to the pre-war or the post-war period.

The basic premise underlying the Ex-School's use of new technologies in the 1960s was the existence of a specific aesthetic programme. This aesthetic view valued the experimental process over the finished product; collective anonymity over personal career; interesting and novel ideas over professional treatment. The Ex-School group was largely opposed to art works marketed as commodities. The individual work of art was often replaced or supplemented by collective processes resulting in impermanent, time and site specific works made of non-durable materials. The Ex-School circle increasingly wanted to communicate to their audience outside traditional institutions (and often had to, since no institutions were interested) and to dismantle the hierarchical relations between art and everyday objects, between high and low (or mass) culture, between the internal elements of the work as well as between artist and public.

Ex-School artists wanted to discard traditional notions of the artist as a special kind of person and art as a special activity. They used varying strategies to achieve this de-mystification of art and the artist. For instance they sought to eliminate subjective choices through the use of rules and constraints, chance procedures or mechanical production. They tried to counter the cult of genius and the traditional positioning in the art world through collective working processes. Or they attempted to open the field of communication by inviting the public to participate in the interpretation of the work — whether by walking through the sculpture as through a passage, by forming one's own version of the visual or verbal cut-up or providing one's own associations to the musical or textual structures.

As the traditional categories of poetry, painting, sculpture or musical composition were dissolved and replaced by hybrid forms, and the distinctions among the art forms were transcended in cross-aesthetic experimentation, an aesthetic situation arose in which anything might be the object and the means of the artistic process. Thus all kinds of not only materials, but also technologies could be introduced into the creative process. It was this aesthetic programme that promoted the particular interrelation between avant-garde and technology in the Danish 1960s. The importance of the aesthetic programme is demonstrated by the fact that experiments often began long before the relevant technologies were fully developed and easily available.

To return to Hans-Jørgen Nielsen's volume of concrete poetry, it is significant that it includes a page of prose produced by a computer — in those days a huge machine requiring a professional programmer and elaborate encoding. Ekbom sees Nielsen's computer text as an instance of serious integration in the electronic era and as "slightly touching or clumsy, rather like children's drawings in which you may trace the first primitive signs of an as yet undeveloped consciousness" (Ekbom 1966). In fact, equally or more interesting results might have been produced by far simpler means. The computer does not really function here in the ways it has been made to do in later instances of computer poetry. In itself, the process of feeding different word classes to the computer and making it generate sentences on its own, according to the then quite new grammatical field theories (formulated by the Danish linguist Diderichsen), was obviously very exciting. And at the time, in the early 1960s, it represented a radical conception of doing away with the emotional and subjective dimensions of artistic creation and approaching the objective conditions of scientific research. The important thing about the inclusion of this text in the volume of poetry is obviously the gesture, the signal value of the computer.

In fact, the avant-garde is rarely much interested in technology as such, but far more in the possibilities involved in using technology for artistic, political, social or utopian purposes or as signals of modernity and change. One of the slogans of ABCinema was "It is easy to make films". Glossy technological solutions are hard to come by among the avant-garde works of this period. What the avant-garde is interested in is not the high-profile, professional technological finish, but the challenge to customary ways of thinking and acting or the visions of other ways to go about things.

To turn the argument full circle, it may, of course, be argued that the aesthetic programme of the avant-garde of the 1960s, which was a necessary condition for its interaction with new technologies, was in itself a response to contemporary changes based to a large degree on the technological development. From this perspective, the response of the avant-garde to the technological, social and cultural changes of the 1960s went far beyond the actual use of new media and technologies. In this wider sense it involved not only aesthetic or artistic preferences, but basic assumptions about the nature of perception, human relations, subjectivity and culture.

BIBLIOGRAPHY

Andersen, Troels ed.
1963   K. Malevic: Om nye systemer i kunsten. Skrifter 1915–1922. Copenhagen: Kunst og Kultur.

Andersen, Troels
1967   *Moderne russisk kunst 1910–1925.* Copenhagen: Borgen.

Bürger, Peter
1974   *Theorie der Avantgarde.* Frankfurt a. M.: Suhrkamp.

Crow, Thomas
1996   *The Rise of the Sixties.* London: The Everyman Art Library.

Ekbom, Torsten
1966   "Nya medier — ny poesi". In: *Vindrosen*, no.3, 71–75.

Foster, Hal
1996   *The Return of the Real.* Cambridge, Mass.: The MIT Press.

Manovich, Lev
2000   "Avantgarde as Software". At: http://www.manovich.net/index.html

McLuhan, Marshall
1964   *Understanding Media.* New York: McGraw-Hill.

Nielsen, Hans-Jørgen
    1965   *at det at*. Copenhagen: Borgen.

ta'
    1967–68   Nos. 1–8. Copenhagen: H.M. Bergs Forlag.

Literature under the Impact of Film: On Dutch Author-Critics of the Avant-Garde and Neo-Avant-Garde

KLAUS BEEKMAN

In the inter-bellum period literature in the Netherlands encountered a tremendous new competitor: film. Soon after its development, films flooded the Dutch cultural market. Most films came from America, some from Russia and from Germany. These two very different art forms both strived for the public's favour. Each was accompanied by its own group of critics, but there were also critics who were active in both cultural fields and who reviewed novels as well as films. It is remarkable that among these critics there were also authors of high literary esteem, such as Constant van Wessem. Van Wessem wrote novels, *vie romancées*, plays, and reviews on literature, music and film. He was best known as the editor of *Het Getij* (The Tide), a literary journal that from 1916 to 1924 offered shelter to Dutch avant-garde authors such as the expressionist Herman van den Bergh and the dadaist and constructivist Theo van Doesburg. Van Wessem also belonged to the editorial board of the film journal *Filmliga* (Filmleague), which was founded in 1927 by the famous Dutch author and critic Menno ter Braak and the moviemaker Joris Ivens, among others. As an author, Van Wessem felt obliged to take up a position towards film. In this paper I will explore how Van Wessem reconciled this new artistic form with the older genre of literature and how he related the filmic medium to literary concepts.

After World War II author-critics classified as "neo-avant-garde" or "experimental" again reacted to the phenomenon of film. Lidy van Marissing is one such author-critic who, in the post-war period, felt obliged to take up a position towards film, just as Van Wessem had done some decades before. However, by the 1970s, when Van Marissing published her experimental novels, contributed to the avant-garde journal *Raster* and wrote literary reviews for *de Volkskrant*, one of the most renowned Dutch daily newspapers, film had undergone radical changes. It is not surprising, therefore, that her assessment of the relationship between film and literature differed considerably from Van Wessem's evaluation forty years earlier, when film was still in its infancy. In this paper I will reconstruct the poetics of these two author-critics. I will demonstrate that while Van Marissing legitimates her position towards film in ways quite different from those of Van Wessem, both critics guide their evaluation and develop their conception of an interface between the arts in a manner determined by strategic considerations. Since Van Wessem was associated with the historical avant-garde and Van Marissing with the post-war avant-garde, a comparison between the two will tell us something about the relationship between avant-garde and neo-avant-garde orientations in Dutch literature as well as film.

Constant van Wessem and film in the inter-bellum period

To Van Wessem, Jean Cocteau was the perfect example of the modern artist because of his ability to express *modern sensitivity*, as Van Wessem formulated it in a paper on Cocteau in the literary journal *De Vrije Bladen* (The Free Papers) in 1925. Cocteau's *modern sensitivity* was derived from the fact that "his character showed something of our times," Van Wessem maintained nearly fifteen years later in his essay volume *Mijn broeders in Apollo* (My Brothers in Apollo: 1941, 5f). Van Wessem made *modern sensitivity* a basic criterion for identifying literature as modern. He described his conception of literature in a series of articles that he published in 1929 in *De Vrije Bladen* under the title of "Het Moderne Proza" (Modern Prose). Here, he defended a certain type of prose written with *modern sensitivity* — a type of prose which is characterised by a "consciousness of modern life" and a "common sense for factualness." This prose could be described as an expression of Nieuwe Zakelijkheid ("Neue Sachlichkeit"). The modern author, he maintained, should take up an objective position towards the object.

Van Wessem played an important role in importing the avant-garde world of ideas to the Netherlands. In the literary journal *Het Getij*, he introduced readers to Marinetti and Van Doesburg. Van Wessem's interest in film tended in the same direction. He compiled a volume of *De Vrije Bladen* in which film as a new medium was brought to the attention of Dutch readers. In this volume, as in his monograph on *Charlie Chaplin* (1927) and *De komische film* (The Comic Film, 1931), Van Wessem demonstrated his admiration for Chaplin, an admiration he shared with many avant-garde artists, as Thomas Vaessens has illustrated (1993).

The volume Van Wessem compiled, entitled *Wij gelooven in den film* (We believe in film, 1926) and to which other well known author-critics such as Menno ter Braak and H. Marsman contributed, carries a fascinating subtitle: "A Confession of Our Generation". The contributions to the volume are polemically presented as the point of view of a "young" generation of artists. The volume opens with a kind of manifesto in which the contributors adopt the position that "We believe in film" and then substantiate this position. They justify their belief by claiming that the medium of film "is young" and "is very dear to the heart of the younger generation, from the conviction that in film a specific 20th century form of expression is growing, which deserves attention, dedication and creative strength" (Van Wessem 1926: 1).

Van Wessem postulated that the younger generation of authors had to defend the new medium of film against an older generation. The younger generation, a member of which Van Wessem considered himself, saw the attraction of film in the fact that "space" and "movement" were the central components of this art form. Van Wessem made a case for the appeal of film by referring to the darkness in which a film is seen, thus allowing the viewer to break away from himself and to experience the film in a more "direct" way. Furthermore, the "silence" of film had enormous suggestive force and the "close-up" enormous aesthetic energy (Van Wessem 1926: 3—4). "The most simple objects", like a telephone or piece of wall, are blown up and "isolated from their surroundings" (Van Wessem 1926: 23). Acceleration in the film can have a comical effect, while slow motion can show all kinds of beauty. "The slow motion functions as a new aspect of beauty, for example in the ballets of Cocteau (*Boeuf sur le toit*, *Adieu New York*, the heraldic dances in black and white of *Romeo and Juliette*)," Van Wessem states (1926: 22). He emphasized that film is a matter of technique — "a technique of sensitivity" that demonstrates the artistic nature of the medium. Film knows how to evoke "emotions." It is not important *what* film is representing, but *how* film is doing so (Van Wessem 1926: 5 f.).

In describing the art of film, Van Wessem is aware that not all products of the film industry stive for its full realisation. His seemingly neutral remark that America exports a lot of cowboy films to Europe is far less innocent than it appears: indeed, Van Wessem later criticised the whole American film genre. In this opinion Van Wessem was not alone. Ter Braak argued in his contribution to Van Wessem's volume entitled "Cinema Militans" that most people go to the cinema not because of the artistic value of the film but to escape reality (1926: 11 ff.). When the Dutch government suppressed the public presentation of Pudovkin's *The Mother* because of its communist content, Ter Braak was one of the first to show the film illicitly. He later founded the "Filmliga" (Filmleague) and an associated magazine, *Filmliga*. The objective of the film league, formulated in the Amsterdam film manifesto of the same name, reads as follows:

> Once in a hundred times we see: film. Otherwise we see cinema film: that of the common herd, the commercial regime, America, kitsch. At this stage film and cinema film are each other's natural enemies. Our belief in the pure and autonomous film, the film as art and as future, is useless if we do not take the case in hand. We want to do so. We want to see what has been experimented and reached in the workshops of the French, German and Russian avant-garde. (Ivens 1970: 17)

The antithesis between film and cinema, between art and popular art, was analogous to the antithesis between Europe and the United States, in which the Netherlands choose the side of Europe (Van Beusekom 2001: 192 ff.) However, the preferences for the "French, German and Russian avant-garde" did not go so far as to welcome the experiments of the French surrealists. According to Ter Braak, a film as a form of art had to be realised on a rational plane: "Just like the other Dutch critics he [Ter Braak] did not like the surrealist experiments, in which the subconscious occupies an important place," Van Beusekom asserts (2001: 203). Films like Walther Ruttmann's *Berlin. Die Symphonie einer Grossstadt* were appreciated unanimously because of their rhythmical montage (Van Beusekom 2001: 228). Ter Braak considered *The Mother* the most important cinematographic masterpiece: it was a successful synthesis of realistic pictures and abstract rhythm, a result of the particular montage concept developed by Pudovkin (Van Beusekom 2001: 224). However, Ter Braak never considered montage as a criterion in his film reviews. He wrote, "the basis of art is never technique, nor a technical dogma, but always imagination" (Van Beusekom 2001: 233).

While the art film and the commercial cinema are seen in oppositional terms, there is apparently no antithesis between the art film and the modern novel. Van Wessem defended his high esteem for the art of film by relating it to literary techniques:

> We can discern the lesson of film in the modern novel: to evoke the drama by means of short, concise suggestions without contemplation or tropes, "sans fil", and in a rhythm directed at tension, at the emotional height, at the unexpected, clear, and overwhelming. The acceleration of the whole does not become, as some claim, an accelerated tempo, as a result of the emotion's refelection of and regulation by rhythmical happening, in which all superfluous "frill" falls away. (1926: 70v)

According to Van Wessem the issue of film is "rhythm". The film artist never sits down "on the chair of his feelings" (1926: 60). The same holds for the dada film *Entr'acte* of René Clair. Van Wessem praised its suggestion of a "subconscious working rhythm" and "its play of associations" (1931: 19).

Modern literature shares with film the "streaming succession of pictures". But this does not mean that authors of the modern novel adopted this streaming technique from the moviemaker. Rather, after defending the art film against the commercial film and arguing that film is a medium of the younger generation, Van Wessem legitimises the autonomy of modern literature vis-à-vis film. Van Wessem maintains that the influence of film on literature is an indirect one. Film and other discoveries of modern life have changed the creative power of the artist, he argues. Modern times have lead to a "new sensitivity" on the part of the modern artist, a sensitivity "for the 'wireless', the rhythmical, the movable" (1926: 69). In other words, this rhythm of the succession of pictures in modern literature springs from the *modern sensitivity* of the author without his being directly influenced by film (1926: 71). Indeed, one finds a succession of pictures in modern literature: one picture is followed by another, and juxtaposing without interrelating them provides rhythm. Thus, modern authors, as Van Wessem puts it, already had *modern sensitivity* when they wrote their novels without detailed descriptions or explanations; film only confirmed the fact that literary authors should continue to write in the manner they did. Similarly, film confirmed the modern novel's abandonment of basic naturalistic assumptions and human psychology:

> Cinema has succeeded in proving that genuine human emotion can be evoked not only by the probable and the similar, and that a whole world of feelings has escaped from logic and psychology, to which cinema, unconsciously, has apparently found the key. (Van Wessem 1926: 72)

Van Wessem has chosen the side of the "young" authors and artists that defended the film as a medium of art. But he does not go so far as to argue that modern literature, for example in its use of montage, has been influenced by film. Behind his point of view strategic intentions hide: Van Wessem creates a distinct profile for himself, Ter Braak, and other members of the group of "young" authors and critics. He characterizes himself and others as defenders of film as a new medium of art, and also as critics and authors of modern literature. He benefits from arguing that, in spite of film, modern literature occupies an autonomous position in the cultural field amidst other modern artistic media.

The conception of literature Van Wessem proposed, however, is not a very consistent one, as Grüttemeier (1995) argues. In his basic assumptions, Van Wessem leaves room for the traditional "idealist aesthetics". According to these, which were proposed in Germany at the end of the 18th century, art is timeless in its transformation of facts to a higher plane, and the work of art is an "organic" phenomenon. In other words, Van Wessem's poetics are akin to an old idealist conception of art associated with the idea that a piece of art is an "organic" unity and a new poetics in which the use of documentary material and the "selecting" and "arranging" of these materials are the central issues.

Lidy van Marissing and film in the post-war period

At the end of her experimental novel *Ontbinding* (Decomposition, 1972), Van Marissing inserted an article discussing her conception of literature, entitled "Notes on a 'difficult' book". In this addendum she defended a "realist" style: "Realist literature shows social patterns and contrasts as movements which are reversible: masters used to be slaves, and slaves can become masters" (Van Marissing 1972: 147). Van Marissing's idea of the function of literature can be characterized as "providing critical information on reality". She focuses especially on contrasts. The technique she uses most to realise this function is montage:

> The split experience of people occupied only with parts and lacking an overall view, their scattered observation of society, their lack of voice, their loss of a sense of time (changeability) and space (unity) – this fragmentation demands a style which tears to shreds the chronological story, the identification of character in a novel, dramatic unity and grammatical rules. Besides, montage is a useful means to disturb the conditioned reader: the reader is not presented with a story in which he gets involved or which introduces him to a sophisticated and harmonious world. (Van Marissing 1972: 145 f.)

Montage thus fulfils two requirements at once: it corresponds to the mode of perception characteristic of modern life, and it establishes conditions for the reception of literature which encourage us to adapt a critical point of view vis-à-vis contemporary reality. Van Marissing turns against those elements that belong to the conventional concept of literature: that reality is surveyable, and that literary reality serves as a haven from a crumbled and obscure reality outside.

When Van Marissing argued that in Dutch literature one hardly finds realist art, she was not at all alluding to the conventions of realist literature of the nineteenth century. Rather, she was referring to the concept of realism as developed in the writings of Bertolt

Brecht. Thus, Van Marissing adopted a conception of literature from an author of the inter-bellum period. She recognized her relationship with Brecht, for whom *realism* meant:

> den gesellschaftlichen Kausalkomplex aufdeckend / die herrschenden Gesichtspunkte als die Gesichtspunkte der Herrschenden entlarvend / vom Standpunkt der Klasse aus schreibend, welche für die dringendsten Schwierigkeiten, in denen die menschliche Gesellschaft steckt, die breitesten Lösungen bereit hält / das Moment der Entwicklung betonend / konkret und das Abstrahieren ermöglichend. (Brecht 1971: 70)

One of the means of achieving these aims of realism in literature was, as Brecht had pointed out in his first full account of the theory of epic theatre, the use of montage. Along with other stylistic features such as intertitles and gestic acting Brecht adopted the technique of montage from film. Van Marissing followed him in this way. In her experimental novel *De omgekeerde wereld* (*The world upside down*, 1975) she advanced her point of view. The novel explores illusions, dreams, and neuroses of the masses of society, and is a parody of literary rules that disguise the relation of literature to reality. In this novel there is no unity, no psychologically consistent characters, and no plot. Van Marissing's novel has been composed from mostly short and autonomous fragments that are separated from each other typographically. Although the fragments may considered autonomous, they can also be seen on a deeper level as connected, because they often deal with identical questions — namely, the issue of appearances and the essence of reality. The fragments are described in the terms of different discourses, such as the scientific discourse ("hypothesis", "fact", "test") and a discourse that is taken from the media of film and television ("montage", "shot", "point of view", "backlighting", "stars"). With the exception of its own discourse, that of the literary text, the novel takes issue with basic assumptions of the concepts of reality implied. What is true and what is false? What is real, what unreal? One often feels inclined to accept for "real" what can be observed. But for many people, " real" is what the media shows:

> Reality as a copy of fiction
> War as a story

Love as a film
I as another. As a hero in a novel .
(Van Marissing 1975: 20)

For some individuals, film pictures are the reference points from which they judge their experience of reality. Some even think that the proportion of reality in film is higher than that of reality itself. One of the fragments in Van Marrising's novel starts as follows: "Some people can kill themselves in a television appearance. In the late evening journal this scene is repeated" (1975: 13ff.). The fragment refers to an actual event in America, in which a television commentator announced she would shoot herself during the transmission, and proceeded to do so. However, not every reader will be aware of the veracity of this tale. The difference between violence in fiction (television, film, literature) and that in reality is, for many people, hard to establish, due in part to the fact that their frame of observation is increasingly determined by the media. In her novel, Van Marissing illustrates this problem by embedding this factual fragment among other (fictional or nonfictional) fragments and by starting the tale with the ambiguous remark that "someone *can* kill himself in a television appearance".

In the novel statements are quoted which go against the conventions of realist illusionism. Emphasis is placed instead on all kinds of technical interventions that create an alternative reality: "One can put the images in another order" (Van Marissing 1975: 18). Mimetic concepts of the representation of reality are at stake here, as Van Marrising emphasises by rephrasing Brecht's famous objection to naive concepts of realist representation:

> *Reproduction.* The direct representation of the observed facts. The magic of the unadulterated document. The hunger for facts as a dislike of abstractions, though nothing is more abstract than a fact: Hundreds of representations of a factory together do not deliver the real meaning of that factory, but remain hundreds of images of this factory's façade. Reality is a construction and thus has to be constructed. What is behind that factory? What interest? (1975: 134)

Van Marissing pleads for a "constructive" style. Only with the help of montage can one present a (critical) image of reality. A complicated historical period such as that of the post-war years does not ask for an unequivocal and one-dimensional representation but instead for a complicated style making use of montage and paradoxes:

> *Construction.* Montage, opposing, cutting and joining images. This method is the result of the experience of the present period as an empty time, full of chaotic happenings and paradoxical forces. By means of this method social and ideological ambiguity is best shown. (1975: 133 ff.)

Conclusions

As a post-war author, Lidy van Marissing does not feel obliged, like Van Wessem did in the inter-bellum period, to legitimate her position towards film. Her preoccupation with the filmic phenomenon stems from something else. Van Wessem had a critical attitude towards a specific kind of film, namely the commercial American movie, which he refused to call "art film". The criticisms of Van Marissing focus on the pretension of film to represent reality adequately and on the way in which film redefines the criteria of realism in its own terms. Like Van Wessem, Van Marissing defends montage. But while Van Wessem legitimises the use of montage via his notion of *modern sensitivity*, a kind of sensitivity that would make it possible for the modern artist of the inter-bellum period to shape the "rhythm" of modern times, Van Marissing makes consistent use of the filmic technique in her novels. Montage becomes an essential means of social criticism by pointing to paradoxes and to the reversibility of statements. In an indirect way she thus makes the point that traditional "realist" literature is not able to portray adequately a complicated world of language and pictures.

BIBLIOGRAPHY

Beekman, Klaus, and Ralf Grüttemeier
    2001   "Constant van Wessem". In: *Kritisch Literatuurlexicon.* Groningen: Martinus Nijhoff.

Beusekom, Ansje van
  2001   *Kunst en amusement. Reacties op de film als een nieuw medium in Nederland, 1895–1940.* Haarlem: Arcadia.

Brecht, Bertolt
  1971   *Über Realismus*, ed. Werner Hecht. Frankfurt am Main: Suhrkamp.

Grüttemeier, Ralf
  1995   Hybride Welten. Aspekte der "Nieuwe Zakelijkheid" in der niederländischen Literatur. Stuttgart: Metzler & Poeschel.

Hanssen, L.
  1995   Menno ter Braak (1902–1940). Voorvechter van de kunstfilm. In: *Jaarboek voor mediageschiedenis* 6, SDU Uitgeverij Amsterdam, 30–40.

Ivens, Joris
  1970   *Autobiografie van een filmer.* Amsterdam: Born.

Marissing, Lidy van
  1972   *Ontbinding.* Amsterdam: Van Gennep.

  1975   *De omgekeerde wereld. Leesboek voor de midden-groepen.* Amsterdam: Van Gennep.

Vaessens, Thomas
  1993   De ster van een ongekend medium. Chaplin als boegbeeld van een nieuwe kunstenaarslichting? In: *Vooys*, Utrecht: Instituutblad van het Instituut De Vooys, vol. 11, no. 3–4, 146–162.

Wessem, Constant van
  1926   *Wij gelooven in den film. Een belijdenis van onze generatie.* Utrecht: De Branding.

  1929   Het moderne proza. In: *De Vrije Bladen*, Amsterdam: S.L. van Looy, vol. 6, 170–175, 204–208, 327–332, 360–364, 389–391.

  1931   *De komische film.* Rotterdam: W.L. en J. Brusse's Uitgeversmaatschappij.

List of Illustrations

27. "Quand on aime la vie on va au cinema". Cinéthique group (1975) 279

28. Graham Percy: *Constable Country*. From: *New Society* (1969)   290

Permission to reproduce the images by Picasso, Duchamp and Warhol was arranged through the Design and Artists Copyright Society (DACS) in London. The editor and the contributors are grateful to the various estates for granting the permission. Special thanks go to the Andy Warhol Estate in Pittsburgh for permitting to use Warhol's *Marilyn Monroe* (*Twenty Times*) as cover illustration.

Index